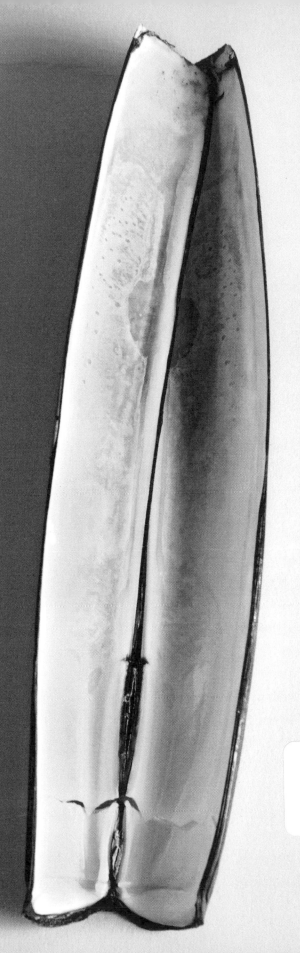

SALT

SMOKE

TIME

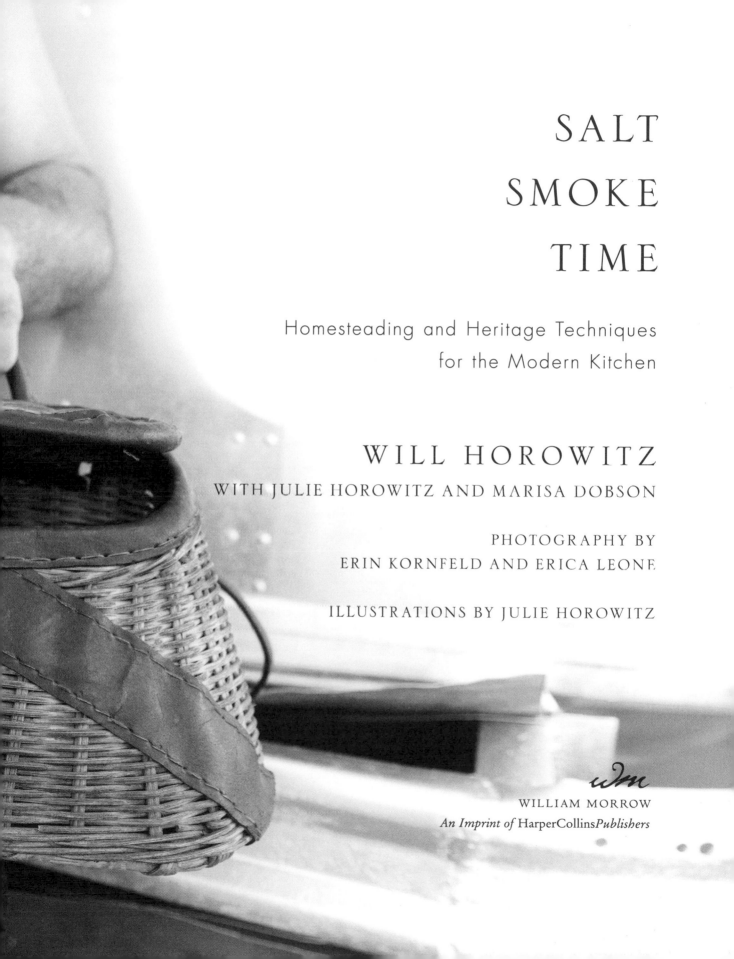

SALT
SMOKE
TIME

Homesteading and Heritage Techniques
for the Modern Kitchen

WILL HOROWITZ

WITH JULIE HOROWITZ AND MARISA DOBSON

PHOTOGRAPHY BY
ERIN KORNFELD AND ERICA LEONE

ILLUSTRATIONS BY JULIE HOROWITZ

WILLIAM MORROW
An Imprint of HarperCollins*Publishers*

Adaptation from *American Indian Society Cookbook,* by the American Indian Society of Washington, DC, compiled December 1975, on page 173.

The information offered in this book is based on experimentation and experience. However, the author is not a trained professional in food safety, fermentation, or any other field; neither he nor the publisher is responsible for the consequences of the application or misapplication of any information or ideas presented herein.

Wild poisonous plants and mushrooms sometimes resemble edible plants and mushrooms, and they often grow side by side. It is the responsibility of the reader to identify and use correctly the edible plants described in this book. Anyone attempting to ingest wild food should seek the help of local experts and groups and consult local authorities regarding legality and safety. The authors and publisher assume no responsibility for problems arising from the reader's misidentification or use of wild plants.

HarperCollins books may be purchased for educational, business, or sales promotional use. For information, please email the Special Markets Department at SPsales@harpercollins.com.

FIRST EDITION

Designed by Suet Yee Chong
Photography by Erin Kornfeld and Erica Leone
Illustrations by Julie Horowitz

Library of Congress Cataloging-in-Publication Data has been applied for.

ISBN 978-0-06-242710-6

19 20 21 22 23   LSC   10 9 8 7 6 5 4 3 2 1

To Benji, Francis, Mac, Molly, and Ed.

You can't begin to know life until you know death.

You truly lived.

Ford the rivers and across the moss-draped streams, through the narrow paths of ancient hardwoods and skyscraping buildings, ribbons of sunlight reflect off glass walls, through mist rising off the bogs and beaver ponds, fading into the subterranean billows of city steam from the sewer-capped streets of the morning's first heat. An old cabin exists, where garlic slowly roasts in a wood stove for a venison stew simmering above. Vessels of wine stand in the corner under chimes of salted fish and dried herbs gently swaying from the fall night's cool breeze. My hands—axe-blistered, ash-rusted—slowly raise my grandfather's copper mug filled with warm broth to my wind-torn lips. The gentle aroma of smokiness fills my nose with memories of sweat lodge bonfires long since past, a rich wave of decadence crashes over my tongue, warmth and understanding pour down my throat. Fat sticks to my lips, as a reminder between sips. The loud ambulance sirens and a taxi cab's halting screech interrupt my contemplation. But, like a revelation, the sounds meld into the mystifying songs of aspen leaves dancing in unison to the loon's morning reveille, hinting at other dimensions. I place my mug back down to gently run my hand through my beard. My eyes, they glow, like northern lights beaming through slices of time and fear. Lifetimes let loose within the infinite nature of this very moment . . . this very smile. Leaning back, I can't help but laugh. Like a child. I am free. Life is here, and we are all still wild.

—Will Horowitz

CONTENTS

FOREWORD

It's become passé of late to advocate a return to nature. Perhaps we find it hard to look at the natural world due to our constant state of war against it. But that incessant vying with nature has always been there, and each age tries its best to educate itself anew regarding the best way to move forward. Thankfully there is always a past to relearn from. Now more than ever do we need to take stock and seriously consider living alongside our planet as opposed to merely exploiting it. This book is an example of that "living alongside," of a culinary "being with the world," of wanting to know more about what the natural world can give us in order to sustain us in the future. This knowledge comes from the past, but it is not contained there. It spreads itself out, greets us, and shows us the way to a more ecological future.

Why preserve? One might argue that we no longer need this ancient method. We have our fridges, our freezers, our ships and our planes; we want for nothing and we have access to everything all the time. But there are serious consequences to this mindset, that of cutting across seasons and seas in the pursuit of all. I believe this cannot continue indefinitely, and sooner or later we'll all have to return to a more local diet that draws on many past methods of preservation. All children should know how to pickle a cucumber or ferment cabbage. They should know how to pick autumnal fruit and how best to preserve it. Do you agree? Why do we always leave food to the last in terms of education? We have our priorities backward, teaching our children about computing before they can even boil an egg.

The recipes in the book promote a new-old way of being in the world. They will help you build a pantry of many foods and flavors. They will release you from the humdrum world of contemporary food and return you to places you never thought you would need to go. From producing your own butter to making your own charcuterie, you'll love the food you make, just as you realize how important you are in relation to it. Food is more than just something purchased in a supermarket. It is found in the woods, on the lakes, among the rivers, and out in the ocean. It is the ecology that keeps us alive. It is our reason for being. We are food.

Following Will's recipes from the growing season to the cold season will help you realign yourself with the seasons—not just in the abstract sense of understanding the four separate divisions that we have given our year, but the almost micro level of how food changes through the days and weeks of the year. When you follow the life cycles of the herbs, fish, mushrooms, and other natural substances in the book, you'll soon understand the whole breadth of each season.

This is the ecological age, when we can no longer deny we are all part of the same planet, the same ecological community. We need to act as individuals and as a community in order to make sure the natural world will be there for our children, their children, and beyond. Will's book is a step in the right direction. It won't solve all our food problems, but it certainly will work toward righting a few of the world's culinary wrongs.

I hope you enjoy this book and the myriad ways it will return you to nature, and yourself.

—JP McMahon, chef, author, and restaurateur

INTRODUCTION

An old pond
A frog tumbles in
The sound of water

—MATSUO BASHŌ

Look closely into nature to find answers. Look at nature from afar to find peace. Surrender yourself to nature to find you already had and turn your back to it to learn it is always there. This is not a book about a chef, a recipe, or a restaurant. This is a book about how nature and history can teach us to best feed ourselves and others, if we allow it to.

Here along the North Atlantic inlets, we are at nature's mercy, whether we are combing the forest floors for mushrooms, raking hard shells from the bays, or fly-fishing the flats. The true power of humility is in its awe of the wild and the unknown. This book is an exploration of our connection to the natural world around us and our place in its beautiful, terrifying cycle.

It is our journey to relearn the art of how to live. By studying our shared history, we begin to carve out our own path toward self-reliance within a microwaveable world of convenience.

The heritage techniques provided in this book are meant to preserve a story as well as an ingredient. These recipes are innovative interpretations of the homesteading and survivalist traditions passed down by our ancestors. More often than not, they involve techniques that have been cast aside in a society dominated by big business and high production. These methods may take time and, consequently, patience, but they involve ingredients and techniques that tend to cost less.

Each preparation represents its own history, through war, immigration, poverty, trade, religion. These are the tales of kitchens that rotated with the moons, rejoiced in the rains, and blossomed in the sun. Where not a single grain could afford to go to waste and the entirety of every animal served a purpose.

It is possible that many of humanity's most important sustainability practices can be found within its homesteading traditions. It's easy to forget that "food waste" is a modern invention. Much of our existence today relies on a rich history of turning one man's trash into another man's treasure. The significance of these old traditions is as important as ever as we're observing our natural resources diminish and our climate rapidly change. It is essential that we look to the past to inspire innovation and technology for a more sustainable future. As our population expands and the environment weakens, it is my hope that these practices in self-reliance will once again find their importance in the modern-day household, one slow-burning campfire at a time. Within our own stillness comes a connection to a universe much larger than ourselves.

SALT

SMOKE

TIME

RELEARNING THE PAST

When human beings lose their connection to nature, to heaven and earth, then they
do not know how to nurture their environment or how to rule their world. . . .
From that perspective, healing our society goes hand in hand with healing our
personal, elemental connection with the phenomenal world.

—CHÖGYAM TRUNGPA RINPOCHE

We were ambushed by a thunderstorm worthy of an ark. It wasn't even supposed to rain, but weather forecasts never carried much weight around the Rockies. The sky broke open to fistfuls of raindrops pounding on our heads. We could see flash floods crashing down off the Eastern Utah mesas, through the narrow alleyways of red cliffs—and headed right toward us. We found shelter by climbing up a rocky canyon wall and into a small shallow-ledged cave. Like castaways, we waited. John sat back to roll a joint and spool his climbing rope as I pulled out a healthy ration of wasabi peas. He was obsessive about his rope after a bad fall a few years back. I was obsessive about wasabi peas.

We looked at each other and nervously laughed. Nobody wanted to state the obvious. As our hangovers quickly dissolved into anxious clarity, we both knew what the next forty-eight hours would look like if the sky refused to let up. John turned to me and said, "Should we put the bowl back where we found it?

Maybe it's some sort of ancient Anasazi curse!" We laughed again, our nervousness unabated.

Completely drenched, I sat down on the ground and leaned against my pack, which was filled with various twine, flares, spikes, brushes, and trowels—pretty much anything resembling an archaeologist's toolkit that could be purchased at a gas station at 2:00 a.m. As I sat on the ledge, my mind began to race. I straightened my spine and decided to meditate. I remember the way the wind felt across my face, drops of water relentlessly crashing against my cheek. I closed my eyes and took in a deep breath, filling my body with space. Slowly, I began to exhale . . . and inhale. My mind filled. Thoughts beat down on me like a drum.

The night before, we had jotted down plans for the expedition over bourbon at a dive bar in Boulder. We had found one of John's old journals from a group mountaineering trip the prior year. In it, he had vaguely described seeing a Native American artifact nestled in the rocks while squatting to take a crap off the side of the trail. An artifact like that is not the sort of thing that one can simply pack out of a canyon, particularly in the presence of others, and somehow John had since forgotten about it until now.

We had made it to the general site after hiking through the night. He hadn't written down anything useful like actual coordinates, but he had recorded distinct observations of the canyon, bushes, forks, twists, springs, boulders, and lightning-struck cottonwoods along the way. In retrospect, it was a bit of a suicide mission. As we sat and waited in that cave, the bar in Boulder already felt like a lifetime ago. Moments and revelations turned into hours and eternities.

Sometime later, I woke up to the storm subsiding. Like rolling up window shades to let in the first beams of morning light, when I finally opened my eyes, it was to a sky exploding with multicolored rays of light in every direction. A labyrinth of dark gray charcoal-sketched clouds was parting. Fear gave way to raw emotion and emotion gave way to clarity, all while a chaos of roaring floods and rapids was still running rampant below us. I looked over at John and smiled; he had fallen asleep.

As the water subsided, we emerged from the cave and began our hike out. It was a rough journey. We marched for hours up what felt like never-ending sand-dune walls only to get hit by another lightning storm, this time while riding big steel-framed bicycles that we had naively locked to a bush on top of the mesas. The next morning, we found my car stuck in a sand bank and debated whether it had just floated in from the floods or if we'd just been that drunk driving in.

Before heading back across state lines, we grabbed a beer at the nearest bar to celebrate.

From that day on, we saw this as a new life for us. Like Indiana Jones, we were going to be treasure hunters—of course, without the archaeology degrees (or, at that time, any other degrees). Calling this dream short-lived would be an exaggeration. Years later, John passed away while doing what he loved best—pushing his limits.

There are people who develop into responsible members of society steadily and formulaically, as if being led up a set of stairs. They are raised, schooled, career-driven, family-oriented—and so it goes. And then there are others—like me. When I was growing up, my education was more defined by learning disabilities and trouble than scholastic success. I was stifled by an educational system that was focused more on producing a carbon copy than an individual. In my teens, I stopped attending high school altogether, finding more opportunities for growth in hanging out with friends and diving headfirst into a pool of psychedelics, lawlessness, and eventual trouble. It's a sad, familiar story, but many of us ended up in jail or didn't make it at all.

Almost every culture has a coming of age, a rite of passage, or a spirit quest to help us find our purpose in life. For many, a deeper understanding of who we are and our relationship to the universe is necessary to ascribe meaning to daily life. There was once more significance—and, most important, time—given in our developing years to quieting our minds, reconnecting to the infinite, and finding our own identity within the natural world.

There is nothing like being struck down by the raw force of the universe's natural elements to put things into perspective. Very quickly it pries our minds loose from the traffic jam of our day-to-day thoughts. When I walk through the woods, I try to let the needling of my own self-consciousness fall by the wayside, identifying it as purely a survival mechanism of my species. Our consciousness is just a tool for our survival, no greater than the spores of a puffball in a deer's path or the acrobatics of a falcon's sky dive. Each step—along the forest floor, along the city streets—like Braille, transcribes a new story. Each step forges our connection to an ecosystem that we as humans cannot escape, even if we foolishly want to.

My happiest memories as a child always revolved around food or nature. It was watching my mother cook. It was eating pâté and rolling out fresh pastas in my grandmother's kitchen, after a long day of fishing or clamming with my grandfather in Gardiners Bay on Long Island. It was roaming the woods in up-state New York with my father as I learned basic orienteering and tracking, while identifying every insect and tree we passed. My mother worked hard to give me and my sister a rich and colorful childhood. She taught us to try everything, to explore other cultures, and to not be afraid to ask questions. When we were learning to drive, she made certain we started out on a manual car—for the sole reason that when, not *if*, we were to travel to or live in other countries, we wouldn't be slowed down for a second.

Both sides of our family had long traditions of working with food. On my mother's side, my grandmother was a French-trained chef and my grandfather was a fisherman. Though they spent much of the year traveling and frequently exchanged homes with a family in Tuscany, they mainly lived in a small house in an old colonial town called Orient on the very northern tip of Long Island. Their house sat on a rocky beach, across from a lighthouse built in the late 1800s. My grandmother's kitchen was lined with beautiful old copper and Le Creuset pots, next to a small glassed-in eating room warmed by an old wood stove. The walls were lined with cookbooks and Native American arti-facts. There was no microwave, and no wedge of cheese, egg, or stick of butter ever saw the inside of a refrigerator.

Harry "Pops" Zinn, 1920s, at the family delicatessen

My father's family immigrated to New York City from southern Hungary, where my great-grandmother had been sold into servitude as a cook at a very young age. She never used recipes; she used her hands and cooked food that told her story. Like so many immigrant Jewish families, shortly after she came to America and to the Lower East Side, she and my great-grandfather opened a delicatessen in Harlem. I grew up listening to stories about their delicatessen. My grandmother used to tell us about the days of brining corned beef and tongues—my father's favorite—in barrels out on a fire escape. To this day I still use one of their old butcher knives to slice my smoked briskets.

RELEARNING THE PAST

In this book, I hope to help further reconnect us to our past so that we may use it as a more sustainable framework for our future. It is not my intent to write a history book or set forth any grand theories. What follows is a very condensed overview of the evolving relationship between humans and food, in order to help connect our history with some of the techniques and processes outlined in this book.

To understand how our food system came to be in its current form, we must start with how it began. Every dish tells a story. Each ingredient represents a culture. As Brillat-Savarin said, "Tell me what you eat, and I will tell you who you are."

When people tell me how much they love food, I often respond with a joke: "Me, too—I've been eating it my entire life!" If you consider cooking food to be an art form, then it's the only one that is biologically necessary for our survival. We—*Homo sapiens*, that is—have been on Earth for about 130,000 years, and for roughly 95 percent of that time humans have been hunters and gatherers or homesteaders. We've always been omnivores, eating just about everything, from insects, plants, bark, and small and large game on land to anything we could catch from the rivers and seas. Early humans began hunting strategically in groups and developed better and better tools that allowed them to follow and catch animals on migratory trails.

Academics suggest that what likely gave us a head start over other species was learning to cook with fire. Heating meat and plants over fire turned raw ingredients into food that both could be easier to digest—and thus consumed in greater quantities for a more consistent and higher caloric intake—as well as preserved if needed. This process also gave us the ability to eat a wider range of food. Nomadic societies have been shown to have been better nourished and less plagued by disease than our later agricultural ones. This was likely due to a multitude of reasons, from a higher caloric diet, to a greater diversity of locally available food, to a dispersed population that made it harder for infestations and disease to spread. Many of the tools, traps, and medicines, as well as foraging and hunting techniques learned in these nomadic times, were passed down, and traces can be found in techniques and cultures across the world today. A species can best sustain itself when its population is in healthy proportion to an ecosystem that can support it.

According to archaeologists, we began farming only eleven to twelve thousand years ago, though recent discoveries have shown possible signs of bread-baking as far back as fourteen thousand years ago, which could indicate we started earlier. With the rise of agriculture came a transition from nomadic tribes to settlers. As villages developed and populations grew, so did monocropping, the trade-rewarded growing of single crops. Property rights hardened and the focus became more centered around profits. We began exporting food products for global trade: Wars were fought over spices, and entire nations of people were enslaved to produce products like sugar, cotton, rum, and tobacco. This drastic shift to monocropping also left us more vulnerable to blights and sensitive to price fluctuations. The industrialized world's reactionary response was to mechanize food.

Despite initial good intentions, it evolved in a way that placed a greater emphasis on higher profits and larger-scale production while sacrificing quality and taste. With no health regulations in place, food production became a free-for-all. Industrialization made it cheaper to strip whole ingredients of their nutrients and add them back in later at addional cost to the consumer. It also became more efficient to process what was perceived to be the most valuable part of many raw ingredients, often discarding the leftovers. This production continues to expand without any connection to nature or ethical boundaries. The poultry industry is a frighteningly good example of this. The ASPCA states, "In 1923, it took 16 weeks to raise a chicken. Today it takes six weeks. . . . If humans grew at a similar rate, a 6.6-pound newborn baby would weigh 660 pounds after two months." While there haven't been enough long-term studies on GMOs yet, there have been plenty of examples of short-sightedness and ignorance that have led us to inadvertently poison our own food supply, so it's only sensible to be cautious.

Recently there's been far more attention paid to evaluating our relationship to food and food production. Many great people—food anthropologists, academics, chefs, writers—have dedicated their lives to this work and have prescriptive advice to offer (see Resources on page 299 for further reading). Most of these experts draw the conclusion that our current industrialized food system is deeply flawed.

The way things currently stand, the romantic idea of waking up and casually strolling to our local farmers' market to source the perfect meal can easily be perceived as a luxurious novelty. In reality, the majority of us simply can't devote the time or the money, or both. Small restaurants and farmers face similar sets of problems. Operating and ingredient costs are so high—and rising—that owners must make untenable choices regarding their suppliers, their ingredients, and the communities they serve. It is nearly impossible to sustain a financially healthy restaurant while keeping your doors open to the 99 percent without making a few sacrifices in ingredient sourcing and quality.

That said, it's important to acknowledge that we also have long-standing food traditions that make the most out of ingredients in order to survive and even thrive during tough times. There's a sort of alchemy in turning what's perceived as "nothing" into "something." From aging pork bellies to fermenting cheese, pickles, and sausages, techniques have been honed to feed us through difficult periods, like long winters, famines, droughts, wars, and recessions. It's no secret that some of our greatest recipes and culinary traditions were developed in these times. Simply pick up any classic cookbook and you'll find the words "peasant" or "poor man's meal" sprinkled generously throughout the text.

I believe we can use these innovative techniques to help solve the problems we face in our modern food system. By simply having a conversation with our farmers or by looking into our own trash cans, we can evaluate our waste and devise a plan of action to utilize the most undervalued and discarded products.

At Ducks Eatery, we use "scraps"—not just our own, but also the scraps from our farm suppliers. We found that many farmers were using cuts like pig ears and goat necks as stew meat, ground meat, dog food, or fertilizer, or even throwing them out. By using techniques such as curing, smoking, and other forms of preservation, we were able to transform these "offcuts" into dishes and products worthy of hard-earned cash and some even of national notoriety. In purchasing these otherwise discarded ingredients at a low cost, we could not only contribute to the farmer's revenue, but also keep our menu at an accessible price point, while still turning a profit. It's a true win-win relationship.

These days the role of the chef is as much a storyteller as anything else. We're connecting the dots between the farmer and the consumer. These same ideas can be applied even without the restaurant or supplier as a middleman. A household cook determined to shop from the local farmers' market can use each ingredient and scrap to its utmost! Incredible and inexpensive feats can be accomplished with a little ingenuity and strategic, intentional scheduling. Our vision of "farm-to-table" may look like harvesting an ingredient and using it fresh for dinner that same night, but that's only part of it; real farm-to-table living is choosing that fresh ingredient to pair with the pickles, cheeses, or cured meat from six months ago that's just now coming into its own.

By no means is this as easy as turning on a switch. It takes a more gradual

shift in our mentality, which I believe begins at our core. But with a firm intention, we can begin to chip away at a broken system and connect the struggling farmer with the struggling restaurant with the struggling community. All by studying the past.

WHERE WE'RE GOING

Observation is at the heart of all traditional sustainability. If we look through a wider lens at food history, we can find some of the best solutions by simply noting patterns already found in nature. This focused observation is the basis of what we generally refer to as traditional homesteading and, more specifically, permaculture.

Permaculture is a sustainable design of living and farming inspired by the symbiotic relationships within the natural ecosystems around us. Examples of this are everywhere. In agriculture, the practice of permaculture is to observe the natural features of an area to better create and manage water retention, light, and the natural production of topsoil through symbiosis. It is the difference between a farm that must be maintained and fed, and one with an ecosystem that nurtures life on its own: to plant a small tree that is known to retain water in an arid area; or to grow a mushroom that helps decompose wood on a plot of land with heavy woodfall; or to grow a canopy of low shade plants among taller ones, creating an entirely new world of biodiversity and growth. Examples within our past can be found through the milpas of the Yucatán and in the crops and techniques of other First Nation groups in North America, where you will often still hear about farming the "three sisters": squash, corn, and beans. The climbing beans are grown on cornstalks in recently harvested cornfields, with squash and pumpkins growing in the shade underneath. . . . You can find examples of this everywhere, some completely natural and some intentionally nursed along by indigenous farmers. You may have observed similar growth without knowing a name for it.

A promising example of applying permaculture to the future of farming is not on land at all, but rather in the exciting frontier of sustainable seaweed aquaculture. Long practiced in parts of Asia, it is now spreading throughout the Western world—and with good reason. Sustainably farmed seaweed shares a zero-input philosophy with small-scale, land-based permaculture, but it's capable of feeding millions without much upkeep. It does not require us to water and feed it and only helps promote new ecosystems around it. While it is still in its infancy in the United States, innovative thought leaders in the Northeast, like Bren Smith of the nonprofit Greenwave, work to develop and teach models of vertical kelp and shellfish farming to start-up farmers and commercial fishing converts all over the world. Over the past few years, I have worked hard to help facilitate kelp farm growth by developing seaweed into recipes and food products that add value while incentivizing both old and new farmers alike. In 2016, I cofounded the seaweed company Akua, creating our first product, a plant-based jerky, from local sugar kelp and discarded mushroom stems.

Homesteading refers more to the philosophy of sustenance living. Surviving off the grid—almost solely off your own land, using only your ingenuity and the work of your own two hands—requires a high level of planning and attention to detail. This intense focus and core belief in self-reliance represents a major departure from mainstream modern life. The phrase "urban homesteading" has often been used to describe households practicing many of the same techniques and ideals, but limited to within more urban environments and neighborhoods. I believe that many of these same principles can successfully be applied to life in city apartments of all sizes, although it may be challenging at times.

I first began cooking seriously while studying primitive survival techniques, traditional homesteading, and Buddhism at Naropa University in Boulder, Colorado. I was interested in cooking, of course, but I had just as much desire to learn how to bow-drill a fire, fix a roof, and farm or build on a small amount of land sustainably. I wanted to relearn how to live, relying on my own skill and creativity. Cooking was a means to an end—making money so that I could one day buy my own land. Over time I fell in love with all the complex and different ways food can be prepared, the subtlety of flavors and taste, and the enjoyment of sharing food as an act of love and friendship. In a way, my life has come full circle as I now work to create a life and group of businesses that are as sustainable and passion-driven as possible. Every day I strive to find ways to incorporate the ideas in this book into different aspects of my personal and professional life, as do like-minded people around the world. This life we work so hard on can be nothing less than a love affair, one that sheds light and inspiration on every moment, and on each other.

Even small efforts to cultivate and enjoy potted herbs or vegetables in one's apartment can evoke these deep feelings of connection and self-sufficiency. I encourage you to read about the many impressive homesteaders and permaculture experts who are currently breaking ground in this area; what follows is my best vision of what a more self-sufficient lifestyle could look like, whether you're off the grid in the boreal forests of the Yukon Territories, living in the suburbs, or making a home in a one-bedroom New York City apartment.

In no way am I suggesting that anything in this book is the exact way you should live, or cook—or do anything, for that matter! My goal is simply for you to use these ideas and possibilities to inspire your own inner vision.

Many people assume "living off the land" as requiring a large piece of land, maybe fifty to one hundred acres. This is probably because our current concept of a farm is set up to sell product via monocropping. In reality, most families can create an almost entirely sustainable food system on just a single acre of land, often producing even more food than they would ever need. I'll address this one-acre model, but let's start off by exploring what's possible on a five-acre parcel of land.

THE FIVE-ACRE FARM

It goes without saying that every piece of land is different, and it's a truism that one could make a lifetime study of a mere quarter of an acre. When buying or leasing land, the most important first step is identifying its ecosystems, history, and basic resources, such as water, wind, soil, and light. By taking the time to observe what is already living on the land, you can adapt the systems of production to coexist in a symbiotic relationship within nature. This saves energy and naturally produces more without depleting resources.

When it comes to the history of the parcel of land, researching and understanding what transformations have taken place can mean everything. A bit of research can identify the type and age of any woodlands, how the land had been stewarded in the past, and whether it's even feasible to grow on it at all without decades of regeneration or introducing prohibitively expensive amounts of topsoil.

It is probably most important to consider the land's natural resources and how it retains water. Is there a source of water? If not, what will it take to drill a well, and will that involve going through bedrock? What are its main sources of energy—for example, is there adequate sunlight? Maybe there's sufficient wind for turbines or possibly even moving water (such as a river or streams) that could be a source for hydroelectricity. Whether the plan is to create a completely self-sufficient home or one that is partially supported by nature, these steps are critical, as they are the foundation of the ecosystem.

When I was younger, I would hear people talking about alternative energy as if there was one solution and we had to pick a side. Now we know that the solution is more likely a combination of many systems, such as solar, hydro, wind, and even methane. All of those systems must be seamlessly worked into the way we design and build structures in order to capture, retain, and circulate energy. One of the most important parts of this evaluation process is talking to people. Simply asking neighbors what they have done or grown best on the land can save you from many seasons of mistakes and loss, and open the door to one of the most valuable tools we have as a community and society: skill sharing.

When designing a homestead, it's useful to map out a property in multiple sections. Start by asking yourself which parts of the farm will require your attention most frequently. Areas that will require daily work are often kept closest to home, whereas orchards, woodlands, and pastures will thrive on the outskirts, where they can be visited once or twice a week as needed. The beauty of having five or more acres is the possibility of keeping more animals and growing more kinds of feed, such as hay and grain. With just an acre or two dedicated to grain, hay, and tubers, a couple of cows can be well fed through most of the year, with enough left over to supply the home with flour and grain. Small homesteaders are often opposed to having cows, as a dairy cow requires hard work and must be milked twice a day. Personally, I think the benefit of having fresh milk, butter, and cheese is worth it, and can be a great luxury for any family.

To reiterate, there are infinite models and variations that can be used when planning a homestead. In this example, I have set up a home using different methods of sustainable construction. I have always been a huge fan of earthbag construction. This method was developed by the architect Nader Khalili and involves building igloo-like structures using recycled plastic or natural sandbags filled with earth, clay, different types of sand, and recycled material. To learn more, check out the Cal-Earth Institute, founded by Khalili, in Hesperia, California. The structures are inexpensive to build and specially designed with solar-retention systems, often as simple as a well-placed window. As with earthships—dwellings built fully or partially underground—the soil's natural insulation regulates and maintains temperature throughout the seasons with far less need for additional heaters or air conditioners.

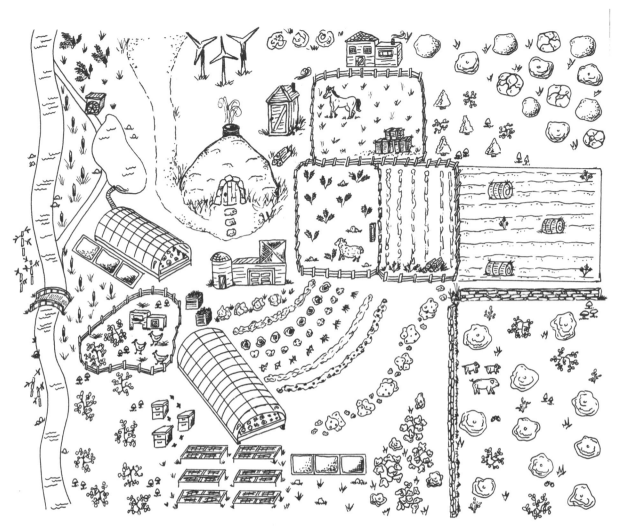

Example of the five-acre farm

As you can see from the illustration opposite, we have rotating pastures with movable fences for animals such as chickens, goats, pigs, and cows. Pigs can be used to till land and chickens to fertilize it. Mixed orchards can incorporate both low-brush edibles such as mushrooms and other vegetation that benefit from having a full or mixed canopy, and edible plants that tend to grow when trees are bare-branched, including wild leeks, violets, trout lilies, and garlic. I've also included a small stream and pond, which can be a home to ducks, crawfish, and small fish, but could also be utilized within an aquaponic greenhouse to grow in colder seasons. There are many ways to propagate berries; some people just plant in excess, expecting that a portion will be eaten by wild animals, but with little effort a structure can be made with a simple wood or bamboo frame covered in chicken wire. You might also consider building an apiary—a great asset for pollination that will also allow you to harvest your own honey. I have set aside an area for chickens, although many people will vouch for the importance of having a mobile chicken coop. Chickens are incredibly productive; in addition to supplying eggs, they can also provide fertilizer. They will also peck for insects on freshly tilled fields—soil turned over either by machine or by simply moving around pig pens. Depending on the grade of the land, the flow of water can be redirected and moisture retained by strategically planting black locust, bamboo, elderberry, autumn olive, sumac, hazelnut, sassafras, and other small trees. Varied woodlands and canopies of maples, birch, spruce, pine, and oak are excellent for syrups, grazing, and timber. This area can serve as perfect ground for fast-growing cover crops or to plant mycelium pads via plugs, root dipping, or spore-filled spray bottles to produce mushrooms. Mycelium can not only be an important source of food and medicine, but it can also promote an efficient and more biologically complex bedrock and soil system, thus improving the natural filtering and composting system in the land.

Around the home area, there are farm buildings for cows, milking, and a stable room, keeping dairy, slaughter, and charcuterie production close by. The root cellar and greenhouse are also nearby for better access in the colder months. I drew our land with a conveniently accessible river. This is not always the case, of course, and in most situations water retention and irrigation plans must begin by studying the natural watershed and determining the best system to slow down or speed up the flow of water throughout the property. At higher elevations, wind turbines can be placed in strategic locations, and in southern-facing areas, solar panels installed with adjustable angles.

The main garden is created using different groups of plants growing and working in unison with each other. There are infinite possibilities for this, but most combinations intersperse larger and smaller cover crops to help create microclimates and build healthier topsoil. Remember to provide multiple solutions for vertical growth—this could be as easy as providing a fence, wall, or living roof for support.

Composting is at the heart of any sustainable system, and the choice of composting system comes down to what it is you plan to compost. Human fecal waste (depending on the end use) can often just be handled in separate barrels that are flipped every few months and mixed with sawdust. Use of human waste requires special care and consideration to avoid the potential for transmission of disease, such as hepatitis. Food or plant-based compost can incorporate insect larvae and worms, which also provides another food source for poultry.

Dead limbs and other structural scraps can be used for mushroom farming or turned into biochar, which has received a tremendous amount of attention in the past decade. It's essentially the controlled burning of dried plant, bone, and wood material that is then sown back into the soil to return organic carbon and minerals. There is research suggesting the potential effectiveness of this practice, though consensus seems to be forming that it's most useful for sandy or degraded soil.

THE ONE-ACRE FARM

The same principles and ideas can also be applied quite easily to a more suburban environment. Of course, the smaller the acreage, the less of a holistic support system that can be created. These days, however, families and communities are figuring out more and more innovative ways to incorporate older homesteading traditions into their modern lives; community-supported agriculture has had a ripple effect. The same rules apply when choosing and working the land, from observing ecosystems to understanding all the natural resources inherent to the area. It is of utmost importance to map out how these resources can be most efficiently used before designing and building structures.

For a one-acre property, a greenhouse is key, and especially nice for kitchen plants, nurseries, and saplings. You can easily connect the greenhouse to an exterior fish or crawfish pond or even build small tanks integrated into the greenhouse itself to save room. Building a separate root cellar is optional, as the main house can often be modified to include one in the basement.

When landscaping a small property like this, be very conscious of how the grades and swales move water through the property, and how well it naturally drains or retains water. Sometimes, in a small neighborhood environment, much of the water drains quickly and directly onto the street. By thoughtful placement of a small pond, swales, or irrigation trenches, you can redirect the pattern of flow to capture its full potential.

In suburban regions that allow farm animals, experts will sometimes suggest a dairy cow, which can be productive but requires bringing in substantial amounts of outside feed. Pigs or goats can work well, but I like the idea of stick-

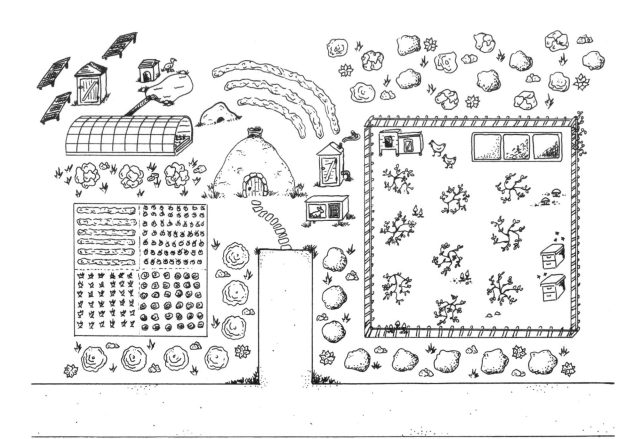

Example of the one-acre farm

ing to smaller animals, such as chickens, rabbits, and ducks. Another question to consider is whether to plant and rotate wheat and grains. This is certainly not always the most useful thing to do on a small piece of land, but it can be a good source of food for livestock and supply the household with the raw materials to make freshly baked breads. This portion of the land can also be used for root gardens, propagating wild edibles or medicinal plants, or simply as raised beds for planting. Even in this small plot of land, a family can grow an abundance of food and continue to produce more year after year. There's also the incalculable benefit of providing engaging activities and learning experiences for families to do together. While full sustainability is unlikely with smaller plots of land, the individual and family experience of designing and working a plot of land and enjoying the fruits of labor creates immeasurable spiritual benefit.

Urban homesteading and permaculture has become a growing practice internationally. For decades, neighborhoods have been slowly turning their alleyways, abandoned building sites, and rooftops into community gardens. These community gardens are useful in mitigating urban blight, but horticulturists will argue that the real focus of cities should be on better connecting them with the support systems of the local farms and food purveyors in their surrounding areas. Many community gardens were built with the primary goal of strengthening communities and the social fabric. The idea of actually producing real food from them was almost secondary. Today, however, we have many urban farms producing enough for CSA programs and even a handful that are able to produce enough to sell back to the community at large. As community gardeners become more familiar with permaculture techniques, these gardens will eventually require less regular upkeep and will be producing higher volumes, potentially enough to reduce the food costs of participating families. With new ideas and technology emerging seemingly weekly on subjects such as vertical aquaponics, solar and fuel cell technology, mycology cultivation, and more, the opportunities to incorporate these insights into urban gardens and urban engineering are almost limitless.

THE ONE-BEDROOM APARTMENT

You can apply the ideas behind many of these homesteading and heritage techniques even in a small one-bedroom apartment—and I say this as someone who lives in Manhattan and knows something about small apartments! With just a little planning, scheduling, and minimal investment, tiny spaces can be made efficient enough to reduce energy bills and allow us to eat better for significantly less money in the long run. Because it's unrealistic for anyone to think that city and urban sprawl will continue to do anything but grow, it has become increasingly important for us to take the time to explore and apply more of these ideas and concepts to apartment living. In fact, many educators believe that figuring out more sustainable systems of vertical communities is a major answer to sustainability at large. At the rate we're going, the amount of farmable land will decrease to below the needed amount to support our species unless we act to change our agricultural practices.

As in the previous examples, there are limitless approaches that can be taken, and each one is dependent on your apartment layout, free time, budget, and goals. In our model on the next page, there's a balcony, which can easily be transitioned into a mini-jungle of abundantly growing food and herbs. Even in the colder months, you can convert it to a kind of greenhouse by taping a single or double layer of commercial clear plastic film to the outside of the railings and diagonally up to the doorframe (nonpermanent/breathable enclosures are generally allowed, but check your local zoning laws). With the right light, you could grow plants year round. This method can also apply to windowsill planters and is no different from setting up cold boxes or light greenhouses in larger-scale models. Besides increasing the solar warmth, it also retains the heat and energy coming off the building itself and can help to insulate the apartment.

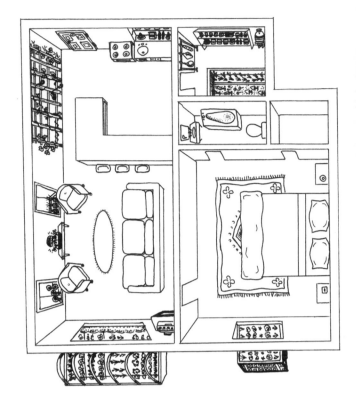

Example of the one-bedroom apartment

On your balcony or directly adjacent inside, you can also set up small aquarium aquaponic systems, though for smaller systems it's often easier to simply place growing trays on top of an average 30- to 200-gallon home aquarium. A small space is ideal for the use of vertical gardens. These can be hooked up hydroponically and aquaponically and can be a huge part of maximally utilizing the space available. A number of companies are now even offering all-inclusive vertical garden sets as complete units. I believe that incorporating plant-, mushroom-, and herb-growing stations will be a more integral part of kitchen design in the future. The idea of building small spaces with "living kitchens" is not so out of reach!

Energy, water, and waste might be some of the hardest areas to tackle for these small spaces. The most obvious and first recommendation must always be: reduce, reduce, reduce. The less waste we produce and the less energy and water we consume, the better for both our wallets and the environment. Small initial investments in sustainable energy systems include passive solar windows, reflecting light, outlet energy monitors, insulation, LED lighting, and energy-efficient appliances. Technology has evolved in recent years and continues to rapidly improve in these areas. Solar paneling (even solar glass windows!) and fuel cell technology are a few bright spots, and companies like Tesla are working to make these advances more and more accessible in configuration, ability, and cost for residential customers. Though some building managers might object to installation, I think small electronics could easily be run off windowsill solar panels at the very least. I also think it's worth exploring the application of single or multiple in-line turbines for spaces as minuscule as kitchen sinks and shower faucets, although there are potential downsides associated with this, like the risk of depleting water resources unnecessarily, especially for those tenants who are not monitoring (or paying) their own water bills.

Controlling climate and temperature is usually a common concern for an apartment or for any small space. Just as in the larger-scale spaces, where it's important to dedicate time to observing natural systems that are already in place, it is important to pay attention to the natural airflow and light in your apartment. A great way of cooling an apartment can be as simple as opening or closing a particular door and strategically placing a fan to amplify an already existing air flow to help circulate air more efficiently. The same can be said about light, and the importance of where we place reflective surfaces and mirrors in our household. Though these might all seem like commonsense things, architects and designers who focus on sustainability can turn them into true art forms. Almost every spiritual discipline in the world has its own philosophy on how to design a home, and often specifically a kitchen! There is a wealth of knowledge available about these concepts if we keep our eyes open to the possibilities. (Check Resources on page 299 for more information.)

Homesteading is a philosophy, a particular mindset. One of the ways I've chosen to illustrate this mindset here is by showing how more traditional homesteading techniques can be incorporated into everyday modern life. There are countless ways to do this and many different entry points. From making your own cleaning detergents, culturing leftover cream into butter, turning milk into cheeses and leftover greens into krauts, converting farmers' market leftover or damaged vegetables into pickles or preserves, and taking meat scraps and leftover grain to make boudin, to drying extra herbs, there are endless ideas to play around with and explore. I encourage you to be fearless. These methods can provide you with a true no-waste kitchen in which you apply the age-old practice of taking things with a perceived low value and transforming them into something great.

2

PRESERVATION TECHNIQUES

What follows are the basic techniques I use to preserve food throughout the year. These can be used whether you're attempting an off-the-grid homestead, urban homesteading, or working as a chef or just as a home cook. I've provided a few alternate methods and basic proportional recipes to get you started.

DRY-CURING AND BRINING

Dry-curing and brining are techniques that generally use salt, sometimes mixed with other ingredients, to change the molecular structure of everything from meats to vegetables and fruits. Brining is similar to a dry cure but is combined with and diluted by a liquid. Brining allows seasoning to flavor ingredients faster than a dry cure, but if done correctly, both create food that has more moisture, juiciness, and flavor. The salting process can be used to pull water out of the ingredients, making them less susceptible to harmful bacteria growth.

When it comes to curing, the most common mistakes are not curing things for the right amount of time, not using the right amount of salt, or not thoroughly covering or submerging the food. If you don't cure it long enough, then the cure won't have time to penetrate the entire protein. If you leave it in too long, the food will dry out, despite being in liquid.

The dry cure and brining amounts that follow are used in recipes throughout the book.

DRY CURE #1

I use this cure for meats, such as bacons, loins, and hams; sometimes for dense-fleshed fish, such as sturgeon or black cod; and for fruits (though without the sugar, if already sweet).

> 1 pound Morton kosher salt
> 7 ounces granulated sugar or 10 ounces pure dark maple sugar (about 1 cup)
> 2 ounces pink curing salt #1 (aka insta-cure #1)

DRY CURE #2

I use this dry cure for some fish and shellfish and when making gravlax. It's a great base to add seasonal herbs to.

> 1 pound Morton kosher salt
> 13 ounces dark brown sugar
> 1 tablespoon freshly ground black pepper

BRINE #1

Typically I like to use this brine for oily fish, such as bluefish, mackerel, shark, dogfish, and eel.

> 1 gallon water
> 1 cup Morton kosher salt
> ½ cup dark brown sugar or ⅔ cup pure dark maple syrup

BRINE #2

This is our standard brine at the restaurants for pork loin, ribs, and chicken.

> 1 gallon water
> 2 cups kosher salt

2 tablespoons pink curing salt #1 (aka insta-cure #1)

⅔ cup pure dark maple syrup

¼ cup fish sauce, store-bought or homemade (page 158)

6 bay leaves (store-bought, or try the lighter wild northern bayberry)

1 teaspoon juniper berries

3 garlic cloves, smashed

½ tablespoon black peppercorns

In our restaurants we use 55-gallon barrels to brine our pastrami and tongue.

Salt is fundamental for our bodies to function properly, and has molded life and society as we know it. It's crucial not to underestimate its importance when cooking. For most of the brining and curing recipes, I use plain Morton kosher salt; if you plan on using a different kosher salt, it is important to go by weight. In this book, a wider assortment of salts are used for finishing and seasoning, such as local sea salts and flavored salts. More and more we are also experimenting with replacing some of our salts with high-salinity ingredients, including wild kelps, dried shellfish, and common seashore plants, such as sea rocket and glasswort.

Pink curing salt is a mixture of salts. There are two main types: pink curing salt #1, which contains sodium nitrite, and pink curing salt #2, which contains both sodium nitrite and nitrate and is typically used in longer-aged, shelf-stable charcuterie. They're dyed pink so that people don't confuse them with table salt. You can purchase curing salts online or at any professional kitchen store. If you are worried about using nitrites even in limited quantities, you can find them naturally in celery juice or celery powder from specialty stores.

ALTERNATIVE CURING METHODS

Ashes, lye, and high-alkaline ingredients like pickling lime are also commonly used in curing foods all around the world, from nixtamalized masa in Mexico to lutefisk in Norway to hundred-year-old eggs in China. We use it commonly in our restaurant for fish, eggs, and even fruit, as these ingredients often have a chemical reaction with the natural pectin in fruit that can harden the outside, making it better for us to cook or smoke. It is one of the secrets to our whole smoked watermelon and cantaloupe burger at Ducks Eatery.

COLD-SMOKING

The difference between cold-smoking and hot-smoking is simple—cold-smoking implies smoking foods at a low temperature, below 100°F. I prefer cold-smoking at a very low temperature: For already cured and dried meats with a low-enough water activity level (see page 31), I usually smoke between 50° and 65°F. For fish, I like to keep it at about 38° to 50°F.

The cold-smoking process is mostly about imparting flavor. It's ideal for working with herbs, creams, dairy—anything you want to keep in a more pristine condition. By keeping the products at a colder temperature, we can safely smoke for longer periods of time, emulating traditional flavors that would come about only after smoking (or burying with embers) for several days or weeks. Common cold-smoked products are katsuobushi (bonito flakes), country hams and bacon, smoked cheeses, and lox.

The methods that follow are used in the recipes in this book.

COLD-SMOKING METHOD #1—ROASTING PANS

Use two hotel or roasting pans (12 x 20 x 4 [or 6] inches each) and one or two perforated half hotel pans, preferably with a rack small enough to fit inside. Place the rack in the half pan and lay out the product so the pieces aren't touching and air can circulate freely. Sit this half pan inside one of the full-size ones, so that its sides are sitting on the rails, keeping it raised off the bottom slightly. Presoak chunks of smoking wood or wood pellets in water 30 minutes ahead of time. Light the wood separately on a burner and blow out the flame so that the wood is smoldering, then place it in the large hotel pan on the open side opposite where the half pan with your ingredients are sitting. Now cover the whole thing with the second full hotel pan. If too much smoke is coming out the sides, you can always seal with plastic wrap or tinfoil. You can also choose to keep the temperature cooler by putting a third hotel pan with ice underneath; to regulate the temperature more evenly, you can buy aerated tubes (see Resources, page 299) for the wood pellets to help direct and control airflow.

Typical hotel or roasting pan with lid

Product placed on inserted perforated pans

COLD-SMOKING METHOD #2—REFRIGERATOR

Clear out a large single-door fridge or mini-fridge. I prefer refrigerators with a glass door so that you can monitor how the smoke is circulating. Drill a 3½-inch hole about two-thirds of the way up one of the non-door sides. (Before you drill the hole, look up the specs of your unit to make sure you're not accidentally drilling into any electrical or coolant systems.)

Use 3-inch piping to build a duct similar to one in an alcohol still (see the illustration). This allows the smoke to cool before it enters the fridge.

Every fridge is different when it comes to air velocity and the fan system. Too much air velocity will heat up the fridge and not enough will inhibit smoke

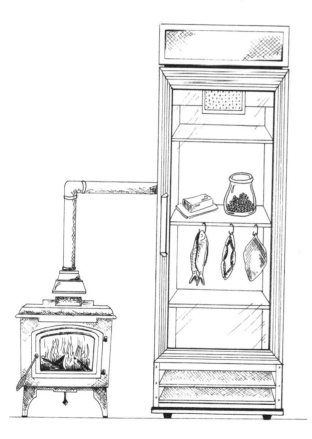

circulation. The smoke must be moving at a high velocity, so insert two in-line duct fans (often used for boats; sometimes these offer variable speed settings) into the piping system. Attach a 3- to 5-inch reducer duct to the end. Several inches below the reducer's duct opening you can place a wood-burning stove, a smoke generator, or a simple hot plate with a pot of barbecue wood 1 to 3 inches away from the duct. Drill a 2-inch hole into the top of the fridge on the right-hand side for exhaust and cover it with a duct or pipe rain cap, which will allow smoke to come out but prohibit liquid from coming in. Light the wood and proceed with the recipe.

Replacing the wood in the smoker with fresh wood often is better for imparting flavor. It's also important to keep the pipes clean in between uses, as resin will build up.

COLD-SMOKING METHOD #3—SMOKE SHACK

The best place to build a smoke shack is on a slight incline or small hill. Any size of building is fine; the illustration on page 27 shows a 4 x 4-foot shack. Build an exhaust with a rain cap, similar to the fridge setup in method #2, or

build perforated vents into the walls of the shack—this is actually best for cross-ventilation.

A 3- to 5-inch-wide pipe can be buried, connecting the shack to your smoke source at the base. For the smoke source, simply attach a reducer 1 to 3 inches away from a wood-burning stove on the opposite end of the pipe.

This shack can be converted into a hot smoker by building a small fire inside the structure or simply by moving the reducer closer to the stove.

HOT-SMOKING

There's a very loose definition of hot smoking out there. Most people are familiar with the terms "low and slow" or "barbecue" and have cooked things via indirect heat. In some parts of central Texas, it's not uncommon to find people smoking brisket up to temperatures of 350°F, and in North Carolina BBQ is done whole hogs directly over hot coals. I define hot-smoking as smoking products between 120° and 400°F over a natural, organic substance (such as corn husks, seaweeds, embers, and/or wood). The original purpose of hot-smoking was for preservation, but now it's primarily used to impart flavor and achieve texture.

Smoke adds depth and flavor to some of the most sought-after products in the world. To enable smoke to better adhere to a protein, you first have to build up the pellicle, a tacky coating that forms on the outside when proteins are allowed to air-dry; this allows the smoke to adhere and permeate the flesh, especially when smoking fish or seafood. The pellicle helps the item you are smoking maintain its structure and texture. When a product is wet, it is more difficult for the smoke to work its way through. The water molecules can create a layer that effectively seals off the food from the full potential of the process. I'd say that the majority of all hot-smoking should begin with a dry product.

I use a technique that involves cooking in multiple phases, varying temperature, time, and smoke. This process allows you to micromanage the flavor, salinity, and texture of the protein. Keeping the temperature on the low side allows the protein to develop flavor through the permeating smoke before cooking causes the fibers to tighten. It also allows the protein to rise in the temperature slowly, which is especially important for seafood. When you first begin to raise the temperature, you're working on developing the bark (caramelizing the exterior sugars). This is perhaps the best time to begin basting with fat or liquid. When you keep a medium temperature (before or after the initial smoke), you are focused on cooking the interior of the protein to its required level of doneness. When you're in the cool-down process, you're giving ample time for the juices to slow down and settle back into the protein, so that you end up with a juicy product.

Following are two different examples that show how we regulate temperature over time.

Brisket

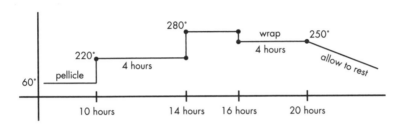

Rainbow Trout

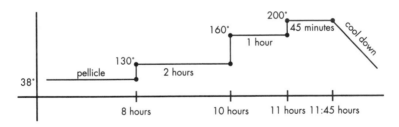

HOT-SMOKING METHOD #1—OVEN

You don't need to buy a hot smoker to try this at home. The simplest way to set up a hot smoker might be to place a steamer insert in a large pot and burn some presoaked wood chips (see page 31) on the bottom. However, in this makeshift system there is significantly less airflow and it's harder to control the temperature.

A much better way to hot smoke at home is to convert your oven into a smoker. The most important thing to remember is that you must maintain decent ventilation and take precautions to prevent a grease fire. Maintaining proper heat, airflow, and smoke is key. An inexpensive yet incredibly important tool to have on hand is a simple oven rack thermometer and wired internal temperature thermometer to keep the results as consistent as possible. Basic convection ovens will supply enough airflow to adequately circulate smoke. If you are working with a standard oven, it might require rotating your ingredients more frequently and being a bit more diligent in making sure your wood stays lit.

Place a shallow hotel pan or roasting pan on the bottom floor of a cold oven—this will be where your put your smoking wood. Place one more pan on the oven rack directly above it to catch grease or liquid before it falls on the wood. Light the wood you're using on a burner or with a torch until a good cherry ember starts glowing. If you're using wood chunks, start with two or three. If you prefer wood chips, add a small handful at a time. You can use a simple metal strainer to place them in over the burner. Blow out any flames so the wood just smolders. Toss these wood embers into the bottom pan and position the protein on the top empty rack. Set the dial to the desired heat and check an oven thermometer regularly, replacing wood as it turns to ash or stops smoking.

HOT-SMOKING METHOD #2—STORE-BOUGHT SMOKER

Store-bought smokers generally come in two different designs: vertical (a.k.a bullet smoker) and barrel. A vertical smoker's fire pit sits on the bottom of the unit and the chips are separated from the food by a water pan. The best ones are stainless steel or ceramic. A horizontal barrel smoker has a similar setup but with an offset firebox. I began on an inexpensive vertical smoker before moving to horizontal, which I think is an easier progression. You can buy a smoker for $90 or you can drop tens of thousands of dollars on it. (I've included a couple of my favorite smoker brands in Resources on page 299.)

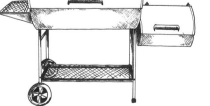

The main thing to keep in mind when shopping around is that you need a thick enough insulation (the best ones are double-walled, with two layers of metal) to keep a consistent, steady heat, which is especially crucial in colder times of the year. The smoker also needs to be large enough for what you want to cook, and with enough airflow, so that the protein isn't crowded. Do your homework, read reviews, and make sure you're buying one that isn't reported to have inconsistent temperatures in different areas. I learned on a smoker that was very poorly made, which forced me to constantly modify it in order to work. That first smoker taught me a lot about the importance of airflow. A crucial element to these types of smokers is learning how to feed your fire and keep a consistent temperature. It's pretty much trial and error, but the best way is to feed it small amounts of wood at a time. Keep it clean and oiled. If well-maintained, a good smoker can last generations.

HOT-SMOKING METHOD #3—CINDERBLOCK OR BRICK SMOKER

One of the ways I first started experimenting with different smoking techniques was when I built my first cinderblock smoker. These cinderblock setups have a long history in the American South, and are often used to smoke whole hogs in North Carolina as well as traditional pit BBQ in other parts of the South. Just as in the store-bought smokers—except for the "bullet"-style smokers outlined on the previous page—most of these smokers have an offset smoke box. The most old-school versions of these involve simply shoveling coal directly underneath a grill without using an offset; make sure you build the walls of the smoker high enough so that you don't end up grilling the protein. If you are using it to smoke whole animals, the idea is to place more coals under the parts of the animal that might take the longest to cook, such as hams and forequarters (over the quicker loins).

The cinderblock smoker can be permanently set into the ground, but one of the beauties of this system is that it's adjustable and you can make it larger or smaller depending on what you are cooking.

An average cinderblock smoker might be 4 feet long by 3 feet wide. Stack cinderblocks to about 3 feet high, then lay 3 or 4 pieces of rebar or steel horizontally over the blocks. This will provide support for the grate, which can be anything from heavy-gauge steel fencing to welded rebar. If you're using it to cook whole hogs, you can stop there and build a top, which can just be another layer of cinderblocks and plywood cut to the dimensions of the opening.

If you're cooking whole hogs, be sure to build the walls high enough so that you can rotate the pig without it touching the burning embers below. If you're cooking smaller items as well, it helps to increase the height of the walls with cinderblocks for a raised second grate. If using direct fire and coals, you should figure out a reliable method of circulating the coals so that they're sitting below the thickest, toughest cuts.

Bolder, harder woods, such as oak, maple, or hickory, pair well with hearty meats. Lighter, fruitier woods, such as apple and pecan, work well for fish and lighter foods. Everybody has their own opinion as to the best wood to work with, but my belief is that the best wood is whatever common smoking wood you find in your own backyard, staying away from sappy evergreens like pine or poplar or beech, which can often get bitter. At our restaurants, we use a lot of local oak, birch, or maple because the flavor is strong but not overpowering and provides a steady heat. You can also use wood chips or pellets or, as mentioned earlier, any other type of vegetable matter that burns slowly. I recommend using seasoned or kiln-dried wood. Green wood can be used if you're an advanced smoker, but you run the risk of imparting too much of the wrong type of smoke (bitterness is common).

HOT-SMOKING METHOD #4—OPEN FIRE

One of the first ways humans ever smoked proteins was by building an outdoor fire and spreading the proteins out on spits far enough away from direct heat to slowly cook. If you're trying this method, be aware that it's easy to accidentally cook the protein at too high of a temperature, so set your protein farther away from the flame than you initially think necessary and be prepared to dedicate much more attention to the process than for the previous techniques I discussed. It's also much harder to direct the smoke in an unenclosed space, but with enough nicely seasoned wood, this process can be effective. A whole hog smoking over a fire does make for a great photo and a fun party centerpiece.

DEHYDRATING

Life needs water to survive and thrive, and bacteria and pathogens are no different. Reducing the water level (or water activity, aW) is an age-old tool for food preservation. We're not sure when humans first began laying out food to dry, but we know it was very early on.

It may sound obvious, but anything that contains water can be dehydrated. Dehydrating removes moisture for preservation without radically altering the makeup of the foodstuff (whereas cooking is about breaking down and altering the structure for flavor, texture, and so on). The benefit of this technique is that

often when reducing the water level, we're also concentrating the flavor. There are three easy ways to dehydrate any type of food.

DEHYDRATING METHOD #1—OVEN

You can easily do this at home if your oven has a low enough temperature setting. The ideal range is 100° to 165°F. But a simple way around this is to turn your oven to the lowest setting and stick a wooden spoon or some other object in the door to vent some of the heat. This is obviously not foolproof, and it can still be difficult to get that low temperature or regulate it in any consistent way. Lay out the ingredient either on a silicone or wax paper–lined baking sheet or directly on a metal rack. Place an oven thermometer in the oven and check it regularly.

DEHYDRATING METHOD #2—DEHYDRATOR

Personally, I'd recommend that you just buy a dehydrator. You can get a perfectly good one for $35 and they don't take up much room (for you apartment-dwellers). Even the entry-level commerical ones can be purchased for between $250 and $450. The store-bought dehydrators generally come with multiple racks and inserts for dehydrating juices. See Resources (page 299) for several of my favorite devices that require simply presetting a temperature and time.

DEHYDRATING METHOD #3—AIR-DRYING

To air-dry outdoors, you can repurpose a laundry rack or construct a rack with 2 x 4s and nail chicken wire to the top. You can also just hang your product by string or rope from tree branches that are high enough. It's important to be conscious of temperature shifts and humidity. In certain regions of the world, it's common practice to dry in the sun, but a cool shady place might have a more consistent temperature. Pick a spot with good airflow. Unfortunately, there's no foolproof way to keep the bugs away. In Thailand, they say that if the bugs aren't eating it, you shouldn't either.

FERMENTING AND QUICK-PICKLING

There's been an explosion of studies and claims in recent years touting the benefits of fermented foods and the common probiotics contained within them. The basic idea is that fermented foods (sourdough bread, for example) are making it easier for our bodies to digest certain foods. They introduce more enzymatic activity to our gut biome, long considered to be destroyed by industrialized foods and heavily overprescribed strong antibiotics.

Generally speaking, the difference between actively fermenting something and quick-pickling is simple. When we ferment food, we're allowing safe bacteria to feed and multiply while avoiding harmful pathogens, often creating a multitude of by-products, from acids and alcohols to carbon dioxide and more. When we are quick-pickling, we're simply souring food by immersing it in a liquid that is already acidic, either naturally or from being previously fermented itself. Both methods are forms of food preservation.

Often, I tend to only quick-pickle ingredients that are more delicate or are not easily fermented, such as herbs, flowers, and many fish. My experience with naturally fermenting some mushrooms, alliums, and seaweeds by themselves is that they often can become more "musty" than desired.

Sandor Ellix Katz, one of the leaders in the United States on lacto-fermentation, wrote, "Fermentation is everywhere, always." It existed before us (and will exist after us)—and yet the word alone seems to elicit fear in people. This is probably due to our overexposure to marketing for bland, industrialized "safe" food products, but that's another book. To me, fermentation is the basis for life. It is the process of bacteria and fungi, like yeasts and molds, constantly transforming everything around us all the time—in forest floors, oceans, in our gut, on our skin, and everywhere else in between. They're symbiotically working to connect the dots of life by eating the waste of one organism and transforming it into what's needed by another. In the food world, this process is responsible for bread, pickles, soy sauce, yogurts and cheeses, vinegars, champagne, beer, wine—the list goes on and on.

It is important to note that the same fermentation is also going on inside us. Our own biome is operating in the same way, billions of flora and gut bacteria working to predigest food for us, and more. It's no surprise that we are cousins of fungi as we operate very similarly, constantly working to convert the world around us. We breathe in oxygen and exhale the same carbon dioxide that yeast exhales to raise bread. Our muscles produce the same lactic acid that is found in our sauerkrauts, and our bodies produce no lack of methanes or other acids. We do it all. It can be suggested that microcosms of flora, from those inside us to the nature and earth around us—when healthy—are all just active symbiotic communities, constantly fermenting and constantly communicating.

Fermenting is an endlessly fascinating subject and one that many respected and knowledgeable people have written books about (see Resources on page 299 for a list of my favorites). Let me be clear—many of my methods have evolved through trial and error, and I am in no way posing as a microbiologist. I'll just give you the basics here to help you understand the recipes that follow and try to reduce some of the apprehension around the subject. As this is meant to be an introduction to fermentation, most of what we will be discussing is lacto-fermentation as it applies to food. I think this is not only the easiest way to get started, but is also a process that allows you to be hands-on and really see, feel, and taste its transformation almost daily.

I've always liked to visualize fermentation as little Pac-Mans eating sugars while expelling everything from lactic acid to carbon dioxide to alcohol. In order for this to work, the art of fermentation is really the challenge of keeping bad bacteria away while good bacteria flourish. The main tools we have at our disposal to manage fermentation are the control of salinity, acidity, humidity, ambient temperature, and time. Just like us, fermentation thrives in some favorable places and environments but struggles in others. Take for example a head of cabbage. If you leave it out for a month on your kitchen countertop, eventually it will degrade into a pool of sludge. If you chop it up, mix it with salt, and place it in a jar, in that same amount of time it'll turn into sauerkraut. The salt is not a fermenter but rather an inhibitor, creating an environment that promotes the right kind of bacteria growth and causes the harmful bacteria to slow down.

There are two types of fermentation: wild and inoculation. Wild fermentation is the cultivation of bacteria that exist naturally in the air and on the surface of products. The other employs laboratory-grown bacteria to inoculate, thus adding an identified "good" bacteria to a product.

The factors that you can control are: time, temperature, acidity, moisture, and salt. When you ferment, you're dropping the pH level and creating some kind of acid (acetic or lactic most commonly). If you're interested in fermenting on a regular basis at home, buy a pH tester. It will quickly become indispensable, especially with meats. Though I can't stress this enough: When fermenting, it is just as important to use common sense and learn to rely on smell and taste. If it smells or looks rancid, it probably is, so don't risk it. There are a lot of variables here, which is another reason why fermentation might be scary to some people. Just remember, harmful bacteria have a hard time growing under a certain pH level (acidity).

TO INHIBIT HARMFUL PATHOGEN GROWTH . . .	PH SHOULD BE LOWER THAN:
Salmonella	3.8
Cl. Botulinum	5.0
Staph aureus	4.2
Campylobacter	4.9
Listeria	4.4
E. coli	4.4
Shigella	4.0
Bacillus	4.3

A BASIC CHART OF MICROBES USED FOR FERMENTATION

Many of these are strains conditioned to better digest different starches and sugars, depending on their intended application, from fermenting grapes for wine or rice for saki to corn or kelp for ethanols, or even digesting some plastics. Many fungi and bacteria are also used symbiotically with each other to make common products like kefirs, coffee, kombuchas, and sour beers. Enzymes work as catalysts to every conversion and reaction, often acting as the threadwork to it all. Each microbe has its own preferences of salinity, temperature, oxygen, and overall environment that it thrives best in!

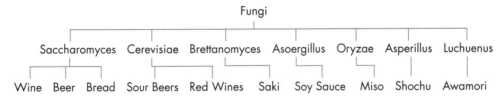

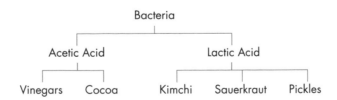

The majority of the fermentation we do at our restaurants involves creating pickles and vinegars. Sometimes the process can be as simple as mixing salt with a few handfuls of berries or flower buds in a jar. Creating a salt-and-water-based solution is generally a little easier if you're trying to keep a larger ingredient submerged. When figuring out how much salt to add to water, first make sure the ingredient is fully submerged and then taste for salt concentration. The solution should be slightly saltier than ocean water.

There's no exact formula to this, but a good rule of thumb is to use 2.5 to 3.5 percent of salt to an ingredient by weight (for example, roughly 2 ounces of salt for 5 pounds of cabbage). When brining, it's important to use just enough solution to submerge the ingredients, keeping in mind that the salt will pull water from the product. Constantly mixing and tasting the ingredients on a regular basis will allow you to make any needed adjustments along the way. It's not uncommon for us to add more salt a couple of days into the process as needed.

In all these things, I want to encourage you to be self-reliant. Fermenting involves guiding living cultures, and every ingredient we handle has its own set of intricacies and variables. When we're in the kitchen, we're not operating a 3-D printer that allows us to replicate anything exactly. We don't want every person to be exactly the same (that would be boring as hell), so why would we want our food to be?

Vinegars can be made from any vegetation with sugar in it, even wood. In fact, much of the industrial vinegar we use is made from wood sugar, the by-product of paper processing. When we make vinegar, we begin by adding yeast or a "mother" to a liquid so that we can turn that liquid into alcohol, and the alcohol into acetic acid. A "mother" for vinegar, or SCOBY for kombucha, is composed of cellulose and different types of yeasts and acetic bacteria. Kombucha mothers can convert directly from tea. Vinegar mothers convert from alcohol. In many cultures, it's a tradition to treasure mothers and pass them down from generation to generation. They typically improve and become more complex as they age.

A discussion of quick-pickling and infused vinegars might not formally belong in this fermentation section, but I'm putting it here anyway. Some people see it as a cheat, but even though we are not dealing with live bacteria, it is a type of pickling that is extremely useful for more delicate items, such as pickled mackerel or herring. This is the process for when you want to maintain the structural integrity of the ingredient. You're using a finished store-bought or homemade vinegar as a base for these.

White Quick Pickle Liquid

This is one of the more versatile pickling liquids and can be made when you need it or ahead of time. Often, I like to add wild herbs or flowers when in season and store in the cellar or refrigerator, just to have on hand. For example, I might prepare elderflower vinegar in early summer and store it for pickling herring in the winter.

Makes roughly 2 gallons

I gallon distilled white vinegar
I gallon water
I cup Morton kosher salt
½ cup sugar
½ cup honey

⅓ cup coriander seeds
⅓ cup mustard seeds
I tablespoon black peppercorns
⅓ cup juniper berries
3 shallots, sliced

In a pot, combine all the ingredients and place on high heat. Bring to a quick boil, then turn off and let cool.

Dirty Quick Pickle Liquid

I tend to use this style of pickle for hardier (in texture) produce, such as okra or parsnips.

Makes 1½ gallons

2 quarts water
½ cup Morton kosher salt
I quart distilled white vinegar
I quart rice vinegar
I quart apple cider vinegar
I cup sugar
I cup pure dark maple syrup
I tablespoon coriander seeds
I tablespoon mustard seeds
I teaspoon dried Thai chiles
I tablespoon sumac powder

8 shallots, sliced
10 garlic cloves, chopped
10 star anise pods
I tablespoon whole black
    peppercorns
I tablespoon juniper berries
I cup fish sauce or garum,
    store-bought or homemade
    (page 158)
½ cup soy sauce
2 bunches dill, rinsed and chopped

In a pot, combine all the ingredients and bring to a quick boil. Cool and store in a cool place or in the refrigerator. If you are using the liquid to pickle something small, it's often better to strain it before using.

PRESERVING WITH SUGARS, FATS, AND ALCOHOL

There are endless variations and examples of jams, jellies, and syrups. The preservation aspect works by lowering the water content (aW) in it and raising the sugar content (for instance, syrups have a greater water content and will go bad before a jam). When you pressure can or jar these products, like most things, it extends the lifespan even more. The most traditional fruit-to-sweetener ratio is equal weight

Typical 8-ounce jelly jar and sugar-coated preserved berries

of each. Bringing this mixture to a boil creates a syrup, and then cooking it down to reduce it creates a jam. (Jellies are made like jam, but solely with the strained juice and no fruit pulp.) The heat activates the naturally occurring pectin and causes the acid in the fruit to react with the sugar, which causes the mixture to thicken when cooled. Depending on the recipe, an additional thickening agent (pectin, gelatin, agar, and so on) or extra citric acid can be added to reach a desired consistency or pH. That being said, I've seen fantastic jams made traditionally by simply mashing strawberries and sugar together in a jar, covering it with cheesecloth, and allowing the mixture to sit for a few days. At Ducks Eatery, we regularly experiment with using smaller sugar amounts than the traditional 1:1 ratio.

Another common way of preserving is with fat and oils, which work to preserve by removing oxygen. The key to doing this right is to maintain very sanitary conditions; because you're creating an anaerobic environment, which then runs the risk of introducing the harmful bacteria *Cl. botulinum*, whose toxin causes botulism. What we've found to be most important (along with a clean environment) is that the ingredient be completely submerged in fat or oil and kept in a cool, dark place. This process is great for everything from medicinal oils to delicious foods like preserved anchovies and classic duck confits. Traditionally, the duck was salted, warmed, and then left to cool in its own fat, which allowed it to be stored throughout the winter. Seafood *conservas* and even simpler confited garlic in oil are also very common examples of this method.

Whether it's preserving venomous snakes in parts of Asia to make homemade Viagra or adding Peychaud's bitters to drinks to help digestion, you will find endless examples of cultures using alcohol to preserve ingredients for medicinal uses or for flavor.

Snake preserved in alcohol

Peychaud's bitters

Another great method of preservation is with alcohol. Common examples are bitters tinctures, which have become a staple in today's modern bar mixology culture and naturopathic medicine. There are innumerable medicinal uses for tinctures, and some speculate that they could have marked the beginning of modern medicine; bitters like Peychaud's were developed by early physicians and botanists as "cure-alls." In their simplest form, tinctures involve adding herbs, spices, or any organic material to alcohol for flavoring or medicinal value. These mixtures usually sit for a couple of weeks to up to several years. When we make them at our restaurants, we use a clear high-proof alcohol with a neutral taste, such as grain alcohol, and try to use dried or dehydrated ingredients with very low water content, such as dried herbs, roots, and seeds. The more surface area that is exposed to the alcohol and the longer you let it sit, the more potent or flavorful the tincture will be.

There are a multitude of techniques for filtering and concentrating flavors in tinctures. For medicinal tinctures, it's very important to refer to published works and recipes, as the simplest of herbs get magnified when added to alcohol and can result in harmful potency.

COLD STORAGE AND DRY-AGING

Whether we're talking about canning, jarring, fermenting, aging, or simply just storing for future use, it's important to keep these ingredients in cool, dark places. In a small apartment, this can be a small closet or a space under a stairwell. In a larger household, this could be a sectioned-off area in a basement. With more land, it could be a dugout root cellar in the side of a small hill. Building root cellars underground has always been preferable, for the same reason that we have historically stored wine in catacombs or built homes such as Earthships into hillsides: The earth is one of the best natural insulators, because it maintains a consistent temperature of 54° to 58°F.

The main factors to keep in mind when building a good root cellar are temperature, humidity, light, and airflow. The difficulty in setup is that different products often require slightly different conditions. A colder room (38° to 45°F) might do well to prolong the longevity of vegetables, but it may not be ideal for fermenting meats, which require a higher range of 55° to 60°F. Higher humidity (90 to 95 percent) can be better for delicate, leafy greens and root vegetables, but will be harmful to ingredients requiring a lower humidity level (such as dried meats, fish, or jarred products). An ideal middle ground would be 50° to 60°F and 70 to 75 percent humidity. Small to moderate airflow is important to avoid a buildup of gases. Light can promote spoilage, so ideally you want to store food in a darker space.

When we store such things as finished fermented sausages, meats, and fish, we're generally not continuing the fermentation process much further, and then they can be stored at cooler temperatures. The pH level has already been lowered and controlled. We're storing primarily to allow the foods to mature in flavor, to preserve them for future use, and to gently decrease their water activity level. A great way of aging meats at home is to repurpose a wine cooler by placing a small, inexpensive humidifier inside for added moisture as an aging chamber. Simply cleaning the interior with some white vinegar will sanitize any unwanted bacteria from the cooler. It's also important to make sure that hanging proteins are not directly touching one another and are clearly labeled with name, date, ingredients, and notes.

Most hard fruits and vegetables tend to store very well through the winter in root cellars. Place tubers and root vegetables closest to the floor and cover them with a light layer of soil or sand. The intention is to trick them into thinking that

The Latin base of *Cl. botulinum* is "botulus," which means "swelling" or "sausage." I find this fascinating because it implies that the Romans might have discovered this after screwing up their sausage.

they're still underground. Remember, they appear dormant but they are still alive. Even the tiniest pinhole in the wall in the farthest corner of your root cellar can cause the potatoes to make a root system and sprout leaves that move toward that light.

Stack cans and jars on the middle shelves of your cold storage. Canning, whether in tin cans or jars, preserves food by creating reduced-oxygen environments (often pressurized or heat-treated). Tinning and metal canning is a bit of a lost art. Most North American canneries are closing or have closed already, and the same thing is happening worldwide. Most of the brands that you see now have farmed out their processing, all to be done by just a few large conglomerates, which I find to be greatly saddening. Canned products have become demonized in this country, but many classic Spanish and Portuguese *conservas* have been developing remarkable flavors by aging in cans for years. Canning in glass containers has experienced a recent resurgence and tends to be more accessible to the home and restaurant cook.

BUILDING A ROOT CELLAR

METHOD #1—SIMPLE HOME CELLAR

Section off part of your basement with plastic sheeting, which you can find in rolls at any home improvement store. If you're in an apartment, the best method is to install a small air vent above the door of one of your closets and tape plastic sheeting to all of the interior walls, excluding the vent, to create a water barrier. This is most important if you plan on aging proteins or anything where you might want to create a more humid space. To make a more permanent—though slightly more costly—option, line the walls with PVC board. The closet should still have a functioning door. As mentioned earlier, you can also purchase and repurpose a wine cooler. In both scenarios, if working to create a more humid environment (for instance, for charcuterie—70 to 75 percent humidity), you can add a small plug-in humidifier for $20.

The French were the first to develop the process of modern canning in glass jars and bottles, but it was in pursuit of military (not culinary) glory. Recognizing the benefit of soldiers bringing their own food supplies on long campaigns, Napoleon offered a cash reward to inventors who were able to find a packable, shelf-stable method of preserving. Confectioner Nicolas Appert claimed the prize after developing the water-bath canning method that we still use today.

It wasn't until more than a decade later that a British inventor named Peter Durand began applying the process to tin cans. However, this would not be popularized for another forty years until a design was made in tandem with a can opener; cans previously required a hammer and chisel to unseal.

In an interesting sequel, the American P-38 can opener (which we sell at Harry & Ida's) became an essential tool in World War II. Developed in 1942, the P-38 is a compact can opener that was issued in the canned field rations of the United States Armed Forces. Historians suggest that the simplicity of its design and the widespread use of canned foods was one of the factors that enabled us to win the war, allowing our military to remain out in the field for an extended period of time without having to restock rations.

P-38 can opener

METHOD #2—OUTDOOR ROOT CELLAR

Dig a small room-size hole, roughly 6 x 8 x 8 feet, into the side of a hill. Then either frame it out with cinderblocks or wood. Run a pipe up to the surface for exhaust. Cover the end of the pipe with a rain cap to prevent water and other obstructions from entering. Build an insulated door to the cellar and cover the roof back up with earth. Alternatively, I've seen people build outdoor root cellars as simply as burying a large cooler (see illustration opposite) or used refrigerators in the ground, or even larger vessels like old buses, shipping containers, and vans. There is plenty of room for creativity. Make sure the walls are built with a water barrier, such as plastic sheeting. Finish by hanging hooks from the ceiling for your proteins and building shelves for your jars and vegetables.

3

THE PANTRY

Nature is not a place to visit. It is home.

—GARY SNYDER

For a seasoned cook, a good working pantry is an indispensable tool. "Pantry" in this book is defined as a home store of preserved wild and farmed produce such as fruits, berries, herbs, spices, and mushrooms. Of course, it is always a treat to use fresh produce whenever possible, but the following pantry items can add depth and diversity to meals (especially in colder months). All the recipes in this chapter produce shelf-stable products.

FORAGING

Like any skill, foraging for wild edibles is not something that's learned overnight. It is a lifetime study. I've been studying and eating wild edibles for more than a decade now, and I'm still a novice and always will be. *I cannot stress enough* the importance of making sure that anything you are even considering eating is identified and cross-referenced with professional foraging and mycology books or with experts themselves. There are mycology groups and meet-ups all over the country, as well as endless online groups to help guide you along your way. It is important to know that when you are eating something in the wild you are risking your life. With that being said, I might feel the same about a few fast-food salad bars I know of.

Harvesting algae at about age thirteen

Every year I forage in nearby woodlands, meadows, coastal areas, and marshes, and with each trip, I learn something new. I discover where particular mushrooms or wild plants prefer to grow, what type of weather condition or soil temperature they most thrive in, and how to identify them throughout the seasons when easily identifiable leaves might have already fallen, and I understand just a bit more about the infinite ecosystems they are a part of. The main responsibility of the forager is to practice foraging respectfully and sustainably. This means taking only what you need, making sure the plant or fungus can continue to thrive, and not damaging the surrounding ecosystem. The more we understand the symbiotic relationship between a plant and its ecosystem, the more we can understand how to protect it. The other main responsibility of the forager is—let me reiterate—not to die. So be mindful of the risks and eat only what you are certain of.

It is helpful to always keep a journal logging what you have found and where, and now, in the days of smartphones, more often than not I geotag every specific location to digital maps.

What follows is a list of the foraged ingredients that are good to begin with in the Northeast and which I commonly use in my recipes. I am not a professional botanist or mycologist; rather I am a passionate chef and hobbyist. *When you're out in the field, it's important to cross-reference with published scientific field guides (see Resources on page 299).*

"There are bold mushroom pickers, and there are old mushroom pickers . . . but there are no old, bold mushroom pickers."

The study of mycology can easily be a lifelong pursuit all in itself. The fungi kingdom is made up of more than five million species, from the shiitakes sprouting out of a log to the green fuzzy stuff growing on our old bread. It is floating in the air. It is in us and what we eat and drink, throughout the ground, ocean . . . it is everywhere, connecting everything. An estimated 30 percent of all healthy soil on earth is made up of fungal matter. A massive network of mycelium threads under the ground connect fauna, send and receive energy, decompose and nurture life—all helping to sustain our planet.

I firmly believe mushrooms have the potential to solve significant environmental problems on a larger scale. From aiding in cancer cures to cleaning oil spills, mushrooms have proven time and again to have significant beneficial applications. The fascinating field of applied mycology, with so many constant new species and discoveries is just in its infancy.

Many experts believe that mushrooms have also helped shape society as we know it, not just inspiring many *Alice in Wonderland*–like fairy tales or video games like Super Mario but potentially even Santa Claus and the story of Christmas. Even in the field of psychology, mushrooms are showing great potential. Outside of being used all over the world for their spiritual use, there have been incredible recent studies showing that small amounts of psilocybin, a mushroom compound, have been effective in long-term treatment of recurring mental health issues like depression. More than ever, people are now taking small doses daily to improve their creativity, productivity, and overall well-being.

Mushrooms are the largest organisms in the world (honey mushroom networks have been found upward of 2.4 miles wide). However, most of what's visible, and what we identify as mushroom, is the fruiting of a much more expansive mycelium pad under the ground. It's important when picking mushrooms to cut them at the base of the stalk, leaving the root so that the mycelium can live to fruit another day. If you accidentally cut too deeply or end up pulling the entire system out of the ground, simply put the base back where you found it and the mycelium network will potentially recover. Collect your harvest in baskets or paper bags with proper ventilation.

In all matters relating to mushrooms and mycology, please refer to universally standard texts to learn the specifics of what to look for and how to differentiate between safely edible and harmful fungi. When done safely and responsibly, mushroom picking can be an incredibly enjoyable activity.

What follows are some good basic mushrooms, with the least harmful lookalikes, to begin with.

WOODLANDS AND MEADOWS

COMMON NAME: Hen of the woods, maitake (illustration opposite)

LATIN NAME: *Grifola frondosa*

DESCRIPTION: Grayish brown caps in large clusters with a white branch-like stalk. Found at the base of trees (usually oak) and on stumps. Note the spot where you harvest it, because it will likely return to the same area. Can weigh up to a hundred pounds!

SEASON: September–November

USE: Choice edible. Flavor can vary from rich and nutty to almost citrus-like. Holds up well to smoking, roasting, and pickling.

COMMON NAME: Black morel (illustration opposite)

LATIN NAME: *Morchella elata*

DESCRIPTION: Black-ribbed, honeycombed cap on whitish hollow stalk. Often found on the ground in sandy soil in mixed coniferous woods, near cottonwoods, elms, and poplars.

SEASON: April–May

USE: Choice edible, with caution. The black morel is excellent in sautés or braises, but it may cause stomach upset, especially if eaten while drinking alcohol. Don't eat more than a handful in one sitting to avoid irritation.

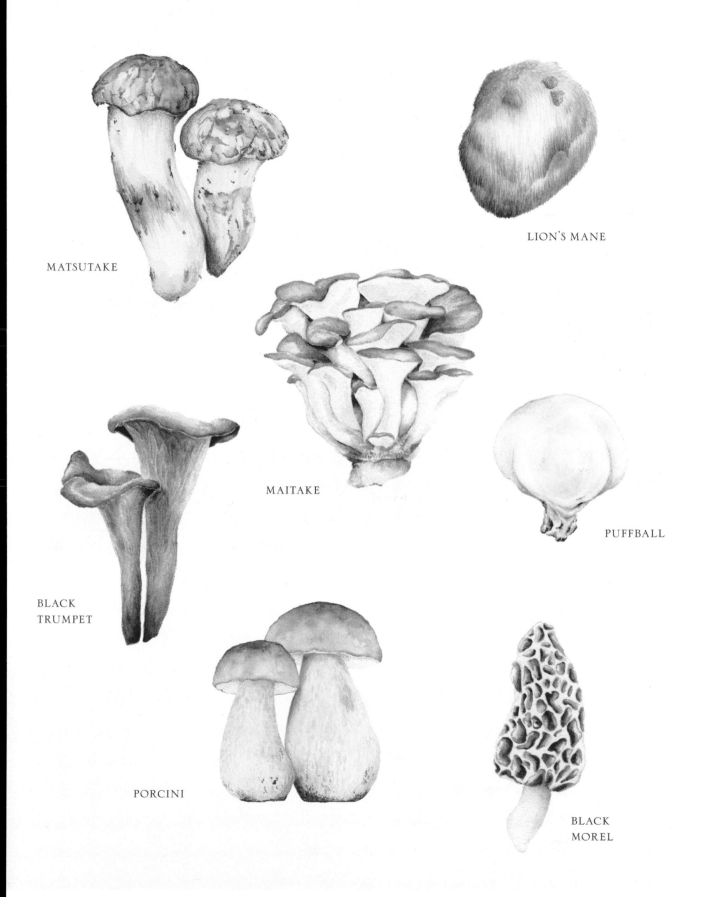

MATSUTAKE

LION'S MANE

MAITAKE

BLACK
TRUMPET

PUFFBALL

PORCINI

BLACK
MOREL

COMMON NAME: Puffball, skull-shaped (immature), and giant (illustration on page 49)

LATIN NAME: *Calvatia gigantea*

DESCRIPTION: Pure white ball, like a smooth golf ball, 8 to 20 inches wide. Most commonly found in parks and pastures in urban or rural areas.

SEASON: Late May to mid-July; August–October

USE: Choice edible when immature. Cut it open to reveal a solid white interior, which means it's good to eat. Excellent grilled, fried, or baked.

COMMON NAME: Black trumpet, horn of plenty, black chanterelle (illustration on page 49)

LATIN NAME: *Craterellus fallax*

DESCRIPTION: Black or dark gray funnels that run into the stalk, with an overall smooth exterior. This mushroom is so fragrant that it's often smelled before spotted. Sniff for it around oak and beech trees. Loves mossy well-drained areas.

SEASON: July–November

USE: Choice edible, excellent in sautés, pickled, or fermented. Flavor improves with drying.

COMMON NAME: (White) matsutake, pine mushroom (illustration on page 49)

LATIN NAME: *Tricholoma murrillianum*

DESCRIPTION: Medium to large bright white mushroom with reddish-brown scales on cap, white gills, and a fat white stalk. Often found in coastal areas or in sandy soil under conifers. Note: Take extra care to identify this mushroom as opposed to its more dangerous lookalikes.

SEASON: August–November in Northeast

USE: Choice edible. Excellent raw, lightly warmed, or grilled but can be prepared in a variety of ways.

COMMON NAME: Porcini, cep, king bolete (illustration on page 49)

LATIN NAME: *Boletus edulis*

DESCRIPTION: Large reddish-brown cap with whitish pores underneath and a fat white or yellowish stalk. Often found on the ground under conifers or deciduous trees.

SEASON: June–October

USE: Choice edible with a very wide variety of culinary uses. This mushroom has many different habitats, colors, and shapes, but all types are delicious.

COMMON NAME: Lion's mane, bearded tooth, pom pom (illustration on page 49)

LATIN NAME: *Hericium erinaceus*

DESCRIPTION: White furry pom-pom-like clusters that tend to grow on hardwood trees or on the wounds of trees.

SEASON: August–November

USE: Choice edible and often used medicinally. Commonly fried by foragers, but we love to roast them whole.

COMMON NAME: Chanterelle, golden chanterelle (illustration on page 52)

LATIN NAME: *Cantharellus cibarius*

DESCRIPTION: Yellow or golden colored with a funnel shape. It has a smooth cap, thin gills, and a straight, smooth stalk. Found on the ground underneath oaks or conifers and commonly along walking paths.

SEASON: July–August in Northeast; June–September in Southeast; September–November in Northwest; November–February in California

USE: Choice edible, excellent in sautés, pickled, or poached. The chanterelle might be the most popular edible mushroom in the world, but beware of confusing it with toxic look-alikes, especially the poisonous Jack O'Lantern (*Omphalotus olearius*).

COMMON NAME: Reishi, ling chih (illustration on page 52)

LATIN NAME: *Ganoderma lucidum* or *Ganoderma curtisii*

DESCRIPTION: The color is rich and shiny with gradients of red, orange, yellow, and white. It grows horizontally attached to the base of living and dead trees.

SEASON: May–November

USE: Choice edible when young and tender; mostly medicinal; good for teas and soups.

Chinese texts have suggested medicinal uses for this mushroom for more than 2,000 years; in the Hanshu *Book of Han* (82 CE) it was called the "mushroom of immortality." Modern studies have shown that Reishi extract is anti-inflammatory, anticonvulsant, and immune-boosting, and may even promote overall brain health.

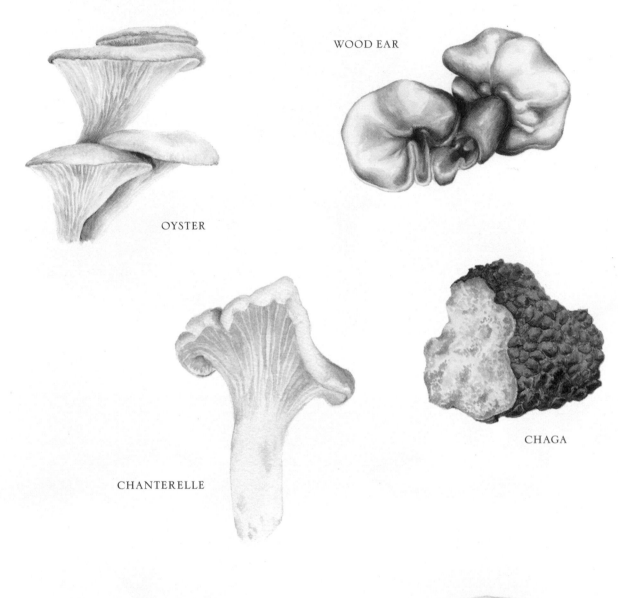

WOOD EAR

OYSTER

CHAGA

CHANTERELLE

REISHI

LOBSTER

COMMON NAME: Wood ear, tree ear, jelly ear (illustration opposite)

LATIN NAME: *Auricularia auricula-judae*

DESCRIPTION: A distinctive ear-shaped reddish-brown jelly mushroom with edges that flop. Overall rubbery texture. Grows attached to deciduous trees and shrubs.

SEASON: May–June; September–December

USE: Edible with mostly medicinal uses. The texture makes it better suited for soups or being dried and ground into powder. It may help to rid the blood of toxins and lower the risk of heart disease.

COMMON NAME: Oyster (illustration opposite)

LATIN NAME: *Pleurotus ostreatus*

DESCRIPTION: Though it can be white, gray, or brown, it always has a broad flat cap, white gills, and white flesh. One of the most common edible mushrooms in the world, it grows horizontally attached to living or dead deciduous trees or can even be found in buried stumps.

SEASON: Year-round

USE: Choice edible with a very wide variety of culinary uses, but especially good grilled and sautéed. A wild oyster mushroom is in a completely different world from anything farmed, and far more delicious.

COMMON NAME: Lobster (illustration opposite)

LATIN NAME: *Hypomyces lactifluorum*

DESCRIPTION: This amazing parasitic fungus grows on common cap mushrooms like Russulas or Lactarious and covers them with a bumpy, reddish orange growth or shell.

SEASON: July–October

USE: Choice edible, with caution. These fungi should be well cleaned and thoroughly cooked. If the host mushroom can't be identified underneath the lobster mushroom, don't eat it. Although there have not been known cases of sickness, there has always been a debated fear of the fungi having taken over a poisonous host.

COMMON NAME: Chaga, clinker polypore (illustration on page 52)

LATIN NAME: *Inonotus obliquus*

DESCRIPTION: Grows into a burned charcoal-like mass on the sides of living trees, preferring birch.

SEASON: Year-round

USE: Mostly medicinal; good for teas and soups. Chaga has been shown to have extremely high levels of antioxidants (beating out other "superfoods," such as açai or pomegranates). There's also evidence of strong immune-boosting and antiviral properties.

WILD EDIBLES

WOODLANDS AND MEADOWS

COMMON NAME: Common nettle, stinging nettle (illustration opposite)

LATIN NAME: *Urtica dioica*

DESCRIPTION: Soft, pointed green leaves on a tall, wiry green stem. Small clusters of numerous green or brown flowers. Often growing close to water. Both leaves and stems are covered in "stinging" hairs, so it's best to harvest with gloves.

SEASON: Spring–summer

USE: Similar flavor profile to spinach. High in protein, vitamins A and C, iron, potassium, and more. Excellent in pestos, soups, and teas. Blanch in hot water to remove stingers.

COMMON NAME: Japanese knotweed, fleeceflower, monkeyweed (illustration opposite)

LATIN NAME: *Fallopia japonica*

DESCRIPTION: Looking like a hardy asparagus with red flecks, this plant grows in groups and pokes up out of the ground. The stalks are jointed like bamboo, and tiny white flowers bloom in late summer.

SEASON: April–May (when shoots are tender)

USE: Excellent in soups, sauces, jams, compotes. It can even be sliced and lightly steamed (peel off the tough rind first). Packed with vitamins A and C, as well as resveratrol (the substance in red wine that is said to reduce the risk of heart attacks). It's also one of the world's worst invasive species, so harvest and eat as much as you like!

ACORN

SASSAFRAS

NETTLE

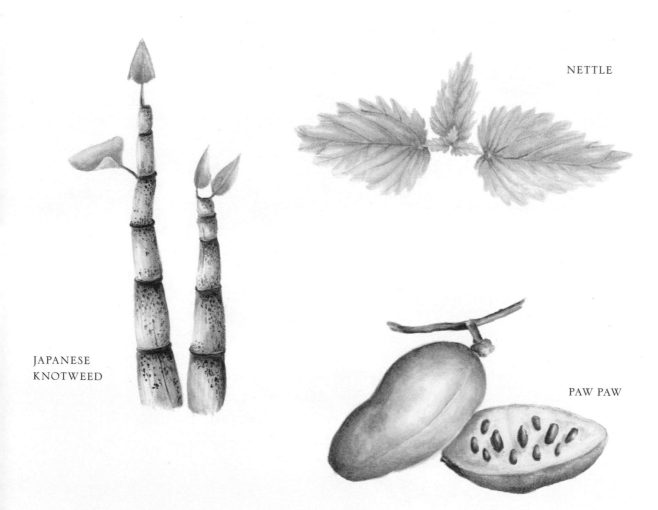

JAPANESE
KNOTWEED

PAW PAW

COMMON NAME: Sassafras, White Sassafras, Red Sassafras, Silky Sassafras (illustration on page 55)

LATIN NAME: *Sassafras albidum*

DESCRIPTION: Medium-size deciduous tree with slender branches. Young shoots are bright yellow-green. Three different kinds of leaves, but never more than three lobes on each leaf.

SEASON: Spring–summer for young trees, otherwise year-round

USE: The leaves, roots, bark, and distilled oil (safrole oil) can all be used for a variety of purposes. The leaves are ground to cure meats and make filé powder (the base of gumbo and Creole cuisine). The roots make root beer. The bark is often used to manufacture safrole oil, which is a natural insect deterrent as well as a necessary chemical compound needed to make MDMA (Ecstasy).

Sassafras albidum was commonly used medicinally by Native Americans in the southeastern United States prior to the European invasion. Some tribes treated lacerations by rubbing the leaves directly into a wound and used many other parts of the plant for medicinal purposes, such as treating acne, urinary tract issues, and high fevers. Sassafras wood was also a favored fire-starter because of the flammability of its natural oils.

COMMON NAME: Pawpaw, poor man's banana, ozark banana (illustration on page 55)

LATIN NAME: *Asimina triloba*

DESCRIPTION: Pawpaw trees grow in clusters of small, slender trunks. The fruits are smooth, large, elongated globes. The flesh looks like a pale, custardy mango.

SEASON: August–September

USE: Best served raw; also excellent in ice creams and smoothies. High in antioxidants and fatty acids.

Pawpaws are the largest edible fruit indigenous to the United States and are prized by bears, raccoons, and other animals. The tough inner bark was used by Native Americans and American settlers to make rope and fishing nets and for hanging game. Chilled pawpaw fruit was one of George Washington's favorite desserts. Lewis and Clark recorded that the fruit saved them from starvation. Mark Twain was also a fan.

COMMON NAME: Acorn, oak nut (illustration on page 55)

LATIN NAME: *Quercus velutina*

DESCRIPTION: Medium-size deciduous tree with large lobed leaves. The acorns are rounded and the cap covers almost half the nut.

SEASON: August–October

USE: After ridding the acorns of the bitter tannins (see following note), the ground flour or meal can be used like any other flour. In Korea, they make edible jellies and noodles from acorn flour. Acorns are also delicious (like any other nut) roasted and eaten whole.

Traditionally, tannins were often removed by storing the nuts in netting or a woven basket set in moving water, such as a river or stream, and tied to the shore or an overhanging branch overnight. An easy way to do this at home is simply to soak them in water for a few days, changing the water each night.

COMMON NAME: Black walnut (illustration on page 58)

LATIN NAME: *Juglans nigra*

DESCRIPTION: Large deciduous tree with a dark gray, furrowed trunk. The long, pointed leaves form in bunches around the fruit (initially green and fleshy, and then ripening into very hard brown nuts). The nuts ripen and fall in October or thereabouts.

SEASON: Year-round

USE: The robust flavor of the nuts make them highly desirable to chefs and bakers, though they are tough to crack. Use like any other hard nut, in baked goods, ice creams, or candies.

COMMON NAME: Black spruce (illustration on page 58)

LATIN NAME: *Picea mariana*

DESCRIPTION: Small, upright coniferous tree with grayish-brown bark.

SEASON: Year-round

USE: Start with the trees at lower elevations and with plenty of sun exposure. The edible parts are the young, bright green, tender tips that emerge from brown papery nubs. Spruce is an amazing source of vitamin C, and tea brewed from spruce tips can be used to treat illnesses, such as scurvy. They hold up well to preservation, but are excellent as a fresh garnish.

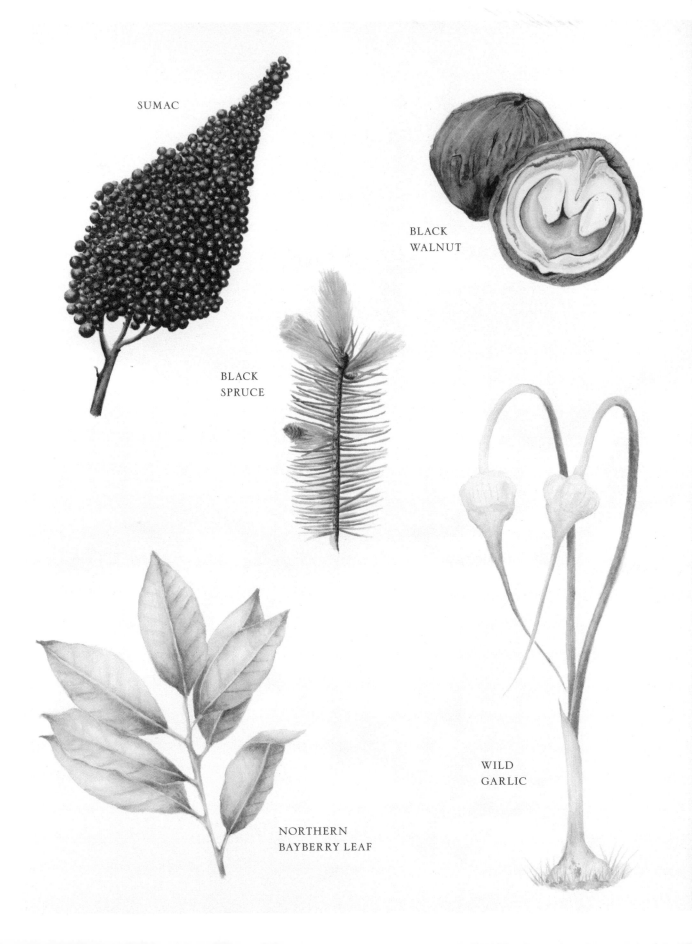

SUMAC

BLACK
WALNUT

BLACK
SPRUCE

WILD
GARLIC

NORTHERN
BAYBERRY LEAF

COMMON NAME: Sumac, staghorn sumac (illustration opposite)

LATIN NAME: *Rhus typhina*

DESCRIPTION: Deciduous shrub with velvety forked branches. The red fruit is clustered and cone-shaped, ripening in late summer. The pointy, serrated leaves are green in spring and summer and turn into brilliant reds, oranges, and yellows in fall. It is important that this plant not be confused with poison sumac. The poisonous species produces white berries, or none at all.

SEASON: Year-round

USE: An excellent source of vitamin C, sumac berries are commonly used to make tea and as a spice. I keep a steady supply of Sumac Syrup (page 96) on hand. Tart sumac berries have a high acetic acid content and consequently are traditionally an important ingredient for anyone living in a climate not conducive to growing citrus fruit. Ground leaves are a great seasoning. The young shoots are also edible, raw or cooked.

Sumac is a common ingredient in the Middle East and along the Silk Road trade route, as well as in many Native American culinary traditions. It is used around the world for its healing properties along with its antiaging, antifungal, antioxidant, anti-inflammatory, and antimicrobial nature.

COMMON NAME: Wild garlic, meadow garlic, wild onion (illustration opposite)

LATIN NAME: *Allium canadense*

DESCRIPTION: Edible bulb with narrow, grassy leaves. Clustered dome of pink or white flowers.

SEASON: Spring–summer

USE: All parts of the plant are edible raw or cooked. Use as you would any other aromatic. Excellent in salads or soups, as a seasoning, or pickled.

COMMON NAME: Northern bayberry leaf, northern bay leaf (illustration opposite)

LATIN NAME: *Myrica pensylvanica*

DESCRIPTION: Attractive deciduous shrub with long, waxy olive-green leaves and wrinkled blue-purple berries.

SEASON: Year-round

USE: The whole leaves are used as flavoring in syrups, sauces, and stews. The leaves can also be ground for marinades, and the berries can be made into candles.

COMMON NAME: Trout lily, yellow dogtooth violet (illustration opposite)

LATIN NAME: *Erythronium americanum*

DESCRIPTION: Small flowering plant with pointy, mottled leaves. The yellow
flowers have bright yellow stamens that bend down to the ground.

SEASON: Spring–early fall

USE: The leaves and flowers are edible and have medicinal properties. The bulb
is only edible in the fall. Slightly sweet when eaten raw, it's a good addition to
a salad. Don't eat in mass quantities, as it's a natural emetic.

COMMON NAME: Common blue violet, purple violet, meadow violet
(illustration opposite)

LATIN NAME: *Viola sororia*

DESCRIPTION: Attractive small plant with heart-shaped leaves and five-petaled
flowers with fine eyelash-like markings.

SEASON: Spring–early summer

USE: The flowers and leaves are edible and are excellent raw in salads, steamed,
or sautéed. The flowers also hold up well to pickling (see page 33).

COMMON NAME: Elderberry (illustration opposite)

LATIN NAME: *Sambucus canadensis*

DESCRIPTION: Medium to large deciduous shrub with drooping clusters of dark
purple berries.

SEASON: Year-round

USE: Both the flowers (in the summer) and berries (in the fall) are edible. The
berries can be made into wine or jelly or eaten whole. Avoid the leaves, stems,
and roots as they are toxic.

COMMON NAME: Black locust (illustration opposite)

LATIN NAME: *Robinia pseudoacacia*

DESCRIPTION: Medium-size deciduous tree with dark gray bark furrowed with
deep vertical lines. The white or purple clustered flowers come forth in May
or June and are very fragrant (like orange blossoms).

SEASON: Year-round

USE: This tree is actually part of the pea family (leguminous), so the flowers taste
like sweet peas. They are delicious raw, fried into fritters, or processed into
syrups and vinegars.

VIOLET

BLACK
LOCUST

REINDEER LICHEN

ELDERBERRY

TROUT LILY

WINTERGREEN

BLACK
BIRCH

COMMON NAME: Black birch, sweet birch, cherry birch, spice birch (illustration on page 61)

LATIN NAME: *Betula lenta*

DESCRIPTION: Medium-size deciduous tree with smooth, gray bark cut by horizontal lines. Scrape the twigs and if you smell wintergreen, you've found it.

SEASON: Year-round

USE: The bark and sap are edible and the trees can be tapped like maple trees. Excellent in teas, tinctures, syrups, and also fermented into beer. The inner bark can be cut into strips and cooked to create "birch noodles."

Birch bark contains the chemical methyl salicylate, commonly called wintergreen oil (though not related to the wintergreen plant itself). The oil was used as a flavoring in chewing gum and candy, though most of what we taste now is synthesized in a lab. Natural methyl salicylate is a powerful medicinal closely related to aspirin and can be toxic in larger amounts. It's been used for centuries; Native American tribes such as the Cherokee chewed the leaves to treat dysentery and drank birch tea to treat colds; the Delaware processed the bark as an emetic; and the Iroquois used it like Bengay for sore muscles. As always, please refer to a naturopath for more information and dosage.

COMMON NAME: Reindeer lichen, reindeer moss (illustration on page 61)

LATIN NAME: *Cladonia rangiferina*

DESCRIPTION: A light-colored green or grayish lichen that forms large branches and lives in rocky soil. Mostly found in cold, open woodlands.

SEASON: Fall–winter

USE: Like acorns and crab apples, lichen should probably not be eaten raw as it has a high tannin content. With proper processing, it can be an excellent and nutritious edible and make for a stunning garnish.

COMMON NAME: Wintergreen, eastern teaberry, boxberry (illustration on page 61)

LATIN NAME: *Gaultheria procumbens*

DESCRIPTION: Small evergreen shrub with red berries. The leaves are shiny and elliptical. The shrub should smell distinctly of wintergreen.

SEASON: Year-round

USE: Like the black birch, wintergreen is excellent in teas, tinctures, and syrups. It also has a long history of being used medicinally to treat a variety of ailments.

COMMON NAME: Dandelion (illustration on page 64)

LATIN NAME: *Taraxacum erythrospermum*

DESCRIPTION: A very common perennial plant with a yellow to red flower, straight green stalk, and strong taproots. When broken, the stems and leaves excrete a milky, sticky substance.

SEASON: Spring–summer

USE: Every part of the dandelion is edible! The leaves and stems are often blanched before being included in salads or stir-fries. The petals are plucked for teas and honey. The taproots can be treated like any other lighter root vegetable.

COMMON NAME: Ramp, spring onion (illustration on page 64)

LATIN NAME: *Allium tricoccum*

DESCRIPTION: A bulbous species of wild onion with broad, smooth, light green leaves, often with a deep purple tint on the lower stem and a scallion-like stalk.

SEASON: Early spring

USE: The bulb, stalk, and leaves are all edible and can be cooked like any other allium. Ramps are considered quite a delicacy because of their subtly sweet onion flavor.

COMMON NAME: Rose hip (illustration on page 64)

LATIN NAME: *Rosa rugosa*

DESCRIPTION: Rose hips are the fruit of rose plants and take on the color of the flower (usually red or orange). They begin to form on rosebushes in early summer and ripen through early fall.

SEASON: Late summer–early fall

USE: Rose hips are slightly sweet and aromatic, like hibiscus. They are excellent in teas, jams, and syrups, and can even be eaten raw (avoid the itchy hairs inside, which can be removed by slicing in half and cutting out).

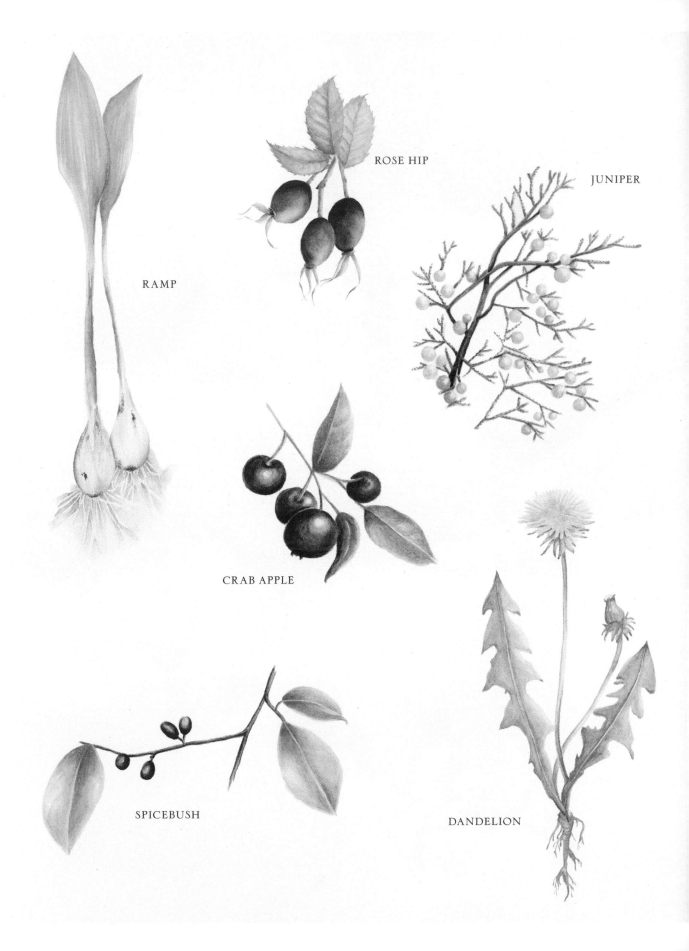

RAMP

ROSE HIP

JUNIPER

CRAB APPLE

SPICEBUSH

DANDELION

COMMON NAME: Crab apple (illustration opposite)

LATIN NAME: *Malus coronaria*

DESCRIPTION: Small bushy tree with reddish-brown, scaly bark. In spring, the pink flowers are extremely fragrant, and the globular fruit ripens in late October.

SEASON: Year-round

USE: Crab apples are high in tannins and so require some processing before eating. Once leeched of most of their tannins, they are lightly sweet or woody and pair excellently with cream or butter.

COMMON NAME: Spicebush (illustration opposite)

LATIN NAME: *Lindera benzoin*

DESCRIPTION: Small deciduous tree with simple oval leaves—very fragrant when crushed. Yellow clusters of flowers appear in the spring with bright red berries.

SEASON: Year-round

USE: Many parts of a spicebush plant can be used. Some people harvest the leaves for tea in the spring to mid-fall. In mid- to late fall, when apples begin to ripen on apple trees, the spicebush berries make their appearance. Spicebush berries are similar to allspice in flavor. These berries can be brewed, pressed, or processed in different ways to treat the common cold. In the fall, pick both the berries and the leaves.

COMMON NAME: Juniper (illustration opposite)

LATIN NAME: *Juniperus communis*

DESCRIPTION: A small coniferous evergreen shrub, with needle-like green leaves. The seeds are berry-like, starting off green and then ripening to a purple-black with a blue waxy coating.

SEASON: Fall–winter

USE: The branches are useful seasoning agents and basting tools when cooking outdoors. Juniper berries have very wide seasoning applications and are commonly ground for flavoring meats, brines, and sauces.

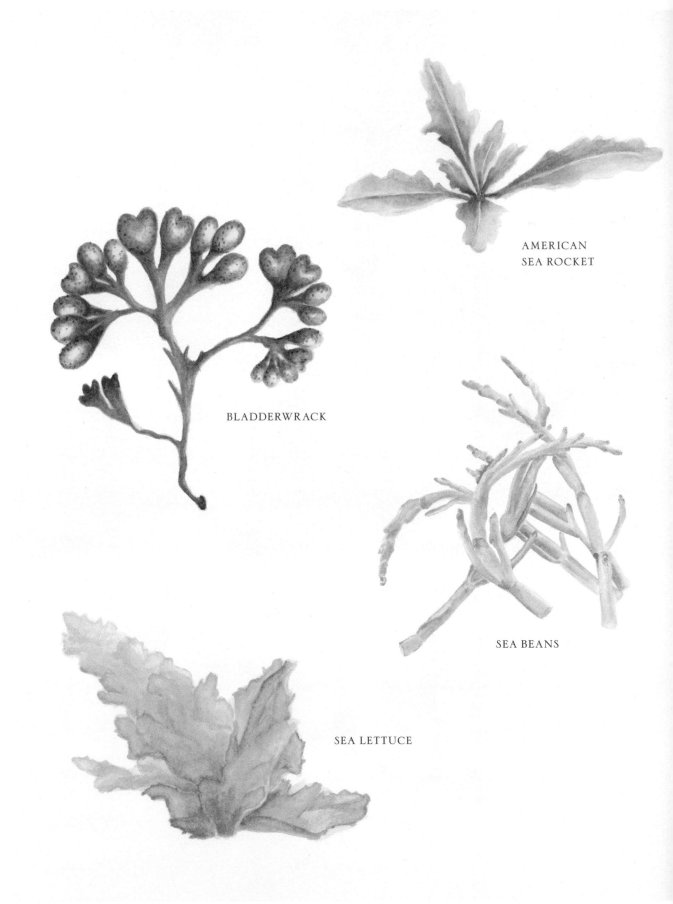

AMERICAN
SEA ROCKET

BLADDERWRACK

SEA BEANS

SEA LETTUCE

COASTAL AND MARSHES

COMMON NAME: American sea rocket (illustration opposite)
LATIN NAME: *Cakile edentula*
DESCRIPTION: Grows like a squat shrub on beaches and shorelines. The green succulent leaves grow alternately on the stem. It produces small colored flowers and fruit in the early summer.
SEASON: Early spring
USE: Similar flavor profile to arugula. The leaves plump after rain and are excellent in salads, sauces, or as garnish.

COMMON NAME: Sea beans, glasswort, samphire (illustration opposite)
LATIN NAME: *Salicornia europaea*
DESCRIPTION: Small succulent bushes with scaly, jointed green leaves. Found in salty marshes or beaches.
SEASON: Spring–summer
USE: A common edible in Europe, it's often cooked like asparagus but can be eaten raw. Its preferred habitat makes it naturally salty, so it's a perfect accompaniment for seafood dishes.

COMMON NAME: Sea lettuce (illustration opposite)
LATIN NAME: *Ulva lactuca*
DESCRIPTION: This thin, flat seaweed has ruffled edges and grows in bunches. It's pale green when young, but gradually turns dark green. It grows mainly in shallow salt water and attaches itself to rocks, shells, and other seaweeds.
SEASON: Year-round
USE: A rich natural source of iron, calcium, and vitamin B_{12}. This antioxidant superfood can be eaten raw in salads but is also excellent in soups, sides, and dehydrated. It tastes very much of the sea.

COMMON NAME: Bladderwrack, popper, sea oak (illustration on page 66)

LATIN NAME: *Fucus vesiculosus*

DESCRIPTION: This brownish seaweed has thick rope-like fronds with bulbous air bladders.

SEASON: Year-round

USE: Excellent for flavoring; can be added to broths or marinades. Perfect for traditional clambakes! The fronds can also be ground for spice, and the bladders removed and sautéed.

Bladderwrack was the original source of iodine and thus has been used to treat a range of medical conditions (most notably goiter and syphilis). Iodine is essential for life and is needed in humans (and other animals) for proper hormone production and regulation. When toasted lightly on a dry sauté pan, it can take on notes of chocolate.

COMMON NAME: Dulse, red dulse, dillisk (illustration opposite)

LATIN NAME: *Palmaria palmata*

DESCRIPTION: This reddish-purple seaweed is flat and leathery, with long single fronds.

SEASON: June–September

USE: Fresh dulse can be eaten directly after sun-drying. It can be ground into flakes or powder, finely diced, or fried into chips. Many use it as a flavor enhancer, much like MSG.

COMMON NAME: Wakame, sea mustard (illustration opposite)

LATIN NAME: *Undaria pinnatifida*

DESCRIPTION: Long, single green fronds with wide, flat leaves and deeply ruffled edges.

SEASON: Year-round

USE: Wakame has a subtly sweet flavor and silky texture. It's excellent in soups (you've probably eaten it in miso soup), salads, or lightly tossed with dressing. It's one of the world's most pervasive invasive species, so harvest and eat as much as you like!

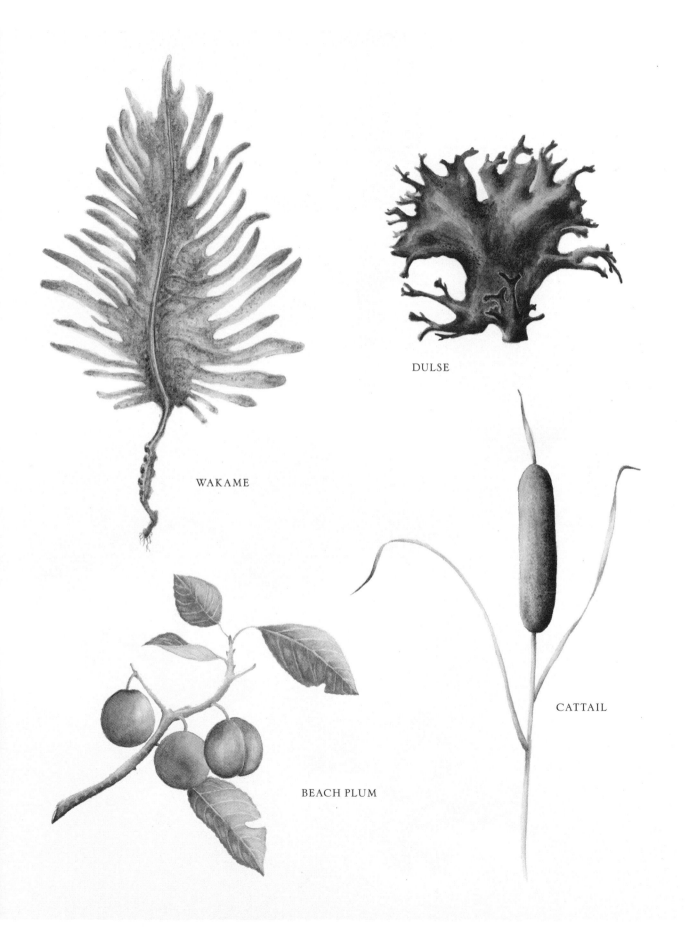

WAKAME

DULSE

BEACH PLUM

CATTAIL

COMMON NAME: Beach plum (illustration on page 69)

LATIN NAME: *Prunus maritima*

DESCRIPTION: A small to medium-size deciduous shrub that grows in sand dunes. It has elliptical green leaves and white flowers with round plum-like fruits.

SEASON: August–September

USE: Excellent in jams, jellies, or syrups. The fruit can be eaten when picked, but are usually only big enough for a couple bites.

COMMON NAME: Cattail, bulrush (illustration on page 69)

LATIN NAME: *Typha latifolia*

DESCRIPTION: Easily identified by the narrow sausage-shaped spike at the top of the stem and the grass-like leaves. Found in or near water, it generally prefers shallow freshwater (or brackish) marshes.

SEASON: Spring–fall

USE: Cattail roots can be dried and processed into flour. The younger plants also make good eating when peeled and boiled. Do not harvest cattails in polluted areas, as they suck up toxic substances from the water.

PANTRY RECIPES

SALT-CURED

Salt-curing is the traditional process to preserve ingredients such as capers, olives, and many citrus fruits. It's now become common practice to apply this same process of curing unripe berries or unopened buds to a wide variety of other more local plants. Within these recipes, there is both a combination of lacto-fermentation and the natural breakdown of fibers from the salt.

Capered Elderberries

Once pickled, pair these berries with smoked trout or turn them into a light caper sauce. This method of "capering" can be adapted to almost any other unripe berry, some fruits, buds, kelp stipes, or seed pods from plants like nasturtiums or milkweed.

Makes about 2 pounds

2 pounds unripe green elderberries
1½ cups kosher salt

3 cups White Quick Pickle Liquid
(page 38)

1. Clean the berries thoroughly and cover them on a tray or in a wide crock with the salt. (Alternatively, for a wet brine, add 3 cups water.) Let cure for 3 weeks in a refrigerator or 2 weeks in a cool root cellar. (If using this technique for fruits or tender pods, it may need only 1 week, depending how soft and sour you prefer it.)

2. Rinse the berries well (drain first if brined) and let them dry. Pour the white quick pickle liquid into a pot and bring it to a boil. Let it cool, then strain over the elderberries. Place in a sanitized jar and let sit refrigerated or in a cool place for a few days before using. The capered berries will keep refrigerated from 6 months to multiple years.

Brined Lemon

At the restaurants we preserve lemons in two main ways: brining with salt and drying (see Note). To use brined lemons, remove the pulp and set aside, cut off and discard the pith, and thinly slice the rind. We use the pulp and brine itself to add salinity and acidity to sauces, roasts, and stocks. Thinly slice or finely chop the rind to add brightness to preserved mussels, other seafood *conserva* dishes, or pretty much anything else you can imagine.

Makes 24 lemon wedges

6 ripe lemons (regular or Meyer)

½ cup kosher salt

4 green cardamom pods

1 vanilla bean, split lengthwise

1 teaspoon black peppercorns

2 northern bayberry leaves

1. Cut the lemons lengthwise into four wedges. Fill a sterilized 32-ounce glass jar with 2 tablespoons of the kosher salt. Place 6 wedges of lemon in the jar and pour 2 tablespoons salt on top. Repeat with the rest of the lemon wedges, 6 at a time, and more salt. Top with the cardamom pods, vanilla bean, peppercorns, and bayberry leaves. Lightly mix and gently press the lemons with the back of a spoon. Add water until the lemons are submerged and the jar is full. Close the jar and shake well.

2. Refrigerate the jar for 3 weeks, flipping the jar over every couple of days to rearrange the contents. As long as the lemons are submerged, they will keep for up to 1 year, but will continue to get softer.

Note: To dry whole lemons or any other citrus fruit, place them in a dehydrator set to 110° to 130°F and let them slowly air-dry until they shrink to about one-third their original size and feel completely dry. This can take anywhere from 10 to 14 hours They're delicious shaved or simmered into soups, stocks, or sauces.

Chive Salt

A perfect finishing salt for salads, roasted fish, and pork. We use chives for flavor in this example, but this method can be applied to a wide array of other flavors.

Makes 3 cups

Handful of chives (or ramps, whole or just the tops)

½ cup water

2 cups kosher salt, plus more if needed

Put the chives or ramps in a blender with the water, then blend until liquefied. Add the salt and blend until consistent in color. The mixture should be bright green. Blend again and add more salt as needed until the texture is like wet sand. Spread the chive mixture on a silicone baking mat and dehydrate at about 115°F until it looks and feels like salt again. Break up any clumps and store in a dry place in a covered container, where it will keep indefinitely. (A perfect way to preserve chives that are on the verge of going bad.)

Dried Rose Hips

In this example, we are simply dehydrating the rose hips, relying on their natural salt and low water content to preserve them. Few dehydrated foods have to be more complicated than this.

Makes about ½ cup

2 pounds fresh rose hips

1. Clean the rose hips thoroughly and place them on a dehydrator rack.
2. Dehydrate at 110° to 125°F overnight. The time will depend on the uniformity of your dehydrator's airflow. Once dried, the rose hips can be further processed by pickling them (follow the recipe for Pickled Violets, page 76) or grinding them into a powder to use as a spice or for teas. Store in a jar in a cool place.

Pickled Elderberries

To pickle elderberries for Hen of the Woods with Elderberries (page 248), use ripe berries; if you use unripe berries you'll end up with a tarter, firmer product. This basic formula is also perfect for pickling early season green strawberries, green tomatoes, and other slightly under-ripened fruit.

Makes 1 pound

3 cups White Quick Pickle Liquid (page 38)

1 tablespoon honey

1 pound elderberries (ripe, or unripe if you prefer less sweet)

In a small saucepan, bring the white quick pickle liquid and honey to a brief boil. Place the berries in a large bowl. If using unripe berries, strain the liquid over them while still hot. If using ripe berries, let the pickle mixture cool first. The unripe berries will need to sit refrigerated in a jar for 1 week. The ripe berries can be used the next day.

Pickled Ramps

We love making pickled ramp cocktails in the restaurants, but pickled ramps can also be paired well with a wide variety of roasted vegetables, meats, and fish.

Makes 1 pound

1 pound ramps, cleaned and
   trimmed
Kosher salt

1½ quarts White Quick Pickle
   Liquid (page 38)

1. Prepare an ice bath. Fill a large saucepan with enough water to cover the ramps by 3 to 4 inches. Add a large pinch of salt and bring to a boil over high heat. Add the ramps and boil until just barely tender, about 1 minute. Drain and toss immediately into the ice bath until chilled. Lay the ramps out on paper towels to dry and let them come to room temperature.
2. Fill as many sanitized glass jars with ramps as you can comfortably fit and pour in the white quick pickle liquid to cover them completely. Seal tightly and keep in a cool, dry place or in cold storage. The ramps can be consumed anytime from the next day to the following year.

Pickled Violets

The process for pickled violets is very simple, and quantities haven't been included here because they'll depend entirely on how much you've foraged or feel like pickling at the time. The same concept can be applied to rose petals (see the Variation below) or other delicate dried buds, inner barks, berries, or fruit.

Violets (or any other ready-to-eat edible flower, such as rose petals or tiger lilies)

White Quick Pickle Liquid (page 38)

Submerge the flowers in enough white quick pickle liquid to cover them completely in a jar. They can be eaten after just a few hours, and then stored in a root cellar or refrigerator for 6 months to 1 year.

Pickled Rose Petals

Pick the flowers and clean them thoroughly. I prefer to remove the petals before I pickle them as it tends to be easier than doing so after. Submerge the petals in premade and cooled White Quick Pickle Liquid (page 38) in a jar and stir once to finish. These petals can be used after just a few hours, and then sealed in a jar and and stored in a root cellar or refrigerator almost indefinitely. I pair these with my preserved Steamer Clams with Rose Hip Brown Butter (page 218).

Pickled Chanterelles

I love mixing these with lightly roasted stone fruit for a beautiful, delicately flavored salad. I have also been known to consume them by the jarful on their own. These mushrooms store great blanched and preserved in one of our smoked oils.

Makes 2 pounds

2 pounds chanterelles

2 tablespoons kosher salt

3 tablespoons good-quality local honey

½ gallon White Quick Pickle Liquid (page 38)

1. Carefully clean the chanterelles by wiping them with a wet towel and picking out any needles or leaves.

2. Prepare an ice bath. Fill a large saucepan with enough water to cover the chanterelles by 3 to 4 inches. Add the salt and bring the water to a boil over high heat. When the water begins to boil, add the mushrooms and cook for about 2 minutes, until just tender. Drain the mushrooms and toss them immediately into the ice bath until chilled. Lay the mushrooms out on paper towels to dry and let them come to room temperature.

3. In a large bowl, whisk the honey into the pickle liquid, then gently add the chanterelles. Pour the contents into a sanitized jar big enough so that the mushrooms are constantly submerged. Seal tightly and keep in a cool, dry place or in cold storage. They can be enjoyed just a few hours after making and kept for months.

Pickled Green Tomatoes with Caramelized Shallots and Cinnamon

As long as people are growing tomatoes, there will always be extra early-season and late-season green tomatoes to pickle. There's no lack of things to do with leftover brine, especially if you like martinis or pickle backs.

Makes 3 pounds

8 shallots, peeled and julienned

1 tablespoon olive oil

2 quarts water

4½ ounces plus 2 tablespoons kosher salt

4 garlic cloves, peeled and smashed

3 cinnamon sticks

1 dried ancho chile

½ cup local honey

3 pounds small green tomatoes, rinsed clean

Leaves from 2 ounces fresh oregano

1. In a small sauté pan, combine the shallots and olive oil. Set the heat to medium and caramelize until dark brown, 10 to 12 minutes, stirring every 1 or 2 minutes. Set aside to cool.
2. In a large saucepan over medium-high heat, combine the water, the 4½ ounces of salt, the garlic, cinnamon sticks, chile, honey, and shallots. Bring to a simmer for 3 minutes, then set aside to cool to room temperature. Refrigerate until cold.
3. Place the tomatoes in a sanitized 5-gallon crock or bucket and pour the chilled shallots over them. Mix in the oregano leaves.
4. Set a plate over the tomatoes. Fill a 1 gallon zip-top bag with water and the remaining 2 tablespoons of salt and place it on top of the plate. This should weigh the tomatoes down enough to keep them covered in brine.
5. Cover the crock with cheesecloth and store it in a dark space with a cool room temperature. After 3 to 4 days, you should begin seeing small bubbles

come to the surface. This is a good sign that there is bacterial activity happening. The brine should begin tasting slightly sour.

6. Now it's just a matter of how sour you want your pickled tomatoes. Normally I like them after 6 to 8 days at room temperature, but the process can be longer or shorter depending on the environment you keep the crock in. A warmer storage space might make the tomatoes pickle faster. As the tomatoes become more sour, the salt and spice will also tend to subside and level out, too.

7. When the tomatoes are to your liking, transfer them into sanitized jars and keep in the refrigerator to slow down the process enough to enjoy eating them for the next couple of months!

Basic Kraut

Once you get the feel of basic kraut, the sky is the limit on how creative you can be. If your kraut gets too sour, don't throw it away . . . drain and stick it into the dehydrator until you have amazing kraut chips to snack on!

Makes about 1 gallon

5 pounds Napa cabbage, cored and finely chopped

2½ ounces plus 2 tablespoons kosher salt

1 red beet, peeled and finely chopped

5 garlic cloves, finely chopped

2 teaspoons whole caraway seed

⅓ cup local honey

1 teaspoon red chile flakes

2 quarts ice water

1. Sanitize your hands well. In a large mixing bowl, combine the cabbage, the 2½ ounces of salt, the beet, garlic, caraway seed, honey, and chile flakes. Use your hands to combine and massage the mixture for 5 minutes, doing your best to squeeze and break down the cabbage.
2. Place the mixture in a sanitized 5-gallon crock or bucket and pour in the ice water. Give it a little stir.
3. Set a plate over the cabbage mixture. Fill a 1 gallon zip-top bag with water and the remaining 2 tablespoons of salt and place it on top of the plate. This should weigh the kraut down enough to keep it covered in brine.
4. Cover the crock with cheesecloth and store it in a dark space with a cool room temperature.
5. Every day, remove the cover and mix the kraut for 1 minute. Replace the cover.
6. After 3 to 4 days, you should begin seeing small bubbles come to the surface. This is a good sign that there is bacterial activity happening. The brine should begin tasting slightly sour.
7. Now it's just a matter of how sour you want your kraut, just like going to the store and picking out a new pickle over a half-sour one. The longer the kraut stays in the brine, the more sour it will become. As it becomes more sour, the salt and spice will also tend to subside and level out, too.
8. When the kraut is to your liking, place it in sanitized jars and keep in the refrigerator to slow down the process. You'll be able to enjoy the kraut for the next couple of months!

Fall Kraut

Using the same general technique as our Basic Kraut, here is an example of a seasonal one we might use at the shop.

Makes about 4 quarts

5 pounds Napa cabbage, cored and finely chopped

2½ ounces plus 2 tablespoons kosher salt

2 tablespoons black walnut meat

½ cup fresh cranberries, roughly chopped

3 shallots, roughly chopped

½ tablespoon finely chopped garlic

½ tablespoon crushed guajillo chile

1 tablespoon chopped fresh marjoram

1 tablespoon chopped fresh oregano

3 tablespoons honey

1. Sanitize your hands well. In a large bowl, combine the cabbage and salt, massaging to break down the cabbage (this is easiest to do with your hands). After 6 to 8 minutes of massaging, add the rest of the ingredients.

2. Transfer the mixture to a fermenting container, either a stoneware or ceramic crock, or a food-grade plastic bucket. Make sure to pour all the juices from the bowl into the container. Pound and pack the mixture tightly to eliminate air bubbles. The goal is to completely submerge it in its own liquid. If necessary, you can always add extra salted water to ensure the mixture is fully submerged. Set a plate over the cabbage mixture. Fill a 1 gallon zip-top bag with water and the remaining 2 tablespoons of salt and place it on top of the plate. This should weigh the kraut down enough to keep it covered in brine. Keep the kraut at room temperature and away from light.

3. The kraut-making process could take anywhere from 1 week to 1 month. It's up to you, but the longer it sits, the more sour it becomes. Test it, mix it, and press it every two days. Once it's at your desired taste, keep it refrigerated for 6 months to 1 year. It can be canned for even longer preservation, but this will, of course, kill any live bacteria.

Fermented Black Trumpets

The end result of these fermented mushrooms is very strong in flavor, and a little goes a long way. Black trumpets have a way of becoming rich and almost chocolate-llike when preserved. They go well with red meats or can be used to flavor a rich cream sauce.

We use this same process for other small mushrooms, flowers, and berries.

Makes about 1 pound

1 pound fresh black trumpet mushrooms

2 tablespoons sea salt

Clean the mushrooms thoroughly, soaking and rinsing them a few times to get any debris out from the crevices. Drain well and transfer to a bowl. Mix in the salt evenly. Place the mushroom mixture in a 32-ounce sanitized jar and cover with cheesecloth. Let the jar sit for about 3 weeks before using the mushrooms; the flavors will intensify the longer the mushrooms ferment. The fermented black trumpets can last almost indefinitely in a cool, dry place.

JAMS AND PRESERVES

This is one of the easiest and oldest ways of preserving fruits and vegetables. From boiling down and canning to simply macerating with honey or sugar and leaving on a forgotten shelf somewhere, there is a wide range of traditional processes to be found across the world. This comes in especially handy in regions where the fruit-growing season is very short, making preservation all important!

Smoked (or Roasted) Strawberry and Cardamom Jam

There will never be a lack of blemished or surplus strawberries in this world, so make jam!

Makes 1 quart

3 pounds strawberries, hulled and roughly chopped
2 tablespoons olive oil
¼ cup honey
½ cup water
Zest and juice of 1 lemon

4 northern bayberry leaves
8 black peppercorns
8 black cardamom pods
1 vanilla bean, split
Kosher salt

1. Arrange the strawberries on a rimmed baking sheet and drizzle with the olive oil. Smoke over hickory or oak at 180°F for 1 hour (see page 31). If you don't have the ability to smoke, you can roast them at 500°F or grill until they have a nice char, 8 to 10 minutes.
2. Transfer the strawberries to a blender, add the honey, water, lemon zest and juice and blend until combined. Pour the mixture into a medium saucepan (if you want a finer consistency, strain the strawberries through cheesecloth first to remove the skins and seeds). Wrap the bayberry leaves, peppercorns, cardamom pods, and vanilla bean in a cheesecloth sachet and place it in the pan. Bring the mixture to a simmer over low heat and cook, stirring often, until you have a jam consistency, about 45 minutes. Remove the sachet and season with salt to taste.
3. Pour into any sterilized jar and let cool down. The jam can be stored in the refrigerator for months.

Beach Plum Preserves

When I was growing up, my grandparents always had beach plums in their yard. This variety is often considered an unwanted species on Long Island. While they are a bit smaller and tangier than the plums most of us are familiar with, they make for a spectacular preserve. Pair with freshly baked country bread, or give jars to friends and family as gifts!

Makes about 1 pint

3 pounds beach plums, cleaned and pitted

2 cups water

½ cup white wine vinegar

3 teaspoons ground sumac

1 teaspoon freshly ground black pepper

2 teaspoons sea salt

½ cup honey

2 teaspoons fresh thyme leaves

1 sheet gelatin (#160–200 strength works fine)

1. Sterilize four 8-ounce jelly (or two 16-ounce mason) glass jars.
2. In a blender or food processor, combine the beach plums and 1½ cups of the water. Add the vinegar, sumac, pepper, and salt and lightly pulse until the flesh of the plums has broken up into medium chunks.
3. Pour the plum mixture into a saucepan and add the honey and thyme. Cook over medium heat, stirring with a wooden spoon and keeping the jam from going up the sides of the pan and burning, until the mixture has reduced by half and has the consistency of a thick syrup, 45 minutes to 1 hour.
4. Meanwhile, in a bowl, pour the remaining ½ cup water over the gelatin. After 2 to 3 minutes, the gelatin sheet should be soft and malleable but not dissolved. Remove the sheet from the water, squeezing out any excess liquid, and stir it into the simmering jam after step 3, making sure it is well combined.
5. Take the jam off the heat and immediately pour it into the sterilized jars. If desired, the jam can be canned, or simply refrigerated for 3 to 5 weeks.

Dandelion Honey

This is one of my favorite recipes, although picking the dandelion petals can be quite time consuming. For me, it is well worth the wait and the end result has become one of my favorite condiments for everything from toast to meat to fish. Since this flower is commonly found in front yards and parks, I am careful not to pick anywhere that a pesticide could have been used.

Makes 2 cups

½ pound dandelion flowers

1 cup cold water

2 tablespoons honey

1 tablespoon sugar

½ tablespoon white wine vinegar

2 teaspoons kosher salt

1 teaspoon citric acid powder
(found in spice shops or at GNC)

One ¼-ounce envelope unflavored
gelatin

1. Break apart the flower heads, picking the yellow petals off the bases. Discard the bases, rinse the petals, and pat them dry.
2. In a medium saucepan, combine the water, honey, sugar, vinegar, salt, and citric acid powder. Bring the mixture to a boil over medium-high heat and cook, stirring occasionally, until it's reduced by about half. Remove it from the heat.
3. Place the gelatin in a small bowl and mix in 1 tablespoon of the warm liquid to bloom the gelatin. Add the gelatin slurry to the saucepan, turn the heat to a simmer, and whisk until there are no lumps, then set the pan aside to cool to 125°F, 5 to 10 minutes.
4. As soon as the mixture has cooled, add the petals and let the mixture cool completely. Cover with cheesecloth and steep for at least 24 hours before using.
5. Cool and store in sterilized jars. This can then be refrigerated for 3 to 6 months, or can for longer storage.

Knotweed Jam

Knotweed is also called Japanese or Asian knotweed, and it's an invasive species with a flavor profile similar to rhubarb. Here's a jam preparation to try with it. The tart quality to the jam makes it an excellent substitute for rhubarb jams, and it can be paired with smoked hams and other meats. Knotweed must be picked in the early spring, the only time when it's tender and edible.

Makes 1 pint

1½ pounds young Japanese knotweed (6 to 12 inches long)

2 tablespoons honey

1 cup water

2 teaspoons apple pectin powder

2 teaspoons kosher salt

½ teaspoon finely ground black pepper

1 tablespoon chopped fresh basil

1. Clean and trim the woody ends of the knotweed as you would with asparagus, then roughly chop it. Add it to a medium saucepan with the honey and cook it over medium-low heat, letting it warm and stew for 6 to 7 minutes, until tender.

2. Dump the mixture into a blender, add the water, and blend until smooth. Slowly sprinkle in the pectin, making sure it doesn't clump; if it does, transfer to a bowl and whisk it with a little water, then return it to the blender. Add the salt, pepper, and basil and blend on high.

3. Return the mixture to the saucepan. Bring to a boil over medium heat and cook, stirring, until the jam is a thick nappe consistency (coats the back of a spoon). Cool and store in sterilized jars in the refrigerator for 3 to 6 months, or can for longer storage.

Smoked Ketchup

If you grow tomatoes at all, the odds are good that you have plenty of unused overripe and late-season ones. A few might have been damaged by pests or have other flaws. Making a jam or ketchup in this case will always be your easiest and maybe most rewarding solution to the problem!

Makes about 1 quart

12 overripe or late-season heirloom tomatoes

½ cup olive oil

⅓ tablespoon kosher salt

½ tablespoon freshly ground black pepper

½ teaspoon ground dried basil

½ teaspoon ground dried tarragon

1 tablespoon pure dark maple syrup

½ cup sugar

½ cup white wine vinegar

¾ cup water

4 tonka beans (or 1 vanilla bean, split)

1. Quarter the tomatoes and toss them lightly with the olive oil, salt, and pepper. Smoke the tomatoes at 220°F for 1½ hours.
2. In a blender, combine the tomatoes, basil, tarragon, maple syrup, sugar, vinegar, and water and blitz for 3 to 5 minutes, until smooth. Pour the mixture into a medium saucepan, add the tonka beans, and cook over low heat, stirring often, until you have a marmalade-like consistency, about 45 to 60 minutes.
3. Cool the ketchup and remove the beans. This can then be stored in the refrigerator for 3 to 6 months or canned for longer storage.

Crab Apple Butter

I have horrible childhood memories of eating crab apples that grew at my father's house. They were often incredibly tannic, and my mouth would pucker up enough to have to spit it all out . . . yet, oddly, every fall I'd try again! Cooking crab apples is a great way of getting rid of, or at least moderating, those puckery tannins. As with acorns, they can also be soaked or brined. The butter can be paired simply with a great sourdough bread, or even with your favorite pork chop. It can also be used in various vinaigrettes.

Makes 1 pint

6 pounds crab apples
2 tablespoons butter
Kosher salt

½ cup apple cider vinegar
Juice of 1 lemon

1. Soak the apples in cold water for 3 days, away from the light on a counter or refrigerate and change the water daily (this helps remove the tannins). Drain and slice the apples into ½-inch-thick wedges, removing the core completely.
2. In a small nonstick sauté pan, melt the butter over medium heat. Add the apples and a pinch of salt and slowly cook until they turn a nice golden brown and have softened (they should be soft enough to cut through easily with a spoon), 8 to 10 minutes.
3. In a food processor, combine the apples, vinegar, lemon juice, and 1 tablespoon salt. Blend until smooth, then pour the mixture into a saucepan. Set over low heat and cook, stirring often, until reduced by half, about 30 to 40 minutes.
4. Cool the butter and store refrigerated for 1 to 2 months, or can for longer storage.

OILS, VINEGARS, SYRUPS, AND EXTRACTS

Humanity has been extracting medicine, flavors, and scents from the wild for thousands of years. Learning to utilize and preserve wild foods in these ways is as important as learning to find them. Many flavors, such as black birch, are my favorite tastes or smells to show people in nature, but can be the most challenging to translate with the same depth or magic in the kitchen.

WINTERGREEN AND BIRCH BARK

Syrups and tinctures (alcohol-based solutions) are a great way of obtaining flavor from natural substances. Wintergreen and birch bark are both plants that contain methyl salicylate, traditionally used to make aspirin, making them natural pain relievers. Always refer to a trained naturopathic physician with regard to proportions and use.

Visit a birch grove with your favorite machete. Peel one single vertical strip (no more than 2 to 4 inches wide and 4 to 6 inches long) from each tree, making certain to keep the inner bark. Be sure to thank the tree. Traditionally, this stripping process was referred to by First Nations people as "windowing." The inner bark of trees has the most oil—a kind of botanical fat. Older trees are more flavorful.

When wintergreen is young it is edible, but most of the time it's too tough to eat. When you peel the bark, you'll notice that it smells just like a stick of gum.

Wintergreen or Birch Bark Extract

We use this at the restaurant in some of our cocktails, though it can be added to buttercreams or cakes or ingested on its own for medicinal purposes.

Makes 2 cups

8 ounces wintergreen or birch bark, with inner bark attached

or

8 ounces fresh wintergreen leaves, with or without berries

1½ cups high-proof neutral-flavored alcohol, such as vodka (80 proof and above)

Combine the ingredients and store in glass bottles or jars for 2 months before using. Keep in a cool, dark place, such as a cellar.

Wintergreen or Birch Bark Syrup

Also perfect for cocktails, but even better drizzled over shaved ice with some berries!

Makes about 2 cups

2 cups raw sugar or honey
1½ cups water

2 tablespoons Wintergreen or Birch Bark Extract (above)

In a medium saucepan, combine the sugar, water, and extract and cook over medium-low heat, stirring occasionally, until the mixture is reduced and syrupy, 60 to 90 minutes. Once cooled, this can be refrigerated for 4 to 6 months.

Wintergreen Oil

This can be a great addition to light vinaigrettes, or used as a finishing oil over lightly warmed matsutake or wood ear mushrooms. I've also finished grilled fish, such as pike and flounder, with a light coating of this oil. This same gentle technique of flavoring oil works well for many other herbs and pods such as bay leaves, vanilla beans, and citrus rinds.

Makes about 2 cups

2 ounces wintergreen leaves, cleaned, with berries attached if you can get them

2 cups neutral oil, such as canola, safflower, or grapeseed

Place the wintergreen and oil in a blender and blend on high for 15 seconds. Pour the mixture into a medium saucepan and bring to a light simmer over medium-low heat. Set aside to cool overnight covered with cheesecloth. Strain. The oil can be stored in sanitized glass jar or bottle in a cool cellar or refrigerator for months.

Sassafras Syrup

I love using this syrup to add a little depth to simple dishes like roasted potatoes. It can also be used in desserts and cocktails.

Makes about 2 quarts

1 pound sassafras root, cleaned and
   freshly peeled
3 cups sugar
1 cup honey

1 tablespoon brown sugar
½ tablespoon kosher salt
1 gallon water

1. Shave off the outer bark of the sassafras root with a small knife or peeler. (It's very important that the bark is used fresh!) If you like, you can take the extra step of shaving the root down into big chips. The more surface area that is exposed, the more flavor that will be extracted.
2. Combine all the ingredients in a large stockpot. Bring to a boil over high heat. Reduce the heat to a simmer and cook until you have a thick syrup that coats the back of your spoon and can drizzle onto itself. As with Sumac Syrup (page 96), the more it reduces, the sweeter the syrup will be and the longer it will last. You're looking for that perfect balance between flavor and longevity. Always store in a dark, cool pantry, root cellar, or refrigerator.

Sumac Syrup

I love using sumac, dried or ground, fresh or preserved. It makes a delicious tea and a wonderful addition to many recipes. At our restaurants, we're constantly looking for more local, fresh ingredients than can offer a flavor profile similar to acidic fruits like lemon or lime. Sumac fits the bill.

Several types of sumac can be found across the United States, but it's most prevalent in the Northeast. It can often be found on disturbed ground, such as on the side of the road or on the outer edges of farm land. The most challenging part of finding and picking sumac is trying to find it in a clean, unpolluted area. I've often gone on extensive foraging trips looking for sumac, only to find it en masse on the side of the highway on my drive home. On a frequently used road, avoid the temptation to pull over and pick it.

Here we're using the long buds of the sumac. It's important to use the bright or dark red variety, as the white plants are poisonous. The buds grow in late spring or early summer, when the plant is maturing, but the best time to harvest is at the end of the summer or early fall, when the buds naturally convert their sugars into acids and begin to develop their identifiable sour flavor.

My favorite use of this syrup is over vanilla bean ice cream, but it can also be used in cocktails and on grilled meats.

Makes about 2 quarts

1½ pounds sumac pods	½ tablespoon juniper berries
3 cups sugar	½ tablespoon kosher salt
1 cup honey	10 northern bayberry leaves
1 tablespoon black peppercorns	1 gallon water

1. Pick the individual buds off the pods. These look and feel like small, furry berries. Submerge the buds in a bowl of water, drain, and repeat two times with fresh water. Thoroughly clean and pick away any debris or stowaway caterpillars.
2. Combine all the ingredients in a large stockpot. Bring to a boil over high heat, then lower to a simmer, and cook and reduce until you have a thick

syrup that coats the back of your spoon and can drizzle onto itself. It's important to note that the more it reduces, the sweeter the syrup will be and the longer it will last. Always store in a dark cool pantry, root cellar, or refrigerator. The syrup can be stored in glass jars or even empty wine bottles.

Smoked Herb Oil

I am a huge fan of smoked herb oils; they're a great addition to anyone's pantry. At the restaurants, I use them to store shellfish and mushrooms and to finish dishes. When making these oils, it's very important that the herbs be carefully and properly cleaned. Since they'll be submerged in oil and in an anaerobic environment, there is a risk of botulism.

Makes 1 gallon

1 pound fresh herbs in whole bunches, such as thyme, lavender, juniper, oregano, or rosemary, thoroughly washed and cleaned

1 gallon organic, neutral-flavored oil, such as sunflower oil

Smoke the herb bunches for 4 to 5 hours at 160°F. Submerge them in a glass bottle or jar of oil and store for 2 to 3 months in a cool, dark place, such as a cellar.

Black Locust Flower or
Spicebush Berry Vinegar

The proportions for this quick vinegar can be adjusted to your liking, and the flavor will depend on the sweetness of the fresh product. This process is an easy way to store and preserve extra household herbs and spices that are lying around, such as basil, dill, or peppercorns. It can also add an interesting acidity to dressings or sauces or to finish raw scallops and other crudos.

Makes 1 quart

1½ cups fresh spicebush leaves and
    berries, or black locust flowers,
    roughly chopped

1 cup rice vinegar
1 tablespoon honey
1 quart distilled white vinegar

In a medium saucepan, combine all the ingredients and bring the mixture to a simmer over medium heat. Simmer for a few minutes, set aside to cool, and pour into a plastic or glass container. Cover and let it sit refrigerated for at least 24 hours and up to a few months, making sure that all the leaves or flowers stay completely submerged.

Concord Grape Vinegar

Very few fruits become quite as sweet as and have the depth of flavor of a good Concord grape here in the Northeast. It's nice to offset the sweetness with a little acid. This vinegar is perfect for use in dressings, to lightly cure raw fluke or black bass, or slathered on smoked skate or over grilled pork in the fall.

Makes 2½ quarts

5 pounds very ripe Concord grapes (harvested at the beginning of the fall)

1½ cups water

1 tablespoon honey

1 tablespoon fresh tarragon leaves

1 tablespoon black peppercorns

Vinegar "mother," or ½ cup raw store-bought vinegar, such as Bragg apple cider vinegar

1. Juice the grapes by pressing them in a large pot with a potato masher or even in a blender set to low, being careful not to break up the actual seeds. Strain the juice into a stone crock or food-grade plastic bucket. (A wider surface area increases oxidization and will help the sugars convert to alcohol faster.) You should end up with about 2 quarts of juice. But a little more or less won't hurt!

2. Combine the rest of the ingredients with the juice. Cover the container well with multiple layers of cheesecloth to keep out fruit flies and store it in a cool or room-temperature area (not a fridge). When working with sweeter substances, you need to be conscious of keeping out fruit flies.

3. Using a hydrometer or gravity tester, which measures liquid density, test the mixture every couple of days or so to see how much sugar there is; the more sugar there is, the denser the liquid will be. You will want to convert the liquid to a minimum of 4.5% and to a maximum of 8% alcohol for vinegar; with a hydrometer this will read .035 to .055. By measuring the gravity (Brix), you can tell how much has converted into alcohol. Depending on how strong the mother (the main buildup of the fermenting bacteria) is, and a bunch of other environmental variables, this process could take between 1 and 3 months to complete (see Note).

4. To finish the vinegar process, you need to put it in a closed container to reduce the amount of oxygen it is exposed to, as this will help it convert

better from alcohol to ascetic acid. One of the signs of a perfectly finished vinegar is a healthy growing mother floating on top. Generally you want a vinegar to be under 3.4 pH for preservation, but with the popularity of different shrubs and drinking vinegars, this can be higher in pH if safely refrigerated. Tasting the vinegar is the best way to determine whether it's done, as how acidic you want it is a personal preference. For testing pH, I use a meter I like from Hanna Instruments that costs about $160. But, especially for vinegars, using a $5 disposable pH test strip kit is just fine.

Note: To jump-start our vinegar, we use an inexpensive aquarium aerator to pump air into the juice, thus speeding up the oxidization process. After it reaches the desired alcohol level, we transfer it to a carboy with an airlock, which then slows the oxidation process.

Morels in Smoked Juniper Oil

When stored properly, preserved morels are a wonderful complement to smoked fish, or they can be enjoyed on their own.

Makes 3 cups

One 6- to 10-ounce branch super-fresh juniper, with or without berries

1 pound fresh morels, cleaned (morels can be tricky to clean; often soaking and drying is best)

Kosher salt

3 cups grapeseed oil

1. Cold-smoke (under 160°F) the juniper branch until it dries out and stops secreting sap. Cut it into manageable pieces, leaving the needles intact.

2. Prepare an ice bath. Fill a large saucepan with enough water to cover the morels by 3 or 4 inches. Add a large pinch of salt and bring the water to a boil over high heat. Add the morels and boil until just barely tender, about 1 minute. Drain and toss them immediately into the ice bath until chilled. Lay the morels out on paper towels to dry and let them come to room temperature.

3. In a large sauté pan over medium-low heat, add the oil, juniper branch pieces, and ¼ cup salt. As soon as the oil comes to a simmer, immediately remove the pan from the heat and set it aside to cool. When the juniper mixture is about room temperature, add the mushrooms.

4. Pour the contents of the pan into a clean jar large enough to fully submerge all the mushrooms. Seal tightly and keep in a cool, dry place or in cold storage, where the morels can be kept almost indefinitely. You'll notice if the mushrooms turn putrid and begin to smell; this will only happen if your storage becomes too warm or if you don't completely submerge the mushrooms in the oil.

Acorn Flour

Acorn flour can be incorporated into bread mixes and used to make johnny cakes or other fry breads.

Makes ¼ pound

1 pound acorns

1. Clean off any debris or dirt from the acorns and remove the caps. Soak the acorns in water to cover for 3 to 6 days, changing the water every day. If you want a speedier process, boil and strain the acorns (dumping the dark liquid) repeatedly until the water stays clear. This will remove the tannins. You'll know the acorns are ready when you taste one and it doesn't make your mouth pucker. Let the acorns dry fully on paper towels for a day.
2. Grind the acorns into flour using a mortar and pestle or a hand mill. Sieve the flour to separate out the fibrous husks. This can be held just like any other common flour, bagged or jarred at room temperature, but is best refrigerated. If it stays dry, it can last indefinitely.

Black Garlic

Black garlic is commonly used in Asian cultures for its antioxidant and medicinal properties. A common misconception is that black garlic is mostly fermented; it's actually very slowly cooked. The flavor comes mostly from a Maillard reaction and a little from the small amount of fermentation that occurs. This process is also well suited to onions and other alliums (see Note); the extensive layers and outer skin help keep it at the correct level of humidity inside.

We make two versions: The soft one is emulsified into sauces and dressings or eaten on its own, and the harder version is used for shaving as a garnish, much like a truffle or a hard cheese. This is one of the most time-consuming recipes in the book, so schedule accordingly!

We are essentially keeping the garlic in an environment that is slightly too warm to allow it to sprout, prevents enough air contact to avoid oxidization, and is too humid to dry it out.

Makes about ½ pound

8 jumbo garlic heads

1. Wrap the garlic in tight packets of 2 heads each in 4 layers of foil. Mark one packet as the test packet (you'll check this one to see how far along you are). We use a dehydrator, but you could also use a rice cooker on the warm setting. Keep the temperature at approximately 120° to 130°F. The temperature should be just hot enough to prevent the garlic from shooting or sprouting.
2. For soft garlic, allow it to slow-cook for 50 to 65 days at this temperature. If it comes out too dry for your taste, make a note to splash a teaspoon of water in the wrapping process the next time.
3. For hard garlic, it generally takes 80 to 100 days to get the right consistency. The challenge with hard garlic is that it needs to sufficiently dehydrate while still remaining large enough to be shaved. If it turns out a bit too acidic for your taste, dark beer or sake can be added during the next wrapping.

4. The garlic can sit out at room temperature indefinitely if dried hard. If kept soft it's best to store it in a sealed container or bag in the refrigerator.

Note: To do this with alliums that have a higher water content, such as onions, dry them at a higher temperature (130° to 135°F) and for less time.

Note: Over the years, I have had a lot of fun using this same technique on other vegetables and fruits that do not have the same sort of layered skin as alliums by soaking them lightly in vinegars in vacuum-sealed bags, or even creating edible skins out of calcium and alginate before the extensive warm storage process. This re-creates the layered skin and pH that helps make more protected ingredients like garlic the perfect natural specimens for the process.

Reindeer Lichen

Reindeer lichen is an incredible edible that's found in boreal and sub-boreal forests in much of the world and often underutilized in the United States. I love to throw it into a white quick pickle liquid or eat it as is after soaking. The texture is so unique. Historically, it was an essential ingredient for survivalists and Native Americans because it could be found year-round and readily growing on rocks, even under snow. It's is also a great source of vitamin C.

Like acorns, lichen should probably not be eaten raw, as it contains a large amount of tannins that could upset your digestive system. Cleaned, dry lichen can be kept for an indefinite amount of time and will be ready for processing whenever you're ready. I recommend processing lichen by soaking it in cold water for two days, refreshing the water each day. This water change also allows the dirt and other hangers-on (such as moss) to fall away.

Lichens work like sponges and can absorb any kind of flavor. This is a great ingredient to experiment with—finish your choice of dish with this lichen to add wonderful texture.

Makes 1 pound

2 quarts water
2 tablespoons white vinegar
2 tablespoons kosher salt

1 pound reindeer lichen (it can be carefully picked wild or purchased from gourmet spice shops)

1. In a medium saucepan, combine 1 quart of the water and 1 tablespoon each of the vinegar and salt. Bring to a boil over high heat. Reduce the heat to a simmer, add the lichen, and poach it for 1 hour. Drain and rinse the lichen, removing any remaining twigs or other detritus. Try to keep the lichen in as large a bunch as possible for ease of handling.
2. Repeat the process with the remaining water, vinegar, and salt, poaching the lichen until it is soft enough to enjoyably eat, an additional 1 to 1½ hours. It can be stored in White Quick Pickle Liquid (page 38) or dried out completely and stored almost indefinitely in sealed bags or jars at room temperature and rehydrated before use.

Fermented Black Beans

This is one of the oldest ingredients in the world. It has appeared in ancient China, Japan, Korea, Malaysia, and other parts of Asia. Black soybeans were traditionally used, but this version calls for common dried black beans, which are a great modern alternative.

There are several ways to create fermented black beans, but we mainly rely on an added enzyme called *Aspergillus oryzae*, the same starter that's used to create soy sauce, natto, miso, and other common Asian ingredients. You can order your own *Aspergillus oryzae*, or simply use quality jarred fermented black bean with live cultures.

Another option is to add salt to cooked beans, leave it out in a warm humid place, lightly covered, and wild-ferment them. For more about wild fermentation, refer to the books listed in Resources (page 299).

Makes 1 pound

1 pound dried black beans
2 tablespoons roasted wheat flour (if you can't find it, lightly toast whole wheat flour in the oven)
2 tablespoon jarred fermented black beans or ½ teaspoon live *Aspergillus oryzae* culture

Rice wine, for spraying
3 tablespoons kosher salt

1. Soak the beans overnight in a bowl with water to cover. Drain the beans and rinse until the water runs clear. Toss the beans into a large saucepan, cover with water by two inches, and bring to a boil over medium heat. Simmer until the beans can be flattened between your fingers, about 60 to 90 minutes. Drain and cool.
2. Dehydrate the beans at 120°F or air-dry on rimmed baking sheets until still just a little moist and warm to room temperature, about 1 hour in the dehydrator or air-dry to feel.
3. In a large bowl, combine the dried beans and flour and toss to coat. Mix in the fermented black beans or live culture.

4. Spread the beans out in a wide woven basket, wood box, or even a glass baking dish to allow moisture to evaporate quickly. Let the beans sit in a cool, dark room, lightly covered in cheesecloth. Each day, lightly mix the beans and spray with a mixture of half rice wine and half water. After 3 to 4 days, you should see significant mold growth. Rinse the exterior mold off the beans, add the salt, and mix well. Finish in the dehydrator overnight at 120°F until dry but still soft enough to eat. The beans should be slightly chewy and extremely rich in flavor.

Fermented Apricots

This is our spin on Japanese umeboshi (made with plums). This method can also be used for plums or any other stone fruit, figs, or grapes. It's a lengthy process, but the end result is well worth it.

Similar to the classic umeboshi, these can be eaten on their own as a sweet snack or served in small amounts over rice or in desserts.

Makes 1½ pounds

2 pounds young apricots (transitioning from green to yellow)

¼ cup barley mead or other grain-based liquor, such as bourbon (white wine will do the trick, too)

½ cup plus ½ tablespoon kosher salt

15 fresh spearmint leaves

1. Soak the apricots overnight in water. This will help separate the flesh from the pit more easily when ready to eat. Remove just the stems for now.
2. Combine the apricots, liquor, and ½ cup of the salt in a medium stoneware or ceramic crock. Place a 3- to 5-pound crock weight on top or just a plate with plastic-wrapped bricks or weights on top. Allow to sit overnight.
3. The next day, rinse and dry the spearmint leaves and mix them well with the remaining ½ tablespoon salt and add to the crock of apricots. Top with a lighter, 1- or 2-pound weight, cover the whole crock with cheesecloth, and let it sit for 3 to 4 weeks. When the apricots are ready for the next step, they should be a bronze color.
4. Drain all of the liquid into a medium saucepan, bring to a boil over high heat, then reduce to a simmer and cook, stirring occasionally, until it is reduced by half, about 30 minutes. Set aside to cool.
5. Meanwhile, dehydrate the apricots at 120°F for 4 to 6 hours, or air-dry them overnight.
6. Mix the cooled reduced apricot liquid back into the dried apricots and store in sanitized jars. If stored in a cool dark place, the apricots will last almost indefinitely.

Chile Ash Paste

A great way to make use of this paste is to expand it into a deep, savory sauce using your choice of stock, and serve it over roasted fish, turkey, or mushrooms.

Makes 1½ cups

8 ounces ancho chiles

8 ounces guajillo chiles

1 medium yellow onion, peeled and roughly chopped

2 garlic heads, peeled and whole

1 tablespoon cornmeal

3 tonka beans (or 1 vanilla bean, split)

10 juniper berries

4 whole cloves

2 black cardamom pods

2 teaspoons black peppercorns

2 tablespoons dried oregano

1 tablespoon kosher salt

½ cup distilled white vinegar

1 tablespoon pomegranate juice

1. Soak the chiles in a bowl of warm water until softened for approximately 20 minutes. Drain and cut off the stems. Set on paper towels to dry for about 30 minutes.

2. Heat a dry, well-seasoned cast-iron skillet over medium-high heat. Slowly char the chiles, constantly mixing them in the pan, until they have a charcoal-like appearance, 20 to 25 minutes. As the chiles begin to release their last bit of oil, they will start to light on fire. While they are on fire, stir with a metal spoon for no longer than 15 seconds. Pour 2 tablespoons water into the pan, remove the chiles from the pan, and set them aside to cool.

3. Add the onion and garlic to the skillet and repeat the same process, cooking over medium heat until blackened but still intact. Remove the onion and garlic from the pan and set aside to cool.

4. Reduce the heat under the skillet to low, add the cornmeal, and lightly toast. Pour it into a small bowl.

5. In a spice grinder, combine the tonka beans, juniper berries, spices, and herbs, and grind them to a fine powder.

6. Remove the seeds from the chiles.

7. In a food processor, combine the chiles, onion, garlic, cornmeal, ground spice mixture, salt, vinegar, and pomegranate juice and blend until you have a paste. Push the mixture through a tamis for a more refined clay-like texture (or use a fine-mesh sieve or a food mill). If there's too much moisture, hang the paste in a cheesecloth and let it dry overnight. This paste is ready immediately and will last indefinitely if kept in a covered jar at room temperature.

MILK

4

THE CREAMERY

Practicing cattle husbandry and dairy production may be out of reach for much of the population, but with a little effort, most of us have the ability to source excellent local milk. Whether it's derived from cows, goats, sheep, camels, or buffalo, the following guidelines and recipes can help you make the most out of whatever type of local milk you have access to. In modern-day America, cows are by far the most popular sources of milk, so naturally, cow milk is widely used and accepted. I encourage you to seek out raw milk from smaller licensed farms and you will notice a drastic improvement in taste.

Quality milk is completely dependent on sourcing from farms using quality cows and milking practices. At our restaurants, we prefer Jersey cows because this breed tends to produce milk with a higher fat ratio. Grass-fed Jersey milk will have a much thicker layer of cream, also called cream line, and a more concentrated yellow color, often seen in the fat on the meat as well. There is nothing for me that rivals the flavor of a retired and fattened dairy cow. Their developed flavor and higher fat percentage makes the meat perfect for cooking and aging.

Though store-bought dairy products are normally purchased in today's society, we might not be as familiar with how the milk is traditionally processed from udder to store. Whole milk is what's produced directly from a cow. If it's processed further, it's often heated and cultured into cheeses or separated by centrifuges into what is sold as cream and fat-free or reduced-fat milks. Even further processing and preservation of the cream may include culturing (optional) and churning it to separate butter from buttermilk.

Not many butters are properly cultured these days, but I think this process creates a tastier product with greater depth. Most dairy cattle are now milked year-round and twice a day, but there are certainly better times of the year for milk. The abundance of tender grass and calving in the spring makes the milk especially rich. Now that we have a dairy aisle in every grocery store, we forget that cheeses, yogurts, butters, kefir, and other cultured and processed products were developed to extend the lifespan of dairy. It's a nice bonus that these methods also produce some of the most delicious products in the culinary world.

Husbandry is a discipline that is both all-consuming and inspirational. I'm honored to call a few farmers close friends and family, as our relationships have grown over years of purchasing for the restaurants and observing their work firsthand. The backbreaking work and expenses of running a small farm are almost unparalleled in the modern world. Farmers begin each day at 5 a.m. to milk the cows, then come the daily feedings, birthing, slaughtering, packaging, selling, and shipping. More often than not, they're also raising and feeding their own families, all the while fending off the increasing pressure from large corporate farms. At any time, the government can implement new and overreaching standards that may fly in the face of generations of tradition. Owning and operating a small farm can often seem like a losing proposition for the passionate small farmers.

I believe one of the ways that small farms—and especially dairy farms—can gain a little more stability and success is by creating more finished products out of raw ingredients. Because of government regulations and startup costs, this can be a very scary prospect for many farmers; but with a little diligence, it's possible, perhaps even surprisingly easy. I recently spent some time with a fifth-generation Jersey cow dairy farmer who, since the 2008 recession, has begun producing some of the most incredible butter in New York State. She told me that her family farm had produced this prize-winning butter on just two other occasions in the past two hundred years. The first occasion was when one of the patriarchs of the family had died in the 1800s, leaving the mother alone with a small family and in charge of running the farm. The second time was during the Depression in the 1930s.

Each time, the prize-winning butter saved the farm and the family's livelihood. The family was able to keep its traditions intact for a new generation and was able to turn a profit simply by using preservation techniques to transform the milk into one of the most incredible-tasting butters I've ever experienced. In separating the milk into the cream needed to make butter, the family was able to turn the excess reduced-fat milk into reduced-fat yogurts, kefirs, and feed, while turning any excess whey into buttermilk that could be sold as is. This, to me, exemplifies many of the central ideas in this book: It is essential that we learn to reexamine our past in order to mine old traditions and apply them to the present. Our future relies on it.

Fermented and Smoked Cream, Butter, and Buttermilk

These smoked creams, butters, and buttermilks have been the centerpiece of countless dishes at our restaurants and others. When given enough time to mature in flavor, they are the star of any show. The yield will be dependent on the fat content of the milk.

2 quarts raw cream

1 medium piece dried kombu (10 to 12 grams)

½ tablespoon raw buttermilk (or the clear liquid/whey that rises to the top of yogurt)

Naturally harvested sea salt or Maldon salt

1. In an open metal container (a half hotel pan is perfect), combine the cream and kombu. Cold-smoke (see page 24) over oak for 2 days, lightly stirring every 8 hours through the process. This basic smoked cream is what we use for many of our recipes in the restaurant.

2. In order to thicken into a spreadable cream and to ferment, add the buttermilk and cover with cheesecloth. Let it sit at room temperature overnight (or if you prefer a tangier taste, let it culture for 2 to 4 days). This thickened product is what we know as crème fraîche.

4. To turn into butter, remove the kombu and pour the cream into a stand mixer with a paddle attachment (best option), traditional butter churn, or food processor.

5. For a softer, spreadable "whipped" butter: Churn at a low setting. Keep an eye on the cream as it thickens, which it should do after a few minutes. This smoked butter can be stored in the refrigerator for 2 to 3 weeks. At our restaurants, we use this in a variety of ways: spread on fresh sourdough bread with herb salt, served on toast with preserved shellfish, and even in some of our desserts.

6. For a harder butter and buttermilk: If you continue churning the mixture for another 10 minutes, the thickened cream will begin to separate into solid and

liquid. The solid mixture is your butter and the liquid is your buttermilk! At this point, you can pour off the buttermilk (see Note) and store in the refrigerator.

7. The butter can be further "washed" by pouring 2 to 3 cups cold water over it and draining. By washing the butter, we're removing any excess milk solids and buttermilk, prolonging its preservation life. Mix in good-quality sea salt to taste, as this will also extend the life of the butter. The end result can be stored in the refrigerator as you would standard butter, either jarred or simply wrapped in wax paper.

Note: The buttermilk can be consumed immediately or used in recipes, such as buttermilk biscuits, or as a culture to start a new batch of butter, or to ferment vegetables.

Seaweed Butter

Seaweed and butter have been best friends for a long time. The duo makes the perfect accompaniment to fresh or roasted root vegetables, for finishing seafood, or simply spread with roasted garlic on good sourdough bread.

Makes 1 pound

2 ounces dried wakame seaweed

Zest and juice of 1 lemon

1½ tablespoons soy sauce

1 pound Smoked Butter (page 116), at room temperature

Kosher salt

Break up the seaweed and grind it to a powder in a spice grinder. Mix the seaweed powder, lemon zest and juice, and soy sauce together in a small bowl and let sit for 1 minute. When the seaweed has spent a mininum of 5 minutes rehydrating, fold the mixture into the butter in a larger bowl. It should have a creamy texture and the color should be close to charcoal. Stir in salt to taste. Cool and store in a ceramic or glass container.

Duck Liver Butter

We make this recipe with more butter than would be used in a traditional pâté so it will melt more consistently with other ingredients. It happens to make for a nicer presentation, too. Duck liver butter roughly spread over a crisp toast with a few flakes of herb salt and a glass of red wine is the perfect predinner snack. For a touch of sweetness, top with Dandelion Honey (page 87).

Makes about 3 pounds

2 pounds Smoked Butter
 (page 116), at room temperature
1½ pounds duck livers, cleaned
¼ cup minced garlic
¼ cup minced shallots
2 tablespoons local dry white wine
 (such as Riesling)

1 tablespoon ground sumac
2 teaspoons ground white pepper
½ tablespoon kosher salt, or more
 to taste

1. In a large sauté pan, melt 1 tablespoon of the smoked butter over medium heat, add the duck livers and sauté. After 2 to 3 minutes, add the garlic and shallots and sauté until the livers are just cooked through, 4 to 6 minutes. Remove the livers when they begin to feel firm and take care not to overcook them, as they can get mealy. Keeping the garlic and shallots in the pan, deglaze the pan with the wine and cook to reduce the liquid by half. Let the livers cool to room temperature, 5 to 10 minutes, then roughly chop them.

2. Transfer the chopped duck livers, and the garlic and shallot mixture to a food processor and add the rest of the butter, sumac, white pepper, and salt. Pulse until roughly blended. Taste and add more salt if needed.

3. Cool and store in a jar, or roll into a log and wrap in wax paper, and refrigerate.

Rose Hip Brown Butter

On the North Fork of Long Island, you will find enormous rose bushes growing just about everywhere. This butter makes a perfect dip for lobster or clams.

Makes 2 cups

1 pound Smoked Butter (page 116) or regular unsalted butter

2 ounces dried rose hips
½ tablespoon kosher salt

1. In a medium saucepan, heat the butter over medium-high heat; as it begins to foam, the milk solids will separate from the rest of the butterfat. Skim off the milk solids until they are no longer produced. This will leave you with clarified butter.
2. Carefully pour the warm butter through cheesecloth into a clean saucepan. Add the rose hips and salt and simmer over low heat until the clarified butter is a nice golden brown color and smells nutty and slightly floral, 20 to 25 minutes. The goal is to impart as much flavor from the rose hips as possible while lightly browning the butter.
3. Let the clarified butter cool to room temperature (it should still remain liquid), then strain out the rose hips. Cool and store indefinitely in a ceramic or glass container in a cool or refrigerated room.

Tarragon Cream

This easy process can introduce any herb to creams, a perfect addition to more acidic foods, such as pickled fish or vegetables.

Makes 1 cup

8 ounces fresh tarragon leaves

1 cup Smoked Cream (page 116) or store-bought cultured crème fraîche

Kosher salt and ground white pepper

Run the tarragon leaves through a juicer. In a medium bowl, use a spatula to fold the juice through the cream. The final product should be bright green. Season with salt and white pepper to taste.

Sage Cream

Another simple process for incorporating herbs into cream, sage cream is perfect for finishing pastas or even on toast with a little brined citrus and cured meat.

Makes 1 quart

4 ounces fresh sage leaves, carefully cleaned

1 quart heavy cream

½ tablespoon buttermilk or whey

1 tablespoon kosher salt

In a blender, puree the sage and cream. Blend in the buttermilk and salt. Pour the mixture into a covered container and punch or create an air vent. Keep the container in a warm place (65° to 85°F) out of direct sunlight; above the stove or near a fireplace is ideal. When the cream has thickened up nicely, you can either pass it through a sieve or leave it rustic. Keep the cream covered and refrigerated for up to 2 weeks.

Black Walnut Crème

Black walnuts are different from regular walnuts in two main ways. First, the shells are a lot harder to crack. Secondly, they have a deeper, funkier flavor than other nuts, which makes them appealing to chefs. If you're foraging for black walnuts, I recommend drying them first and using a large stone, hammer, or commercial cracker to break them open, or you can purchase the meat already picked.

If you're cracking your own nuts, dry the nut meat on a silicone baking mat or dehydrator sheet in the dehydrator at 140°F overnight. Store-bought walnuts do not need further drying. Black walnuts have a very oily texture, so a second drying process is needed. Shake them around a bit and dry again for 2 to 3 hours, until they break apart easily. At this point, they should be in good shape for the grinder.

Makes 1 cup

4 ounces of black walnut meat
1 cup Smoked Cream (page 116)

½ tablespoon buttermilk or whey
1 tablespoon kosher salt

Use a grinder or a food mill to grind the dried nut meat into a powder. In a bowl, fold 2 tablespoons of the black walnut powder into the smoked cream and whisk in the buttermilk and salt. Pour the mixture into a covered container with holes punched for ventilation. Keep the container in a warm place (65° to 85°F) out of direct sunlight; above the stove or near a fireplace is ideal. When the cream has thickened up nicely, taste to see if more salt is needed. Keep the cream covered and refrigerated for up to 2 weeks.

Crab Apple Cream

Crab apples used to be eaten more commonly, but most people today find them too tannic to enjoy on their own. This process brings out their natural flavor with a less challenging, more delicious end result.

Makes 1 cup

2 small to medium crab apples, peeled, cored, and cut into ¼-inch-thick slices

½ tablespoon butter, melted

1 cup Smoked Cream (page 116)

1 tablespoon kosher salt

1 teaspoon filé powder

1. Preheat the oven to 350°F.
2. Toss the crab apples with the melted butter on a baking sheet and roast until soft, 12 to 15 minutes.
3. In a bowl, whisk the apples into the smoked cream and add the salt and filé powder. Pour the mixture into a nonstick sauté pan and slowly—very slowly—reduce it over low heat, stirring frequently with a spatula, about 12 to 15 minutes until the apples begin to caramelize and naturally break up. The mixture will turn into a dark, flavorful paste. Let it cool to room temperature. Store covered and refrigerated for 2 to 3 weeks.

CHEESE

The production of cheese is an age-old preservation process. Though many fresh cheeses are made by simply adding a little vinegar or citric acid to milk, the vast majority of cheeses are made with rennet, an enzyme found in the stomach of ruminant mammals (e.g., cows, goats, and sheep) that helps their young digest milk when nursing. Since stomachs and bladders were some of the early vessels used to store liquids, it's been conjectured that early cheese production may have been accidentally discovered when raw milk reacted to the digestive enzymes in these vessels.

Since then, humans have spent centuries refining the art of cheesemaking. Anyone interested can easily buy hundreds of specialized animal- and nonanimal-based rennets, as well as mold baskets, presses, surface bacteria, and countless other pieces of equipment and books. The real experts have devoted a lifetime of study on this subject. I have done my best to simplify some of the basic ideas here and point those interested in the right direction.

It's easy to find good commercially prepared rennet, but if you practice husbandry or are close with your farmers, a local and decent animal-based rennet can be made and stored for personal use. It's best when taken from the stomach of a very young ruminant mammal, no more than a few days old. Often farmers will harvest rennet when the animal doesn't survive the birthing process or in the days shortly after. The stomach is thoroughly cleaned, then kept whole or cut into 1-inch squares. It must then be kept packed in salt for 10 to 14 months before use.

After aging, if using squares, remove the number of squares that you need (each square is equal to 2 to 3 drops of liquid animal rennet) and rinse off the salt. Soak for 20 minutes in water, tying the pieces to a string to allow you to dip them into milk. Alternatively, if using a whole salted stomach, rinse until any visible salt is removed, add it to 2 quarts of water or whey, and store it in a cool place out of the light for 4 days. Strain and discard the stomach, and the liquid that remains will contain usable rennet.

Any excess whey produced by cheesemaking will also contain rennet and can be used to start other cheeses or culture dairy as well as to ferment vegetables or make soups. It can also be dried completely to be used another time.

Basic Farmer Cheese

The quickest and easiest way to begin making soft cheeses at home!

Makes 1 pound

2 gallons whole milk
(preferably raw)

¾ teaspoon homemade rennet
(see opposite) or ½ teaspoon
store-bought rennet

1 tablespoon kosher salt

1. In a pot set in a bain-marie, gently heat the milk over medium-low heat until it reaches 86° to 90°F. Add the rennet, stirring it in gently and keeping the milk warm. The milk will begin to coagulate into curds and the surface will thicken in 8 to 15 minutes. A good way to test its readiness is by spinning a small, buoyant object (a small Tupperware bowl works great) on top of the milk; when the milk is thick that the bowl stops spinning, the milk is ready to be cut.

2. Take a knife or wire and run it through the curdled milk, cutting 1-inch squares along the entirety of it, thus releasing the whey. Set cheesecloth over a bowl. Pour in the curds and drain off the whey. Lifting up the curd by the cheesecloth, give it a good squeeze and pour the excess whey from the bowl into a separate container to be stored in the refrigerator for another use. Pour the curds back into the bowl, removing the cheesecloth, and season the mixture with the salt.

3. Take a small cylindrical pasta strainer, basket, or tin can (with holes drilled through) 4 to 6 inches wide and no more than 5 to 7 inches deep. Line the inside of this "mold" with a large square of cheesecloth—with enough overhang that you can fold it over and cover the cheese. Pour the curds into the lined mold and pack them in. Fold the excess cheesecloth over the cheese.

4. Using a precut round of wood the diameter of the top of the mold (or a reasonably tight-fitting pot lid), press down strongly on the cheese to expel the remaining whey and moisture. (You could also purchase a cheese press, or

make your own with a frame built out of untreated 2 x 4-inch pieces of wood with a hinge connecting one corner and a hook connecting the opposite side. Bricks or other weights can get the job done, too.)

5. Take out the cheese, flip it over, and press again to help form a shape and prevent air bubbles. A farmer cheese like this is typically more moist and requires less pressing than a harder aged cheese.

6. You can also mature it in flavor and turn it into an aged cheese. Dry for 3 to 5 days uncovered in a high-humidity aging room, turning it over two or three times every day. After this round, you can wax the cheese with food-grade wax and place it in an aging room with a temperature range of 55° to 65°F and at 80 to 90% humidity for a minimum of 5 weeks, until it reaches the desired flavor.

Smoked Ricotta

Homemade ricotta is easy to make and a perfect accompaniment to just about any dish. We cook it into our grits and serve it on waffles and charcuterie boards, and even in desserts.

Makes 2 cups

1 gallon whole milk (preferably raw)

1 quart heavy cream

1 tablespoon kosher salt, or more to taste

¼ cup distilled white vinegar

Juice of 1 lemon

1. In a saucepan, combine the milk, cream, and 1 tablespoon salt and bring to a rolling boil over medium-high heat. Let it boil for no more than 2 minutes, turn off the heat, and add the vinegar and lemon juice. As soon as you see the mixture start to curdle, after about 30 to 45 seconds, take it off the burner and let sit undisturbed for 5 to 10 minutes to curdle.

2. With a slotted spoon or spider colander, remove large clumps into a shallow hotel pan. (It's okay if they bring along some liquid, too.) Pour the remaining milky liquid through a sieve or regular colander and add those clumps to the rest of the curds in the pan. Taste and season with more salt as needed. The leftover liquid can either be discarded or used as a great addition to soup broths. We love adding it to our leftover mussel or clam juice and cooking it with a dash of lemon.

3. Place the pan into a smoker for 2 hours at 190° to 210°F. Every 30 minutes, mix the ricotta lightly so that it doesn't get more than just lightly caramelized on top. Let the mixture cool, store it in a covered container, and refrigerate for up to 2 weeks.

Yogurt

The best yogurts take time (flavorful bacteria need time to develop!). Begin by using a small amount of store-bought yogurt with live cultures. Then after you make a batch, you can save some to make the next batch. The beauty of this method is that the more times you process from a single starter, the more developed and complex the characteristics and taste will become.

Makes ½ gallon

½ gallon whole milk (preferably raw)

½ cup plain probiotic yogurt (easy to find at most natural food stores)

1. In a pot, bring the milk to a simmer over medium heat. Let it cool to room temperature until it is just warm to the touch, about 100°F (or set the pot in an ice bath to speed things up). Whisk in the yogurt and pour the mixture into a ceramic pot or glass jar and cover with a tight-fitting lid.

2. Leave overnight at room temperature so that the cultures multiply (this is called "setting up"). The longer you leave it out, the thicker and more sour it will typically get. Once finished, you can infuse with flavors (see Tarragon Yogurt, opposite). Before flavoring the yogurt, save at least ¼ cup to make a future batch. The liquid runoff (or whey) can also be used to make more yogurt or other products in the future.

Chestnut Yogurt

We were fortunate enough to open our first restaurant with a Brazilian cook who grew up on a dairy farm specializing in yogurt. Infusing flavors in yogurt is easy and a great excuse to add yogurt to savory dishes.

Makes 3 cups

10 chestnuts
2 cups Yogurt (opposite)

1 to 2 teaspoons kosher salt
Ground white pepper

1. Crack the chestnuts and remove the meat, making sure to peel off any inner skin. Crush the chestnut meat and dehydrate it overnight at 140°F. Throw it into a food mill or spice grinder and process to a fine powder.
2. In a bowl, fold the chestnut powder into the yogurt, cover, and let it sit overnight in the refrigerator. Season with the salt and white pepper to taste.

— *Tarragon Yogurt* ——————————————————————

Infusions can be as simple as adding a few whole herb stems and refrigerating the yogurt overnight. I love making tarragon yogurt: Add 8 to 10 fresh tarragon leaves to ½ gallon of yogurt and refrigerate overnight. Or for a more intensely flavored yogurt, juice the herb first and mix in the bright green liquid and then refrigerate for a few hours. These methods can also be done with common flavorings like vanilla, maple syrup, or honey, or whatever else you would like to experiment with.

ICE CREAM

Though I never had a sweet tooth as a kid, I have always been a sucker for good ice cream. The better the milk and the eggs, the better the ice cream—it's as simple as that!

Black Walnut and Smoked Cream Ice Cream

Black walnut is one of the most interesting flavors of the Northeast. Unfortunately, the walnuts can be quite challenging to process, so many people buy them already broken down. Their richness, depth, and funk make them perfect for ice cream!

Makes 1½ quarts

¾ cup chopped black walnuts

2 cups Smoked Cream (page 116)

1 cup whole milk

½ teaspoon sea salt

1 vanilla bean, split

6 large egg yolks (from local eggs, bright orange yolks preferred)

⅔ cup maple sugar

Pure extra-dark maple syrup, heated, for serving

Chopped fresh mint, for serving

1. In a dry sauté pan, lightly toast the black walnuts over medium heat until you begin to see a little color, about 3 to 5 minutes. Remove from the pan and set aside to cool.

2. In a medium saucepan, combine the smoked cream, milk, salt, vanilla bean, and ¼ cup of the walnuts. Gently heat over medium-low heat, stirring often, for 15 minutes; do not let the mixture burn.

3. In a bowl, whisk together the egg yolks and maple sugar. Whisk rapidly (or use an electric mixer on medium) until thick and pale in color, 5 to 7 minutes.

4. Strain the milk and cream mixture into a separate large bowl. While it's still hot, whisking constantly, slowly pour in the beaten egg yolk mixture, to temper. Let the mixture cool completely in the refrigerator, then add the remaining ½ cup walnuts.

5. Churn the ice cream in an ice cream machine or an old-fashioned ice bucket churner. Alternatively, to make an ice cream with a rougher consistency, place the bowl in the freezer or set in snow and rapidly mix every 4 or 5 minutes to incorporate air until frozen.

6. To serve, drizzle each portion with 1 tablespoon hot maple syrup and sprinkle with ½ tablespoon chopped mint.

5

RIVERS, LAKES, AND OCEANS

Some of my earliest memories revolve around fishing the rivers, lakes, and oceans of the Northeast. Starting when I was very young, my father would take me hiking through the woods to show me his favorite childhood fishing holes, with freshly dug up night crawlers in hand. I can picture the fallen logs where the best bass would live, the catfish bubbles telling us exactly where to cast and how deep to drop the hook, and the way that one particular monster perch looked jumping into the air—the same one that nearly pulled me in. Years later, while living in the Rocky Mountains and exploring the rivers and mountains of the Northern Yukon Territories, I took up fly-fishing, which has become a lifelong passion.

On my mother's side, seafood was more than just a love—it was a birthright. My grandparents lived right on the water, and my grandfather was an avid fisherman, scalloper, and clammer. He also kept traps out in front of the house for crabs, lobster, and eels. When it came time to pull them in, I would follow him deep into the bay, feeling around the sandy floors with my toes for clams while just barely keeping my mouth above the water. To this day, I still use many of his original rods, clam rakes, and nets—the same ones that he used to teach me as a child.

Netting bait fish with my grandfather in Orient, New York

My family's longest-standing tradition, starting well before I was born, is the annual clambake. From building a fire to scrubbing clams to harvesting fresh bladderwrack seaweed along the shore, there is a job for everyone. At the heart of it used to be my grandmother, who would oversee each task until the feast was complete—one giant pot made up of everything the ocean had to offer. Without these early experiences, I am confident that I would not have become a chef.

So much of this book is based on the importance of awareness and observation. Fishing is no different. From a survivalist point of view, there is no such thing as being a specific type of fisherman, though the art of fishing requires learning a wide variety of disciplines, from fly-fishing, spin casting, trolling, trapping, and netting to spearfishing, depending on the type of fish and environment. Understanding what signs to look for and following how each species moves, feeds, and lives is learned from years of observation and from

Playing with an anchor rope in Orient

Fishing with my father in Shenorock, New York

listening carefully to fishermen more experienced than yourself. When I'm out in the bays and oceans, I prefer the challenge of abstaining from viewfinders or other expensive technology and relying on my gut instinct; watching for different types of birds, bait fish, ripples, and tides. Experienced fly fishermen must know their flies and the cycles of their fishing holes down to the week, as changing temperatures, water levels, fish, and insect spawning dictate everything.

Even a passionate fly fisherman will admit that there are times when a fly rod just isn't the most efficient way to fish an area. There is nothing worse then going into a stream with an overpriced fly rod and watching the person next to you pull your fish with a fifteen-dollar push button spin rod, a can of worms, and a bobber. I once heard that in an average fly fisherman's career, they wind up spending an average of $400 per fish, based on equipment alone. I make a real effort to keep my rods pristine for longevity; I managed to hold on to the same 5-weight rod for about fifteen years (up until a slight mishap in Maine one recent summer). One of my close friends is a professional guide and hunter down in Louisiana. He swears by inexpensive light fishing tackle when he's shore-casting for monster sand sharks, and enjoys the added challenge of it.

If you aren't able to get out there and fish for yourself, spending the time talking to your local fishermen or fishmonger to better understand what is in season and sustainable can fundamentally change the way that you cook. Our oceans, rivers, and lakes not only provide us with food but also help regulate the climate. It's hard to overemphasize the importance of these systems on our collective way of life. The Monterey Bay Aquarium Seafood Watch and their state-specific consumer guides are a great resource. At the restaurants, we take pride in sourcing and preparing what most would refer to as "trash fish," which are often invasive species, as well. Spider crab, mackerel, eel, giant hardshell clams, squid, sea robin, dogfish, and bluefish are all local examples that we work with regularly. It's not uncommon for us to see fifty pounds of fresh bluefish show up at the restaurants, because it was excess for a local fisherman and is still misconceived as an inferior-tasting fish.

When curing seafood, it's important to work with the freshest possible fish and shellfish. We do everything we can to work directly with our purveyors to shorten the time between when the fish is caught and when it reaches our kitchens. That said, not all fish tastes best fresh. This depends on the species, the preparation, and the season. Just as butchers often recommend hanging meat to allow it to rest before preparation, most experienced sushi chefs know that some fish require a certain amount of time out of water to develop and mature in flavor. Similarly, other factors, such as the manner in which an animal is killed and when the innards are removed, can affect how quickly the flesh becomes rancid. It's important to take note during these steps, as harmful bacteria can linger despite how the ultimate product is prepared— aged, cured, or consumed fresh. You may be familiar with the Japanese art of *ikijime*, a technique of quickly killing and cleaning fish. They start by thrusting a thin rod through the brain and spinal cord, instantly killing the animal and preventing the body from producing any postmortem lactic acid that could sour the meat. They then immediately drain the blood so as not to discolor or alter the flavor of the flesh. I utilize a version of this method every week when I'm breaking down fresh eels for the

restaurants, before butchering and smoking them for service. When preserving fish, it is important to keep in mind what process will work the best with which type of fish. We tend to use more oily fish to cure, pickle, or smoke, while more delicate or lean fish lend themselves better to being eaten raw or lightly cooked.

Most people know the general signs to look for when buying fish: clear eyes, firm to the touch, and a fresh "nonfishy" odor. Skate, rays, dogfish, and shark must always be consumed within a day or two of catching if being prepared fresh, as they excrete uric acid through their skin, making them ammoniated and off-putting. If preserved within that short window, however, cured skate can be intensely flavorful and delicious after many months of aging unrefrigerated.

Shellfish should also be eaten very fresh. We look for oysters and clams with strong shells and firm flesh, an indication that they've lived in good, clean, fast-moving waters, which forces them to develop stronger, more flavorful muscles. In my family, there is no bigger pleasure than simply sitting by the water, slurping down fresh oysters and steamer clams by the bucketful with a glass of chilled prosecco or ice-cold beer. Even when my grandfather was well into his nineties and wheelchair-bound, he had us bring him fresh shellfish with every visit. There was little else that would light up his face more than being at home with all of us eating littleneck clams on the half shell. I'm happy to include in this chapter the recipes for seafood feasts that my family has enjoyed for generations.

Something to appreciate as you consider these recipes: Each one will result in a product that can be stored for months. Be sure to attend carefully to the details. For example, when hanging fish to dry, do your best to make sure the temperature is controlled; fish heads can fall off if it gets too warm and you can lose your product altogether. Opening up a smoker to a hundred headless eels lying in soot on the bottom of the oven is not a good feeling. Rig the fish up and process thoughtfully for the best (and safest) results.

DRYING AND SMOKING

Dried and smoked foods are at the heart of all my kitchens and menus. Even my pantry at home is filled with countless different dried ingredients that I can pull from anytime to rehydrate and pair or cook with small amounts of fresh produce from the market each week. This way of cooking and looking at the kitchen adds both depth and value to meals: It plays an integral part in how I cook. This ranges from a few dried chiles added to fresh pastas to rehydrating rock-hard game meat for a stew.

Smoked Bluefish or Mackerel

Many local fishermen in the Northeast still throw bluefish and mackerel back or give them away. Both of these fish are fantastic to eat fresh, but their oily texture makes them the perfect fish for smoking!

Makes 1½ pounds

½ cup kosher salt

1 tablespoon chopped garlic

½ cup granulated maple sugar or
   brown sugar

1 gallon water

2 pounds bluefish or mackerel,
   filleted, with the skin on

1. In a large stockpot or bucket, whisk the salt, garlic, and sugar into the water. Add the fish and let it marinate in the refrigerator for 12 hours.
2. Let the fish air-dry in a cold smoker or refrigerator uncovered for 3 to 4 hours to build the pellicle.
3. Smoke over oak, birch, or maple at 130°F for 3 hours. Increase the heat to 150°F and smoke for 2½ hours. Then increase to 180°F and smoke for 2 more hours. From here you can remove the fish from the smoker and set aside to rest for about an hour until it has reached room temperature. Wrap in plastic and refrigerate. The most important part of smoking fish is taking your time and not letting the fat inside the fish heat up too fast. As soon as you see pearls of fat on the surface of the skin, you know you have ruined a perfectly good piece of fish!

Pickled Bluefish or Mackerel

Not only are these fish perfect for smoking (see page 140), their oily nature also makes them perfect for pickling. Pickled mackerel (which I prefer to the bluefish) is one of my favorite things. This recipe also lends itself well to other smaller, bait fish like herring and bream.

Makes 2 pounds

1 quart White Quick Pickle Liquid
   (page 38)
2 teaspoons allspice berries
2 shallots, jullienned
1 bunch fresh dill

1½ tablespoons Dijon mustard
3 garlic cloves, peeled and smashed
2 pounds bluefish or mackerel,
   filleted, with the skin off, and
   sliced into 2-inch strips

In a large-enough jar or bowl, combine the pickle liquid, allspice, shallots, dill, mustard, and garlic. Add the fish (it should be submerged in the liquid) and brine it in the fridge for 2 to 4 days. To test the fish, slice through a piece. You should see where the liquid has soaked through the meat all the way and the middle should still be a little pink. The fish can be kept in a covered container in the refrigerator for up to 3 weeks. It can be served in the brine as is or drained and tossed in a few tablespoons of sour cream and tarragon and served on sourdough or rye for a wonderful appetizer.

Smoked Trout

This is a basic dry cure that I use primarily for trout.

Makes 4 trout (about 3 pounds)

4 whole rainbow trout, cleaned
and butterflied, with head and
skin on

Dry Cure for Trout (recipe follows)
¼ cup Birch Bark Syrup (page 93)
or maple syrup

1. Cover the trout completely with the dry cure. Cover the trout and let sit overnight, in the refrigerator, then rinse off the cure. Air-dry the fish for 4 to 6 hours.

2. Smoke the trout over seasoned oak or maple at 130°F for 2 hours. Increase the temperature to 160°F and smoke for 1 more hour. Use a paintbrush to coat the flesh of the fish with the birch bark syrup. Increase the temperature again to 200°F and smoke until the flesh becomes caramelized, about 30 to 45 minutes. (Refer to the multiphase smoking chart on page 28 for details.)

— Dry Cure for Trout

1 cup kosher salt
1 cup lightly packed brown sugar
2 tablespoons pure dark maple syrup
2 teaspoons ground black pepper
1 tablespoon minced garlic
½ tablespoon minced shallot
1 teaspoon cayenne pepper
1 tablespoon juniper berries

Mix all the ingredients in a medium bowl; the dry cure is then ready to use.

Cured or Smoked Trout Roe

This process can be modified for any roe that you want to cure separately from its surrounding fat, whether it's the roe from steelhead trout, salmon, or any other fish that comes inland to breed. For this process, you need to source very ripe roe. Ask your fishmonger when this comes in (for us, it's generally in the spring). Curing roe was one of the first major challenges we took on at the restaurants, and after learning how to cold-smoke it, that method ended up being our go-to technique. Not only is the taste incredible, but curing and smoking allows you to stretch the lifespan of the roe from mere days to several weeks. Cured roe also makes for great fishing bait, likely because of the fat content, but you don't need to smoke your roe for trout fishing unless you're feeling particularly beneficent.

4 trout roe sacs, rinsed
¾ teaspoon kosher salt

1. The trickiest part of this process is extricating the roe from its fatty casing. The roe will be covered in a membrane, usually with one vein resembling a fishy "umbilical cord." It's easiest to remove the thin sac-like membrane by carefully slicing it open in a bowl of water, as you might with a pomegranate. Use extremely cold water and wear gloves to protect the roe from the heat of your hands. Next, gently strain the roe and place it in a bowl over an ice bath. The more carefully you handle it, the better the roe will keep its structure intact.

2. While the roe is still in the bowl over ice, gently mix the salt into the roe, being careful not to overhandle it. After a few hours, the cured roe will be ready to eat as is, or you could take it one step further by cold-smoking to preserve it longer and intensify the flavor.

3. To cold-smoke the roe, carefully spread it out on a rimmed baking sheet. Load up a smoker with lighter-burning substances, such as grapevines or light-flavored woods, such as pecan, birch, and oak. Unlike most other smoking applications, you want as little air moving over the delicate roe as possible. If your smoker has a strong internal fan, it might even be

worthwhile to loosely enclose the baking sheet in a cardboard or foil housing; you can also coat the roe in a very light layer of olive oil to help protect it, though you risk modifying the flavor. Very gently move the roe around with a paddle or lightly spritz with cold water to prevent it from developing a skin or pellicle.

4. It's also very important to keep the temperature between 36° and 39°F. If you don't feel confident about the reliability of your cold smoker and think it might run warm, place the roe on plastic wrap set over a rimmed baking sheet filled with ice to be safe.

5. Depending on the amount of smoke, the cold-smoking process could take from 30 minutes to 1 hour. You don't want to overwhelm the natural flavor of the eggs; you're looking for a gentle partnership of smoke and brine. When it's ready, the roe will likely look the same, or take on a slightly darker, more golden color. Store in a tightly sealed container in the fridge for 2 to 3 weeks.

Smoked Eel

My grandfather was an avid eel fisherman, and my grandmother would beautifully prepare his catch for us. Smoked eel was considered a true delicacy then, and is making a comeback today. My grandfather would keep the live eel in a bucket of ice water before processing; the ice made the eel more dormant, making it easier to kill. There are many ways to begin butchering eel; when I'm processing large quantities, killing them with salt can be a brutal but more efficient practice, and it dissolves the eel's mucous membrane, which you need to do anyway. If I'm working with only a handful of eels, as in this recipe, killing them one by one out of an ice bucket with a knife is preferred and more humane as it expedites the process.

Makes about 4 pounds

5 to 8 live eels, each ¾ to
    1½ pounds

2 cups kosher salt (if using salt to
    kill eels)

2 gallons Brine #1 (page 22)

2¼ cups pure dark maple syrup

½ cup soy sauce

½ cup apple cider vinegar

1. Place the eels in a container or cooler with a strong lid and cover with the kosher salt. Close the top quickly as they will try to escape. After about 30 minutes, you can open the container, wash off the eels, and begin to process them.

2. To process the eels, start with a sturdy, wood cutting board and hammer a square flooring nail at the top of the board, then remove the nail. This hole is how you will anchor an eel to the board.

3. Place the eel on the board, lining up the small space between the head and the gill with the premade hole. You want the eel's spine or back facing you. Carefully hammer a clean nail through the eel's head into the hole. Once secure, your first step is to butterfly the eel down the back (instead of through the stomach, as with other fish). With a short knife or a specialized unagi knife, make an incision just behind the head and move across the body, pulling toward yourself; be careful not to cut too deep or you risk separating

the spinal cord from the head. Do not let the innards break open, especially the green bile. Next, with your other hand holding the belly side, run your knife from the original incision along the top of the spine all the way to the end of the tail. It is important not to insert the tip of the knife further than the spine, and to feel it run along the bone the entire way, so as not to cut into any of the meat or organs.

4. Next, place the knife *under* the spine and carefully pull the blade to the tail again, this time removing the spine completely and as many of the ribs as possible. In smaller eels, the ribs are considered edible pin bones, so it's not essential to remove them all. Discard the head and very carefully remove the offal. (If you're cleaning a large amount of eel, it's worth keeping the dark orange liver to make pâté out of it. The eel's rich diet makes for an extremely

decadent pâté. I also like to wrap the intestines around skewers for grilling.) Rinse the meat off gently and repeat to prepare the rest of the eels.

5. Pour the brine into a large container, pour in the brine and whisk with 2 cups of the maple syrup. Submerge the cleaned eels, cover, and refrigerate overnight.

6. Rinse the eels thoroughly under cold water, then lay them skin side down and fully opened up on rimmed baking sheets. Place them back in the refrigerator and let air-dry for another 24 hours, or until a pellicle has formed.

7. In a bowl, combine the remaining ¼ cup of maple syrup, the soy sauce, and vinegar. Transfer the glaze mixture to a standard 32-ounce spray bottle and top off the bottle with water.

8. Smoke the eels at 140°F for 1½ hours. Spray the meat side of the eels with the glaze mixture after the first 30 minutes and every 30 minutes to follow. Increase the heat to 175°F and smoke for 2 hours more. Spray the glaze on one last time, and smoke at 200° to 210°F until the meat is lightly caramelized about 1 hour.

9. Let the eels cool, then cover or tightly wrap in plastic and refrigerate for up to 2½ weeks, or freeze.

Shad, Cod, or Scallop Roe Bottarga

When making shad bottarga during shad's early springtime season, look for pristine sacs that haven't been punctured. You should clearly see individual roe within the sacs. Traditional bottarga is made with a specific species of grey mullet or bluefin tuna, but this process can be used with other species of fish with similar roe sacs found in the Northeast. If you can't find shad roe, you can use cod or scallop roe. My personal favorite is diver scallop roe.

Makes 1 pound

2 cups water

½ cup kosher salt

4 fresh shad roe sacs, cod roe, or sea scallop roe

Good-quality olive oil

Sea salt

1. In a saucepan, combine the water and kosher salt and bring to a boil, then let it cool completely. The salt must be completely dissolved for this brine to be effective. Cool the brine and pour into any shallow glass or plastic food-safe container, then the submerge the roe sacs in the brine, cover, and refrigerate overnight.

2. Dip the roe in olive oil; this helps it dry more evenly and delicately. Gently roll it in sea salt.

3. Cold-smoke the roe at under 60°F for about 1 hour. Throughout the process, you will need to resalt it lightly once or twice before it's done smoking. As the moisture leaves, it will take some of the salt with it. This is a delicate balance to strike, as you don't want the end product to be too salty.

4. Tie up the sacs or wrap the roe in cheesecloth and hang in a cool, dark place with good airflow for up to 3 months. A small quantity of roe might be ready in only a couple of weeks. You will know it's thoroughly dried when the sacs are firm to the touch all the way through. (Instead of hanging, you can also dry the sacs or roe in a dehydrator, turning carefully, at 115°F for 10 to 12 hours. This will speed up the process dramatically but doesn't give you as delicate of a product.)

5. The end product can be sliced, shaved, or grated and kept in the fridge for several months.

Dried Monkfish

When a fish becomes too expensive to serve whole or as fillets, it's important for me to find a new way of approaching its preparation in order to make the most out of it and keep our food and prices accessible—no different than the added value of making a country ham. By drying the monkfish tail, what was once one or two portions now becomes something beautiful and flavorful that we can shave onto fifteen portions of vegetables or starch.

Makes 2 pounds

RUB
1 pound brown sugar
1 pound kosher salt
4 garlic cloves, crushed
½ tablespoon crushed black pepper

4 whole monkfish tails (4 to 6 pounds total)
Sumac syrup, store-bought or homemade (page 96)

1. To make the rub: Combine the brown sugar, salt, garlic, and pepper in a bowl. Pack the mixture around the fish, covering it completely. You can set the tails on a rack to help drain the moisture, or place them in a zip-top bag for less airflow and a slower, more intensified cure. Refrigerate the fish in the cure for at least 24 hours, but no longer than 3 days. You'll know it's ready when it turns a deep ruby red.

2. Rinse off the rub; the fish should feel stiff to the touch. Tie the fish with twine and hang it in a cold smoker for 4 days, keeping the smoker under 45°F . Every day, add small amounts of smoke; use fruit or nut wood (such as pecan, applewood, or cherry). On the second day, brush with a light layer of sumac syrup. After 4 days, let the fish hang and dry-age in the smoker or in a dry-aging room for 2 weeks or 3 to 4 weeks in a refrigerated room or cellar, until it's hard enough to slice paper-thin like prosciutto.

Smoked Scallops

These are perfect for eating as is, or as part of a larger composed dish. This recipe can be used with smaller bay scallops, as well—both considered prized treasures on the North Fork of Long Island.

Makes 4 or 5 servings

15 large sea scallops

BRINE
2½ cups water
1 cup kosher salt
1 cup lightly packed brown sugar
2 tablespoons pure dark maple
    syrup

2 teaspoons ground black pepper
1 tablespoon minced garlic
½ tablespoon minced shallot
1 teaspoon cayenne pepper
1 tablespoon juniper berries

1. Clean the scallops and trim them if you like, by peeling off the foot and side muscles, saving the odd bits for future chowders and stews.
2. To make the brine: In a pot, combine the brine ingredients and bring to a boil, then set aside to cool.
3. Cool the brine and pour into any shallow glass or plastic food-safe container, submerge the scallops in the brine, cover, and refrigerate overnight.
4. Drain the scallops and air-dry them on racks for 6 to 8 hours, until they're tacky to the touch. Smoke them at 160°F for 2 hours, then at 210°F for 20 minutes, or until they're beautifully golden brown on the outside and perfectly cooked on the inside. I prefer them a little undercooked or on the raw side.

Smoked Cod

Cod fishing in the Northeast is an integral part of why we are all now here at all. It is the reason early Scandinavian expeditions began exploring our coasts. When smoked right, cod can be one of the most decadent fish we have access to.

Makes 2 pounds

BRINE
2 quarts water
½ cup Birch Bark Syrup (page 93)
1 cup kosher salt
1 cup lightly packed brown sugar
2 teaspoons ground black pepper
1 tablespoon minced garlic

½ tablespoon minced shallot
1 teaspoon cayenne pepper
1 tablespoon juniper berries
2 teaspoons pink curing salt #1
(aka inta-cure #1)

2 pounds wild Atlantic cod, filleted

1. To make the brine: Combine the brine ingredients in a bowl and whisk together. In a hotel pan or a large plastic container, add the brine mixture and the cod. Make sure the cod is fully submerged by weighting it with a zip-top bag filled with water. Brine the cod for 24 hours in the refrigerator.
2. Rinse the cod with cold water and let it air-dry uncovered in the refrigerator for 6 to 8 hours to build its pellicle and until it feels tacky to the touch.
3. Smoke the cod in three phases: at 140°F for 3 hours, at 180°F for 1 hour, and at 210°F for 30 minutes. Let cool to room temperature.

Smoked Mussels

We've been serving smoked mussels since we opened our first restaurant. These have always been a favorite for us. Mussels are inexpensive, plentiful, and when prepared well, as addictive as candy.

Makes 2 cups

4 dozen Hollander mussels or similar large mussels

1 cup safflower oil

1. Scrub the mussels and let them sit in fresh, cold water for 30 minutes. Set up a stovetop steamer over high heat. This can consist of simply a steamer insert in a pot or three hotel pans, one filled with water on a hot burner, one perforated pan above it for the seafood, and one pan on top working as a cover. Steam until they just open, then immediately remove the mussels from their shells. Lightly toss the mussels in ½ cup of the oil until coated.

2. Place the mussels in a cold smoker, keeping the temperature below 100°F for 3 hours, carefully mixing every 30 minutes so as not to oversmoke. Use oak or any fruitwood.

3. Cool down, fold in the remaining ½ cup oil, and then store in a jar, refrigerated, for up to 1 week.

Preserved Cockles in Smoked Thyme Oil

Hardshell clams in the Northeast are often classified by age and size but are actually the same species, cockles being the youngest, then littlenecks, medium topnecks, cherrystones, and quahogs. These are excellent by themselves or with bread and butter.

10 dozen cockles (baby hardshell clams), cleaned

1 quart Smoked Herb Oil (page 98), made with thyme

1. Prepare a large steamer and steam the cockles just until they open, taking care not to overcook them. Shuck the cockles from the shells; they should slide out easily and keep whole.
2. Place the clams in small jars, then pour in the smoked thyme oil to fully submerge, and seal. Let the jars sit unopened for 1 to 4 months. The longer they sit in the oil, the more flavor the clams will take on.

Pickled Oysters

The trick to this recipe is simple: Use fresh, excellent-quality oysters. We use wild-foraged ones from Rocky Point, Long Island, New York. I feel it's important to find an oyster that exemplifies the incredible heritage of oyster eating and oyster farming of the region. Pickling works best with a slightly sweet and mildly briny oyster, such as any medium to small variety of Blue Points.

Makes 24 oysters

1 quart White Quick Pickle Liquid   24 medium to large oysters
   (page 38)

Pour the pickle liquid into a 2- or 3-quart glass or plastic container. Shuck the oysters and submerge them in the liquid. Pickle for at least 24 hours. These should last about 1 week, but we've had pickled oysters last well over a month. You'll know they're bad if they smell fishy or are slimy to the touch.

Shrimp Paste

When I was a kid, my grandfather had an old seine net that I loved using every time I stayed with him. It was and is the best way to collect small shiner fish and krill for bait. Slowly dragging that net up onto shore is just as fascinating to me now as it was when I was young. You never know what you'll pull in.

Shrimp paste on its own can have an extremely off-putting smell and taste, but as a flavor-boosting ingredient in other dishes it can add tremendous depth. Fermented small shrimp recipes can be found all over the world and are used in everything from sauces, marinades, and dressings to fermented vegetables and more! Krill, similar to shrimp, are an incredibly important part of our ocean's ecosystems, and it's no surprise that they've become a staple of many kitchens. It's important to use fresh shrimp or krill.

Makes 2 pounds

2 pounds fresh small shrimp (with or without their shells) and/or krill, rinsed

4 tablespoons kosher salt

½ tablespoon minced garlic

1 shallot, minced

1 teaspoon cayenne pepper

1. Toss the shrimp with 2 tablespoons of the salt. Air-dry for 2 to 3 hours, if outside temperatures are above 50°F, or dry in the dehydrator at about 110°F for 1 hour. Remove the shrimp and crush to a paste with a mortar and pestle or in a food processor, adding the garlic, shallot, cayenne, and the remaining 2 tablespoons salt.
2. Press the shrimp paste into squares or rounds 1 inch thick and 3 to 6 inches wide. Place them either on a drying rack for 5 days or in a dehydrator at 90° to 95°F for 4 days. (There are many traditional finishing techniques that involve burying the paste underground to increase the fermentation process, giving the end product a more intense, funkier taste.)
3. The dried paste can be wrapped well in wax paper and stored in the pantry.

Fish Sauce or Garum

Garum is an oilier version of fish sauce, originally prepared and used in North Africa and ancient Greece and later popularized in Rome. We call this "fish sauce" in house, but the product is really a cross between fish sauce and garum. This sauce is a fundamental part of many of our sauces, cures, and brines. We've found that it adds complex layers of briny depth to smoked meats and other proteins but also as a companion to many vegetable dishes. We have discovered that this same process can be used to make sauces out many different meats as well, opening the doors to more interesting products of food waste.

When selecting fish for this process, use a small oily fish, such as herring, sardines, or shiners. Even though you're purposefully rotting the fish, it must be very fresh to start.

Makes 1½ pounds

5 pounds small oily local fish, cleaned

½ pound kosher salt, plus 1 tablespoon if needed

3 tablespoons sumac syrup, store-bought or homemade (page 96)

8 northern bayberry leaves, dried or fresh

½ tablespoon juniper berries

1 tablespoon black peppercorns

1. Mix the fish with the salt and place it in a ceramic container or crock large enough to hold up to 2 gallons of liquid. Tie cheesecloth over the top. Let it sit for 24 hours, then open and stir. The salt should have extracted enough liquid so that the fish is fully submerged. If it's not completely covered in its own liquid, add 1 tablespoon salt and 1 cup water and let it sit overnight again.

2. Lightly mix in the sumac syrup, bayberry leaves, juniper berries, and peppercorns and pour in 1 gallon water. Cover with cheesecloth again and let the mixture sit in a cool, dark room for about 3 months (and up to 6 months), stirring it thoroughly every couple of days until the fish breaks down and settles on the bottom, leaving you with a brown oily liquid. The intensity of the smell varies, though for the sake of your loved ones, keep this

in a separate room or enclosed cabinet. Once the fish is broken down, strain the fish solids out of the fish sauce, pressing to get the last bits of flavor out of the fish. (You can hold on to the drained fish solids, combine with a handful of salt, spread out in a dehydrator, and dry completely at 120°F for 5 to 7 hours until completely dried—and presto, you have shelf-stable fish salt to use for seasoning in future dishes!)

3. Transfer the fish sauce to a small 3-gallon barrel (we use small whiskey barrels, which can sometimes be found at home brew stores or online). Age the fish sauce in the barrel for an additional 1 to 3 months, depending on what you have the patience for and how strong an end product you're looking for. From this point, it can be used and stored in jars and refrigerated for several years.

North Fork Clambake

"Granny would conduct the family as if composing a symphony. All the youngest would be on seaweed duty, while Papa Benji would take me raking for clams. You usually just find 'em with your toes. It was our family's greatest feast, and everyone knew their job. The seaweed would crack, smoke, and burn over the hot sand-covered coals. I remember the smell well . . . it meant that piles of lobsters and clams were sure to come. Lobster roe was fought over like a gang of vultures over a kill."

—ANDY SOKOBIN, MY UNCLE

This recipe defines a good portion of my childhood and some of my favorite early memories. The clambake is without question the biggest family event of the year, the one we all look forward to most. When we were growing up, my grandparents engrained every step of this process into us; it became second nature. When it came time for them to step back from the hands-on cooking, it felt only natural for me to assume that role. It's because of them that I know how to dig out every last bit of lobster meat, from underneath the head to behind the lungs and at the tip of each claw; how delicious the green tomalley can be; and that uncovering a strip of bright red roe is like finding gold—and should be eaten quickly and quietly.

Makes 10 to 15 servings

4 dozen topneck or cherrystone clams

I dozen quahog clams

5 dozen steamer or soft-shell clams

4 dozen large local mussels

15 pounds bladderwrack seaweed ("popper"), sprayed with fresh water

2 whole Pekin ducks, cleaned and quartered

2 dozen small red potatoes, new potatoes, or Yukon Gold potatoes

8 lemons, halved

15 local live lobsters (1¼ to 1½ pounds each)

15 ears local corn, shucked

I large russet potato

I quart Rose Hip Brown Butter, melted (page 120)

PREPPING THE INGREDIENTS

1. Scrub and clean the clams and mussels and
   rinse the seaweed. Cut 8 x 8-inch squares of
   cheesecloth and use them to wrap small
   packets of each type of clam (except for
   the quahogs) and the mussels, so that each
   is of equal size and separated by type of
   shellfish. Create the same few packets for
   the duck and then again for the small potatoes,
   which should fit 4 or 5 in each bundle. Wrap each
   lemon half in a small square of cheesecloth, to allow you to
   squeeze out lemon juice without the seeds (save this for the end!).

LAYERING THE POT

2. Place about 5 inches of cleaned seaweed in the bottom of a large stockpot
   (about 60 quarts/15 gallons).

3. Distribute the quahog clams around the pot, followed by a thinner layer
   of seaweed. Do the same with the bags of duck and potatoes, followed by
   another thin layer of seaweed. Repeat by layering the remaining ingredients
   in this order: topnecks and steamers, another layer of seaweed, mussels, then
   more seaweed.

4. Nestle the lobsters into the pot with seaweed tucked around the edges (to
   protect the lobsters from the edges of the pot). Add more seaweed, and then
   the corn.

5. Top off the pot with any remaining seaweed and finish by placing the sole
   russet potato at the top center. Cover the pot lightly with the lid and place a
   brick or weight on top.

COOKING

6. Place the pot over a large propane burner or hot coal bed. The clambake will
   take anywhere from 45 to 90 minutes, depending on the temperature outside
   and the heat level. Use your single russet potato on top as an indicator: As
   soon as it is fork-tender, your clambake is ready to serve!

SERVING

7. Spread the seaweed over the table as a base for serving. Cut open the bags and pour out the contents over the seaweed; cut down the center of each lobster. Serve everything with the melted butter and the lemons. Quahogs—referred to as bacon of the sea—are traditionally used for flavor, but are often too tough to eat out of a bake.

— Tomalley

Most people get turned off by lobster tomalley—which means more for me! The tomalley is the green gunk that lines the inside of the lobster, a combination of its insides: backfat, liver, roe, and other unmentionables. One of my favorite things to do with the tomalley is to turn it into what I call "Long Island Guacamole."

Makes 2½ cups

2 cups tomalley (from 6 to 8 lobsters)
4 tablespoon Smoked Cream (page 116) or store-bought crème fraîche
4 or 5 roasted garlic cloves (see Note, page 190), mashed
Pinch of cayenne pepper, salt, black pepper, sage (or any fresh herbs)
Zest and juice of 2 limes
2 shallots, minced

Mix together all the ingredients in a bowl and serve with chips.

Crab Boil

Unfortunately New York isn't known for its crab boils. We are close enough to New England that the tradition here and in my family leans more toward lobster and clambakes. We still, however, hold one of the larger populations of blue crabs, which usually get shipped off to places like Maryland where they tend to be more popular. Blue crabs are native to the Northeast, all the way down to the Gulf. While they are beginning to face issues with other invasive species like spider crabs, they are still bountiful and absolutely delicious.

Makes 8 to 10 servings

2 to 3 pounds smoked andouille sausage, cut into ½-inch slices

½ cup minced garlic

1 tablespoon cayenne pepper

2 red onions, roughly chopped

½ cup ground black pepper

3 tablespoons miso

½ cup soy sauce

8 to 12 fresh or dried northern bayberry leaves

½ cup canola or vegetable oil

½ cup picked fresh thyme leaves

½ bushel live jumbo blue crabs

1 pound butter, at room temperature

3 lemons, halved

1. Fill a large steamer pot (60 quarts/15 gallons is ideal) with about 8 quarts of water (one-quarter full). Add the andouille, garlic, cayenne, onions, pepper, miso, soy sauce, bayberry leaves, oil, and ¼ cup of the thyme. Bring the mixture to a boil over high heat and let it boil for 10 minutes. Add the crabs and gently mix and boil until they start to turn bright red.

2. Carefully remove the pot from the heat and add the butter. Cover the pot and let the crabs steam for another 10 minutes or so, until the butter has completely melted, and mix. Strain off any excess liquid and pour the crabs and sausage onto a butcher-paper- or newspaper-covered table.

3. Char the lemons on a grill until the flesh has blackened and blistered a bit. Shake the remaining ¼ cup thyme over the crabs. Serve with the charred lemons and whatever other sides you love—grilled corn and roasted potatoes are our favorites.

6

MEAT, BUTCHERY, AND CHARCUTERIE

Just as with seafood, it's important to find a sustainable and ethical source of meat. Although we use meat in many of these recipes, I feel that it's important to note that I do not believe there is a sustainable future for the world's population to depend on meat as a main protein source. With that said, we have been on a path over the past two years to greatly reduce the amount of meat on our menus, making sure that what we do serve can be not just more sustainable in less volume, but as focused and delicious as possible.

This chapter explores butchering, curing, smoking, and basic preservation techniques. Similar to the last chapter, I provide recipes for larger, whole animal feasts traditionally used as a form of appreciation for the animal, and to bring people together for communal dining. Preserving meats, like all preservation techniques, grew out of the need for survival, but is now done primarily to impart a deeper and richer flavor.

No matter how we choose to live, we are all part of a larger system that involves harming other forms of life in order for us to survive as a species. Though it can be emotionally painful to think about it in this manner, I feel it's delusional to try to frame it in any other way. Every living thing wants to continue living. A flock of ducks will flee from the sound of a gunshot. A possum will play dead. An octopus will camouflage itself against the ocean floor. A plant will grow toward the light. A human will engage in fight or flight in an emergency. We all share an inherent drive to live. We as humans have a tendency to judge whether one form of life is more acceptable to kill over another, based on how closely we feel its anthropomorphic or emotional responses resemble our own.

We simply do not have enough information to determine whether any one life is more valuable than another, making it essential that all life be treated with respect and humility. It is also our shared responsibility to take on the reality of death and its inevitability. In doing so, we allow ourselves to appreciate the quality of each moment and breath taken by every life form.

We are largely disconnected from this practice and responsibility. Grocery stores fill their aisles with the most aesthetically pristine produce, while anything less perfect-looking goes to waste. Packaged meat and seafood are precut, vacuum-sealed, and often dyed more appealing colors or pumped full of water and phosphates. Some are even renamed in such a way that it's often difficult to determine whether they've come from something living at all. Many of these animals are overmedicated with antibiotics and fed GMO feed, most of which has not been responsibly tested and has likely helped drive many of the modern health concerns we now face as industrialized nations.

What we choose to eat is every individual's decision. If we can acknowledge that no matter what we choose to eat, we are taking life in some form, it is important to truly experience what this actually means. As a chef, the most important tool I have is my connection to the ingredients. Every chef who cooks with meat should have the experience of killing an animal at close range. Even many hunters are disconnected from this important experience, when shooting a whitetail deer from hundreds of yards away and then walking up to claim an already lifeless body. More than anything else, seeing another being go from living to lifeless, feeling its spirit surrender, commands respect more powerfully than any other experience I have ever had. It is not something to be taken lightly or that gets easier—nor do I think it should.

In the same way that the earth naturally composts and decomposes organic material for minerals and nutrients, our digestive system works to break down food. Life and energy keep moving through the whole system, never lost but constantly twisting, turning, redirecting, and dispersing. In death, there's life.

TRACKING AND HUNTING

One of the ways I developed my passion for cooking was by practicing primitive wilderness survival skills, from as young as six or seven. It is an art that relies on making oneself vulnerable and humble in nature. I truly believe that these skills, this kind of re-education, may be the only way we can save the wilderness. I have met some extraordinary trackers, survivalists, guides, and hunters over the years. I learned a tremendous amount from each of them, but without dedicating the rest of my life to it, I could never come close to matching their breadth of knowledge. As my life and career progress, I circle back more and more to those early days and months in the woods: hand-drilling fires, weaving fish traps, and later learning to bake acorn flatbreads over stone and ash. These were the experiences that really led me to take cooking more seriously. I suppose it's not so strange that so much of the cooking we do at the restaurants now uses fire and smoke as major components.

Deer

Like many subjects in this book, the most important skill for tracking and hunting begins with observation. Learning to open our senses fully to our environment becomes critical. Good hunters can tell just as much about an animal by the trail it leaves as they can by making visual contact with it. When it comes to tracking, the common assumption is that this refers only to the footprint of an animal. It's true that the footprint can certainly reveal a lot, but more often than not the real narrative is what surrounds each print. Each animal leaves behind a history of its behavior in its trails.

A good way to begin understanding this is by simply spending the time to examine a single square foot of grass, allowing yourself to become immersed in each little micropath, trail, and mark, noting an unusual direction of a few blades of grass, the scraps of an acorn, or an intricately made path of leaf-cutter ants. In a relaxed state of mind, walking through the woods becomes a practice of constantly widening and narrowing one's vision. The goal is to see your entire surroundings in one gaze while at the same time searching for signs of trails and wild edibles on the ground beneath you. A footprint can first and foremost help you identify what animal you're following; but its contour, depth, direction, and the spaces in between each track can also tell you what that animal was doing at that moment.

Bobcat

When foraging, we tend to spend a lot of time following deer trails, with the understanding that many kinds of mushrooms and edibles are spread by animals as they brush along plants and spread spores or by eating and eliminating fruits and berries with seeds. Chanterelles are a great example of mushrooms that grow alongside trails for this reason. Deer are ritualistic creatures; they tend to follow the same routes over and over to watering holes, feeding grounds, and beds. It is easy to spot a deer trail because the damage they do is proportional to their size. From clipped, directional grasses and other ground cover, scat, snapped twigs, or small patches of hair left behind to tree scraping made by bucks in rut, you can see the signs if you are relatively observant. Smaller animals leave trails that require a much more careful eye. Similar patterns on a smaller scale can tell you whether a rodent or a bobcat had been grazing, hunting, panicking, and so on. These tracks can give us clues to an animal's size, how fast it was moving, and often even its sex.

Moose

Once a year, I go down to the Louisiana bayous to learn about hunting boar and gators. Tracking in that environment has taught me to look for many other types of signs—from disturbed alligator grasses to how fast different spiders weave their webs—that can allow you to gauge the busyness of a trail or boated waterway. Whether we're trapping, hunting, or foraging, the first step is learning how to read and understand these signs in the natural world.

Squirrel

Smell and sound go hand in hand in all of these scenarios. In urban areas, the constant sensory overload can numb these senses. When I was younger, I spent a few months living in the rainforests of Central America. One morning while hiking, a friend and guide, who had been a poacher and was now an educator, abruptly stopped on the trail because he had smelled a deadly fer-de-lance viper ten meters down in a bush. The whole experience left me in awe. As I got older, I found myself occasionally being able to smell that same reptilian scent and to listen for that consistent sound of movement that only something slithering could make. Shortly after, that same friend stopped me again while walking on a different trail because a very faint sound had tipped him off to two medium-size tapirs almost exactly 150 meters northwest of us. Sure enough, there they were.

Coyote

In college, I spent some time traveling in the Northern Yukon territories, mountaineering and running rapids down the Hess River. I still remember very clearly what it's like to walk into a small clearing of dug-up roots and be overwhelmed by the musky "wet

Mountain
Lion

Fried Locusts

(adapted from American Indian Society Cookbook,
by the American Indian Society of Washington, DC, compiled December 1975)

In the early summer, catch the locusts when they first emerge from grub (before they can fly). Melt enough butter to fill at least one-quarter of the way up a cast-iron skillet. Pour the live locusts into the pan and shake them around, frying them until they stop moving and are crisp and browned. Drain and empty into a large bowl. Toss with salt and eat, holding them by the wings.

—Raphael Gonyea, Oneida

Snapping Turtle

(adapted from American Indian Society Cookbook)

Catch a live turtle about 12 inches wide. Hold it by the tail and offer it a stick to bite on. Have someone else hold on to the stick while you carry it to the chopping block. While the other person pulls on the stick to stretch his neck out, cut off the head with an axe. Very carefully, using a sharp pointed knife, cut around and under the shell until you free the meat. Dip it in boiling water to take off the thin outer membrane. Cut the meat into serving pieces and boil it in salted water for another hour or more. Then, take each piece and roll it in flour with salt and pepper. Fry it in hot fat until golden brown on both sides. You can fry a younger turtle like chicken. The meat will continue to twitch for a while, which is normal.

—Bertha Jennings, Ottawa

Moose Nose

(adapted from American Indian Society Cookbook)

Cut the nose off the moose head, with the hair and all. Poke a stick through the nose. Cook over an open fire, keeping it about 1 to 2 feet away from the flame. The hair will burn off by itself. When it looks done, turn it to the other side and cook until tender. About an hour total.

—Katherine Peter, AFN

dog" smell of grizzly bears. When you are by yourself in those situations, there is nothing that will make the hairs on the back of your neck stand up straighter . . . but at the same time, there's little more that's as exhilarating.

Some of these experiences felt almost telepathic at the time, as if there was something higher than just instinct and a mastery of the senses. Most indigenous cultures carry oral or written histories that discuss the different levels of awareness, their effect on us as hunters, and our connection to the natural world within our daily lives. It's often expressed as a level of "oneness" in its deepest sense. Thus, the awareness lends itself very well to many meditation and spiritual practices. Even after all of these years, there are things that I have seen from very experienced woodsmen and trackers that seem to extend beyond the rational world.

BUTCHERING FOR CURING

POULTRY AND WILD GAMEBIRDS

Processing wild birds requires a specific and tedious step-by-step. Once the bird is killed, the first step is to remove the feathers. There are two main ways to defeather a bird by hand. One is to pull off the tail feathers and any of the colored plumage that easily separates, then hold the bird by its feet at least 12 inches away and use a blowtorch to singe off the rest of the feathers. Char them slightly, being careful not to accidentally cook the skin. The other method is to hold the bird by its feet and dunk it into a pot of boiling water. Both methods make it much easier to pull the remaining small feathers out, which can be done with pliers or by wrapping the bird in a towel and rubbing with your hands. Rinse the bird in cold water to ensure all feathers and debris are cleaned off.

Use the butt of a heavy chef's knife or a cleaver to remove the head at the base of the neck and the feet from the ankles.

Locate the bird's oil gland, a fat-filled sac at the very tip of the tail, and cut it off using a sharp knife. Follow by making a shallow incision along the length of the belly, beginning from the tailbone all the way up to the wishbone at the base of the breast. Be very careful not to slice too deep or you will puncture the intestines. Then, make a small incision around the throat where the neck connects to the body to loosen the esophagus and windpipe. Using your hands, pull off the loosened neck. Reach inside the body at the tail end and carefully pull out the innards, saving any hearts, gizzards, or livers for cooking later. In many cultures outside of the United States, every single organ is used. Consider what you might do with these innards.

Lay the bird on its back and carve out the wishbone from the chest cavity. Separate the drumsticks and thighs from the carcass by gently pulling at them to see where the natural seams are. You should see a gap between the thigh and breast and be able to run your knife through that space, from the inside of the thigh and down to the spine. When you're cutting a bird, you should never be cutting meat—you should just be cutting cartilage and sinew. Hold the drumstick and thigh as one piece in your hand and pull it back until you hear it dislocate from the hip joint.

Turn the bird onto its breast with the back facing up. Run your knife along either side of the backbone and remove. There is a little dimple along the inside of the spine, where the legendary "oyster" meat sits (I think it's overrated, but it's important to mention it). Carefully peel away the skin and pop out the oyster so that it's still attached to the thigh. When separating the thigh pieces from the spine, there should be no resistance. You could do this with your bare hands, but using a knife makes it that much quicker and easier.

Flip the bird over again and run your knife between the breast and the center breastbone, removing each side of meat completely and taking care to keep the tenderloin attached. (At the restaurant, we usually set aside the tenderloins and roast them as snacks for the kitchen staff.) Remove the wings and prepare separately. If the meat is going to be cooked in the next day or two, I suggest putting it immediately into a brine.

It's important to note that when you're cutting protein, you want the blade angled slightly toward the bone to avoid cutting into the valuable meat. In most butchery, the animal will tell you how to cut it, even if you're not familiar with it. As you remove a leg or breast, for example, you can follow the lines of the muscle and the structure of the animal as a guide.

Always remember to keep the carcass for stock. And, it's always, always better to be generous when cutting into and around skin and fat while butchering—you can trim away but you can't put back on!

If you're eating wild game, make sure to search very thoroughly for leftover shotgun pellets.

VENISON

Breaking down deer is different from the method for other animals if you want to keep the skin whole and intact for tanning. What follows is a brief overview of how to field dress a deer, but this process could be modified for any animal whose skin will be saved and used later. (There's a list of hunting and survival guides in Resources on page 299 that give much more detailed information.)

Begin by hanging the deer upside down. I believe the best way to bleed out a deer is to cut an incision at the throat and hang the deer over a large bucket. Add ½ to 1 cup salt or vinegar to the bucket and stir; this is a traditional way to prevent the blood from coagulating.

When the bleeding has mostly stopped, tie the carcass by the head, with the legs splayed. Working from the belly side, cut from the anus up to the top of the breast bone, right under the base of the neck. A hooked knife is ideal but a boning knife works, too. Use your hands to carefully remove all the intestines and innards (if the bile sac bursts, you could ruin your meat). Run the boning knife around the base of each of the animal's hooves then inward to meet the initial incision that runs the length of the body. Use your hands, or carefully pull with pliers, to peel off the skin. Set the skin aside to be scraped, cured, stretched, and tanned. Use a knife to cut away the head until you get to the vertebrae. When you get to that point, use a bone saw to remove the head with strong sure strokes.

Remove the tenderloin and backstrap—the muscles on either side, traditionally the most prized possessions for many hunters because of their inherent tenderness, though we know now they are not always the most flavorful. (See Venison Gravlax on page 183 for a great recipe to get the most flavor out of these cuts.) Move to the back of the animal and run the knife along the spine, peeling off the backstrap. Holding the muscle firmly in one hand, use the other knife to cut and trim away any silver skin or cartilage. Flip the carcass around and going in from the belly-side cavity, run the knife from the top down along the spine, removing the tenderloin using the same motion as for the backstrap.

Next, I cut off the hams or legs. Run your knife through the tissue between the hip plate and the spine. Pull the hip bone toward you to dislocate it, then run your knife through the tendons to remove the leg from the body. You shouldn't have to use a bone saw here. Repeat with the other leg.

Working on the legs now, use a bone saw to separate the shin from the upper thigh, then run your knife around the hooves and use the bone saw to cut off the hooves. The shins can be used for stock or any kind of roasted preparations. The upper thigh or ham can be used for a wide variety of other preparations.

Untie the deer and place it on a clean work surface. Remove the two front legs, repeating the process of cutting along the seams and dislocating the limbs from the carcass. Remove the hooves and shins.

Hooves can be cleaned carefully, then blanched and boiled. This stock will create pure natural gelatin.

Return to the main carcass. Cut straight down the center of the breastbone to separate it into two halves. Starting from the outer tips of the ribs, measure 4 to 6 inches down; with a boning knife, cut a light line here, moving horizontally across each rib. This will be your guide to separating the short ribs. Next, using the bone saw, cut away the short ribs following your precut lines and remove.

Cut vertically through the remaining ribs down to the spine in pairs of two, then use the boning saw to finish the cut through the spine to separate. These make great saddle roasts. Alternatively, you can then saw down the middle of the carcass on either side of the spine to create two whole beautiful racks for roasting.

Venison heart is great for tartare. If you use any innards, be conscious of worms and bacteria that affect hooved animals. More information on potential risk factors can be found in any local hunting guide.

Mounting a deer head may be fun for sportsmen, but for a survivalist it is a waste. The hides from the head are perfect for brain tanning, a method utilizing the animal's own brain as a source of oil for the tanning process, which yields high-quality, soft, absorbent leather. There is also no shortage of edible meat in the head, such as the jowls, face, and tongue. Even the antlers can be essential in things like tool-making, while the "velvet" encasing the antlers has long been used for naturopathic and medicinal preparations. The stomach can be used as a water vessel, if not as a natural casing for sausage, and tendons and sinews are great for using as string, or thread, and for making tools.

FARM ANIMALS

Butchers may think in terms of certain cuts of meat, but there's no right way to break down an animal—many of the cuts that we think of as "correct" are simply those that companies and consumers consider the most saleable. With the disappearance of local butchers and a general lack of communication between industrial meat packers and chefs, most cuts that are distributed to restaurants follow generic standards from the 1970s and 1980s (often renamed and rebranded). With a few exceptions, most industrial meat packers and supermarkets are focused only on selling, and will go above and beyond to trick customers into thinking a cut of meat is worth more than it is. A classic example of this is the "prime rib," which is not actually graded prime meat. It is very important whenever possible to work with small local butchers who care enough to genuinely discuss what it is that you're buying—what part of what animal it's from—and even offer preparation tips. Don't be afraid to break the rules a bit. While Western tradition considers tenderloin, chicken breast, or filet mignon to be choice cuts, there are cultures that consider them the least flavorful.

If you'd like to learn the basics of butchery, I suggest starting with the pig. If you can learn how to break down a pig, you can break down just about anything. When we butcher a pig, we tend to do it with our specific needs in mind. The jowls, hams, fatback, bellies, tenderloins, hocks, and front legs are cut specifically to be cured in different ways and are often aged. The rest of the head is used for head cheese, and many of the innards end up in terrines and pâtés. The ears and tails can be braised and served cold or fried up for a snack (same goes for any excess skin). The stomachs, shoulders, blood, and intestines are all used when making encased meats, such as sausage, and the lower ends of the intestines are for chitlins. The collar and rib eye can be cooked on the grill and the ribs (of course) get split up for smoking. For additional butchery information, see Resources (page 299).

CURING AND SMOKING

Maple-Smoked Bacon

There are very few things in my life that I love more than maple syrup. It's one of the most authentic tastes of the Northeast region, as it's one of the few locally cultivated ingredients still produced today that was widely used by indigenous groups before us and not brought over by colonists. Maple trees are tapped toward the end of winter, when the starches in sap begin converting to sugar.

Though it's often considered inferior because of its poor clarity, I prefer the darkest maple syrup I can get my hands on. We recently began smoking our syrup at the restaurant with dried maple wood. I've even begun bringing maple water on long hikes for that extra bit of short-term energy. If it were up to me, everything would be drenched in maple syrup.

Makes 7 or 8 pounds

CURE
1 cup kosher salt
½ cup lightly packed brown sugar
3 tablespoons ground black pepper
2 tablespoons Hungarian paprika
1 tablespoon pink curing salt #1
  (aka insta-cure #1)
1 tablespoon allspice berries
¾ cup pure dark maple syrup
5 or 6 garlic cloves, crushed

Two 4- to 5-pound pieces pork
  belly, skin removed*

LACQUER
1 cup pure dark maple syrup
½ cup soy sauce

---

* There is an ongoing debate on whether to smoke bacon with the skin on or off. I prefer removing the skin before curing the pork, then drying the skin and frying it on its own to make cracklings as a snack. When you remove the skin, you build a nice layer of smoke and caramelization on the cured bellies themselves. The fat content in pork belly is so high that there's no risk of the meat drying out.

1. To make the cure: In a bowl, combine all the cure ingredients.
2. Place the pork belly in a nonreactive container. Generously rub the cure over the pork bellies. Cover and refrigerate. Let the bellies sit in the cure until they take on a darker red color and are stiff to the touch, 8 to 10 days (see Note), depending on thickness. Flip them every few days, redistributing the cure if needed. The bellies may release quite a bit of water—that's fine.
3. Rinse the pork bellies thoroughly, then air-dry for 3 days.
4. When ready to smoke the bellies, make the lacquer: In a bowl or a spray bottle, combine the maple syrup and soy sauce.
5. Place the bellies in the smoker and heat the smoker to 160°F. Cook to 145°F internally for 10 to 12 hours, depending on their thickness, brushing or spraying the meat with the lacquer about every hour. (You can take more time to smoke the bellies, but don't let the interior temperature exceed 155°F. I've seen traditional smokehouses smoke bacon for up to 3 days, and I've also observed a higher-temperature smokehouse cook it in just a few hours, both with very good results.)
6. Let the bacon cool before slicing. When cooking it to eat, I recommend removing it from the pan before it crisps up, so you can appreciate the texture you worked so hard to achieve. In a cool place, the smoked bacon can last for a few weeks, or you can freeze it for even longer.

Note: You can also age the pork bellies in an aging room for up to 3 weeks. If you do so, I recommend letting them sit in the cure for no longer than 8 days, as the dehydration during the aging process will concentrate the flavor and saltiness. If the bellies cure for too long during this first step, a 3-week aging process will leave you with an oversalted belly.

Beef Jerky

This process can easily be modified for other proteins, such as venison, buffalo, or moose. We like to use fattier cuts of brisket for this recipe, though the leaner cuts work just fine. Whatever cut you use, make sure to slice across the grain.

Makes 1 to 1½ pounds

1 whole flat of brisket (4 to 6 pounds)

4 ounces dark brown sugar

¼ cup fish sauce or garum, store-bought or homemade (page 158)

¼ cup soy sauce

1 tablespoon pure dark maple syrup

2 tablespoons freshly ground black pepper

2 teaspoons ground celery seeds

2 teaspoons garlic powder

2 teaspoons onion powder

2 teaspoons sweet paprika

1 teaspoon finely ground dried Thai chiles

1 teaspoon ancho chile powder

1. Remove the silver skin from the brisket (little bits left on there are okay, as they grab on to the seasoning and can be very flavorful). Cut the brisket across the grain into ¼-inch-thick strips and toss them in a large bowl.
2. In a separate medium bowl, add all the other ingredients and mix well until they turn into a paste. This will be your marinade.
3. Add 1 tablespoon of the marinade at a time to the beef, tossing until each strip is fully coated in a medium-dark gloss. Once they're covered, you can add as much of the remaining marinade as you want, using a little less for a more beef-forward flavor or a little more if you prefer a more concentrated, spicy kick.
4. Lay out the jerky strips in a dehydrator so that they're close but not touching, or you'll end up with one solid sheet of jerky. Turn the dehydrator to 150°F and dehydrate the strips for 3½ to 4½ hours. Use the shorter time for jerky you're going to eat right away or put into cold storage; use the longer time if you're taking the jerky camping or it needs to hold at room temperature or higher.

— Hot Jerky for a Late-Night Drinking Snack

Living in Kathmandu during a time when access to electricity was staggered throughout the day, I learned to appreciate the depth of flavor and the necessity of cooked or rehydrated dried meats. The traditional Nepali dish sukuti is a perfect example of that, often consumed late night around a mug of hot fermented millet wine.

Makes 2 to 3 portions

I tablespoon mustard oil

2 tablespoons fennel seeds

I tablespoon cumin seeds

½ tablespoon chile flakes

½ tablespoon chopped garlic

½ tablespoon minced shallot

Kosher salt

½ pound Beef (page 181) or other jerky, store-bought or homemade, cut into
    I- to 2-inch lengths

½ tablespoon soy sauce

I tablespoon chopped fresh cilantro

2 medium tomatoes, each cut in eighths

Juice of I lime

In a cast-iron skillet, heat the mustard oil (a pressed oil, easily found at Middle Eastern stores or a nice grocery) over medium heat. Add the fennel, cumin, chile flakes, garlic, and shallots. Sauté until the spices are lightly toasted and the garlic and shallots are fragrant and translucent, about 2 minutes. Add a few dashes of salt. Add the jerky and soy sauce, stirring constantly. Remove from the heat, add the cilantro, tomatoes, and lime juice and toss. Serve with toothpicks to share, or heap into bowls for larger portions.

Venison Gravlax

I was first inspired to apply the Scandinavian process for gravlax to meat by watching some traditional farmers in Norway make a gravlax version of pork loin, which gave it an amazing translucent hue. I first began testing it out while cooking smaller wild venison with some chefs in the Yucatán in Mexico. I was amazed at the intense flavor and bright rose color this process yielded. It's an excellent way to get the most out of a lean, smaller cut of meat.

Makes 8 to 12 servings

2 to 3 pounds venison loin (can also use the backstrap)

RUB
2 cups kosher salt
1½ cups lightly packed maple sugar (or light brown sugar if you can't find maple)
½ tablespoon allspice berries
½ tablespoon juniper berries
½ tablespoon black peppercorns
1 teaspoon pink curing salt #1 (aka insta-cure #1)

GLAZE
2 or 3 apricots
1 cup pure dark maple syrup

1. Clean the silver skin off the venison loin.
2. To make the rub: In a small bowl, combine the kosher salt, maple sugar, allspice berries, juniper berries, peppercorns, and curing salt.
3. Rub the mixture into the loin with your fingers, making sure all the sides are completely coated. Wrap the loin in plastic wrap and refrigerate it just until the meat starts turning cherry red, 2 to 3 days. Rinse off the rub with cold water.
4. To make the glaze: Juice the apricots to yield about ¾ cup juice. In a small bowl, whisk the juice with the maple syrup.
5. Hang the venison in a cold smoker and cold-smoke it under 44°F for 10 hours, depending on the thickness of the loins, brushing it with maple-apricot glaze every few hours.
6. I recommend refrigerating the gravlax for 2 days before eating it to allow the flavor to settle. This gravlax process extends the venison's edibility from a matter of days to up to 3 weeks! When you're ready to eat it, slice it very thinly with a sharp knife.

Smoked Duck Breast

Long Island has a rich history of duck farming, with the oldest farms originating in the mid-1800s. Today, Crescent Farms is the oldest duck farm still remaining, and it's owned and operated by the original family. We grew up eating duck from Crescent Farms, so it feels only natural to use their products at the restaurant.

Makes 2 to 2½ pounds

1 cup soy sauce

1 cup fish sauce or garum, store-bought or homemade (page 158)

1 teaspoon pink curing salt #1 (aka insta-cure #1)

1 cup honey

½ cup pure dark maple syrup

6 large (8 to 10 ounces each) Pekin duck breasts, boneless and skin on (Crescent Farms preferred)

1. In a small bowl, combine the soy sauce, fish sauce, curing salt, honey, and maple syrup. Pour the mixture over the duck breasts in a small container or large zip-top bag and brine in the refrigerator for 16 to 24 hours. The breasts should be a little stiffer and cherry red or brown in color.

2. Rinse the duck breasts thoroughly, place them on a rack, and air-dry at room temperature (but no higher than 65°F) for 3 to 5 hours, until the surface becomes dry and tacky to the touch.

3. Smoke the duck breasts over oak, fruit, or nut wood at 160°F for 1½ hours. Turn the smoker to 180°F and smoke for 1 additional hour, then increase the temperature to 220°F and finish cooking for about 30 minutes. You want a caramelized exterior while the inside stays bright and medium-rare (135°F). Check the duck every few minutes during this last high-heat period to ensure it does not overcook. If you don't get the caramelized exterior, cool down the duck and refrigerate it, then brush it with a little oil and torch the outside until richly browned. You do not want to render the fat or the skin (no crispy duck here), but you do want that added flavor.

CHARCUTERIE

Charcuterie is the practice of preserving meat through fermenting, salting, curing, drying, jarring, smoking, and confiting. What began as survival techniques for hunters and families who depended on every last bit of their animals to feed them through the year is now practiced more for its delicious splendors. There is still no better way to stock up your pantry than with homemade salumi, bacon, patés, confits, lardos, and hams! The passed-down traditions and timeline of slaughtering and preserving animals are still very much responsible for how we eat today and come together with family, from big maple-glazed holiday hams to warm bacon on a winter day.

Duck Prosciutto

Learning to make duck breast prosciutto is a great first step to understanding the varied processes involved in charcuterie. Once you master this recipe, it's easy to add and explore more intricate and deep flavors. At the restaurants, we have versions that incorporate everything from freshly ground Madras curry powder to locust flowers to roasted kelp.

Makes 4 breasts

2 cups kosher salt
2 cups lightly packed brown sugar
6 thyme sprigs
5 garlic cloves, crushed
1 teaspoon black peppercorns

1 teaspoon juniper berries
4 large Pekin duck breasts, boneless and skin on (Crescent Farms preferred; see the headnote on page 184)

1. In a nonreactive container, combine the salt, brown sugar, thyme, garlic, peppercorns, and juniper berries. Add the duck breasts and press the dry rub into the surface of the meat, making sure all sides are equally covered. Let them sit in the refrigerator for 12 to 14 hours.

2. Thoroughly rinse the breasts in cold water, then cold-smoke them with oak or another fruitwood, keeping the temperature below 100°F, until the flesh is a light rose color and the breasts are slightly firm to the touch, 7 to 9 hours.

3. Hang the smoked duck in a cool, dark room for 7 to 10 days. When it's ready to consume, it will have attained a prosciutto-like consistency. You can store the duck prosciutto wrapped and in the refrigerator for several weeks.

Boudin Noir (Blood Sausage)

Sadly, blood boudin is a disappearing tradition along the Louisiana boudin trail, along the outer areas of Lafayette. This recipe is my own version of a boudin sausage, but is in keeping with the traditional methods and is the perfect recipe to use up any leftover rice and meat scraps.

Makes 8 to 10 pounds

1 bundle (about 10 ounces) salted small to medium hog casing, 29 to 32 millimeters wide (can be purchased online or at any local butcher shop)

SEASONING MIXTURE

1 cup kosher salt

½ cup dried oregano

⅓ cup ground black pepper

5 tablespoons ground coriander

¼ cup dried sassafras or filé powder

2½ tablespoons fennel pollen

½ tablespoon pink curing salt #1 (aka insta-cure #1)

½ cup roasted garlic paste (see Note, page 190)

SAUSAGE

3 pounds boneless pork butt (shoulder)

3 pounds pork fatback

3 pounds smoked pork scraps (such as leftover smoked ham, rib ends, and so on—ask your butcher)

12 cups cooked barley, rice, or similar grain

1 quart fresh pork blood (from any Asian specialty food store or your local butcher—they may have to order in advance), refrigerated

COOKING AND SMOKING

White wine

Apple cider vinegar

1. Soak the casing in cold water and refrigerate for 24 hours. (If you have casing left over after making the sausage, salt it again and store for later use.)
2. To make the seasoning mixture: Combine all the seasoning mixture ingredients and set aside.
3. To make the sausage: Cut the pork butt and fatback into chunks and freeze them for 1 hour. You do not want to actually freeze the meat, but it will be easier to grind if it is very cold and a little stiffer.
4. Grind the meat in small batches using a meat grinder or finely by hand. As you are exposing the meat to much more surface area it is critical you wear

gloves and keep the die and bowls cold (we keep them in the freezer before using). It also helps to also keep the bowl over a larger one filled with ice while grinding. By keeping the fat cold this will also lead to a juicer finished product!

5. Roughly chop the smoked pork scraps with a very sharp cleaver, making sure to remove any bone shards or cartilage. Place the scraps in a large bowl set on top of another bowl filled with ice, to keep the meat cold while you're preparing the other ingredients.

6. Working in small batches so as not to heat up the meat (the grinder will give off slight heat once it begins processing), put the pork butt, fatback, and scraps through the grinder. Place the ground meat in the freezer while you finish processing the rest; do not leave any meat sitting out at room temperature.

7. Put on a fresh pair of gloves. In a large bowl, combine the ground meat, barley, and the seasoning mixture and mix by hand. When it's thoroughly mixed, gradually pour in 2 cups of the cold pork blood. You're looking for a loose, porridge-like texture; add the remaining blood if needed.

8. Take a small spoonful of the raw sausage and fry in a pan to taste for seasoning. Adjust the seasoning as needed until you're happy with the result.

9. Attach the casing to a sausage stuffer or funnel and begin to fill with the mixture, careful to avoid any air bubbles. This is easier to achieve with a product like blood sausage, which is wetter and looser, but less air will make for a more professional result. As soon as the mixture starts to come through the nozzle, tie off the casing as close to the meat as possible, using string or butcher's twine. The meat should be nice and evenly taut in the casing. Don't overstuff or you'll break the casing; don't understuff or you'll have shrinkage and gaps. (We often don't even tie off blood sausage, but allow it to spiral whole onto a baking sheet to cook. If there is a break, simply tie off both sides around the tear and keep going.)

10. To cook the sausage: Fill a large sauté pan with 3 to 4 inches of water, or enough to just cover the sausage, and a splash of white wine and bring to a simmer over medium heat; don't let the water boil. Add the sausage and bring the internal temperature up to 140°F. Once the meat has started cooking, you can very gently turn it over in the pan, taking care not to tear the casing. Remove the sausage to a surface and let it dry on both sides, flipping after a couple of hours. Let the sausage dry overnight in cold storage or the fridge.

11. To smoke the sausages: In a sprayer, make a 1:1 mixture of water and apple cider vinegar. Cold-smoke the sausage at 140° to 150°F, spraying it lightly with the vinegar mixture every 30 minutes. Keep it moist so that the casing doesn't shrink. Smoke until the internal temperature is 140°F, 4 to 5 hours. Don't let the smoker get too hot, as it may render the fat and dry out the sausage.

12. Let the sausage cool, then it's ready to eat! It will hold for several weeks in the refrigerator or it can be frozen for future use.

Note: To make roasted garlic paste, slice a head of garlic horizontally about ½ inch from the top, exposing the cloves. Place on a sheet of foil large enough to wrap the head of garlic completely. Drizzle olive oil on top and sprinkle on a pinch each of kosher salt and black pepper. Close the foil package, twisting the top. Roast in a 300°F oven for 2 hours. Set aside to cool. Remove the garlic from the foil. Turn the garlic head upside down and squeeze for paste!

Hunter's Sausage

This version of sausage or kielbasa is one of my favorites. It is rich in depth and flavor and has the perfect bite and texture, if made correctly. As in the previous recipe for blood sausage, it's important to keep the meat very cold (rotated in and out of the freezer) and that all surfaces are very clean. You can make this without a starter, but we use it because it gives a better consistency to the sausage.

Makes 3 pounds

1 bundle (about 10 ounces) salted small to medium hog casing, 29 to 32 millimeters wide

SEASONING MIXTURE
1 cup dry milk powder
3 tablespoons brown sugar
2½ tablespoons kosher salt
1 tablespoon pink curing salt #1 (insta-cure #1)
1 tablespoon dried oregano
½ tablespoon ground juniper berries

½ tablespoon ground allspice
8 garlic cloves, minced

SAUSAGE
3 pounds venison, elk, or similar lean game (shoulders or hams are best)
2 pounds pork fatback, cut into ½-inch dice
2½ ounces Fermento (culture)
2 tablespoons water, plus more for the sprayer

1. Soak the casing in cold water in the refrigerator for 24 hours. (If you have casing left over after making the sausage, salt it again and store for later use.)
2. To make the seasoning mixture: Combine all the seasoning mixture ingredients in a bowl and set aside.
3. To make the sausage: Working in small batches so as not to heat up the meat (the grinder will give off slight heat once it begins processing), grind up the game meat using a meat grinder with a medium die or quickly chop by hand. Combine the ground meat, fatback, and seasoning mixture.
4. In a bowl, whisk together the Fermento and water until completely dissolved. Mix it into the meat mixture.
5. Attach the casing to the sausage stuffer or funnel and pack the sausage in tightly. Tie off into links every 6 to 8 inches. When you've finished stuffing,

use a clean thumbtack or an actual store-purchased sausage pricker and poke small holes around each link, looking out for any air pockets and puncturing them.

6. Set the sausage in a warm, moist place, ideally 70° to 85°F. A closet with a humidifier works well. The lower the temperature, the longer it will take to ferment, but as long as you keep it above 50°F, the fermentation process will take place. Spray the sausage with water every few hours to keep it moist, so the casing won't dry out faster than the meat mixture inside.

7. After several days, begin testing the sausage. If you have a pH tester, the ideal range is between 4.3 and 5.1, depending on how far you want to take the fermentation process. Transfer the sausage to a dry room, or a designated aging room to hang until finished. This space should be 54° to 58°F at 75 percent humidity, with low and even airflow. Once the sausage is in cold storage, the fermentation process will slow down until ceasing; this last step serves to simply concentrate and mature the flavor. Generally, the sausage will be ready for consumption in 6 to 8 weeks, but it will reach its maximum flavor in 3 to 5 months.

Goat Prosciutto

This prosciutto is a great addition to cured and preserved boards, is incredibly flavorful when eaten alone or added as an accent to other dishes, and is the perfect protein snack for hiking.

Makes 4 pounds

CURE MIXTURE
3 or 4 fresh juniper branches (4 to 6 inches each)

1 cup blanched bladderwrack seaweed, roughly chopped

½ cup kosher salt

⅓ cup chopped roasted garlic (see Note, page 190)

3 tablespoons maple sugar

2 tablespoons cracked black pepper

8 rosemary sprigs, needles plucked off the sprigs or roughly chopped

1 tablespoon dried or fresh juniper berries

2 teaspoons fennel pollen

GOAT
1 goat leg (7 to 10 pounds)

1½ tablespoons honey

2 tablespoons fat (goat, duck or pork) or olive oil

1. To make the cure mixture: Remove the juniper needles from the branches (discard the branches). Combine with the remaining cure ingredients in a bowl and mix.

2. To prepare the goat: Brush the goat leg with the honey, taking care to coat the whole leg. Rub the cure mixture all over it, making sure to get into any nooks and around the bone.

3. Prepare a sheet pan with a rack. Set the goat leg on the rack and place another sheet pan over it, adding a weight on top of that. Lightly cover the two pans with plastic wrap or a cloth and leave in the refrigerator or cold storage for 2½ weeks.

4. Thoroughly rinse off the leg in cold water and hang it in dry storage or an aging room. Let it age for about 35 days. Goat leg is a relatively lean cut of meat, so it will not take too long to dry. Test the leg after 25 days, being careful not to let it overdry or you'll risk the meat becoming stringy.

5. When it's ready, lightly coat the leg with the fat or olive oil, then cold-smoke it over oak or nut wood for 3 days at about 60°F.

6. Thinly slice the prosciutto at an angle parallel to the bone and serve. This will hold in the refrigerator for 4 to 5 weeks, or you can freeze for longer storage.

Butchering a Goat

When you break down a goat, I find it easiest, after the animal has been dressed, to make the first cut right above the hip plate—where there's a gap between the thighs and bottom of the pelvis. Take your knife around the gap and finish the cut about 2 inches above the tail. Pop the leg out of the joint and carve away the cartilage between the bones.

SMOKING AND COOKING WHOLE ANIMALS

Preparing whole animals is not an act of survival but rather celebration. For many cultures it is a way to celebrate with one's community, from the blessing of a good harvest, to a wedding, birth, or new year. From the *léchons* of the Philippines, hangi in New Zealand, *cocinita pibils* of the Yucatán, or traditional boucheries of the Cajun parishes of northern Louisiana, these traditions are still at the heart of every deep-rooted culture in the world.

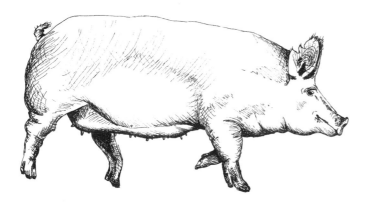

Whole Charred Rabbit

"Pop grew up farming in Puglia. Growing up here near the Sound, we kept a rabbit pen out back. They were my pets and it was my job to feed them. I'd even gone and named them. Though come fall, they began to run away . . . sometimes one a week. One day, I came home early from school and Ma had Thumper tied up above the sink. . . ."

—VITO FASCILLA, MY CHILDHOOD FRIEND

Vito and I grew up together, and still to this day we joke about poor Thumper, but it wasn't until recently that I really began to appreciate the significance of this story. It captures the exact moment of culinary transformation from the Old World to the New World. Though many families moving here to New York tried their best to hold on to their traditions, all too often it was a losing battle to modernization and convenience.

This rabbit—which is brined, cold-smoked, confited, and grilled—is incredible with just about anything you serve it with, though I prefer a bright chimichurri.

Makes 2 to 3 servings

1 whole head-on rabbit or wild hare
   (2 to 2½ pounds)

BRINE

3 quarts cold water
2 tablespoons kosher salt
2 tablespoons brown sugar
1 tablespoon honey
1 teaspoon pink curing salt #1
   (aka insta-cure #1)

CONFITTING

3 quarts duck fat (or enough to
   just submerge the rabbit), at
   room temperature, plus more for
   basting
1 tablespoon juniper berries
2 teaspoons allspice berries
2 teaspoons black peppercorns
4 garlic cloves, peeled

1. Clean the rabbit, carefully removing all of the innards. (Save the liver for a quick pâté—makes a great snack while cooking the rabbit!—or use it as a substitute in Duck Liver Butter, page 119.)

2. To make the brine: In a large, clean container, combine the water, kosher salt, brown sugar, honey, and pink salt. Place the rabbit in the container and top it with a small plate to keep it submerged. Let it sit overnight in the refrigerator.

3. Rinse the rabbit thoroughly and cold-smoke it over oak or hickory for 2 hours at about 100°F.

4. To confit the rabbit: Preheat the oven to 225°F.

5. Place the rabbit in a hotel pan or roasting pan with the duck fat, juniper, allspice, peppercorns, and garlic. Transfer to the oven and confit the rabbit until right before it's fork-tender, about 2 hours. Let the pan cool to room temperature, then remove the rabbit from the fat.

6. Cook the rabbit on a wood-burning grill, basting with duck fat as needed. When it's charred to your liking, take it off the grill and serve.

Whole Chicken

A well-cooked, local chicken can be simple to prepare and one of the most comforting, delicious meals to serve. With a little bit of age and smoke, the result of this process has brought people back to it time after time—myself included.

Makes 4 to 6 servings

BRINE
1 gallon water
1½ cups kosher salt
1 cup pure dark maple syrup
½ cup honey
2 tablespoons fennel seeds
2 tablespoons black peppercorns
2 tablespoons dried oregano
1 teaspoon pink curing salt #1
 (aka insta-cure #1)
½ tablespoon cayenne pepper
2 lemons, cut into ¼-inch slices

2 whole chickens (3½ to 4½ pounds
 each)

LACQUER
½ cup honey
⅓ cup soy sauce
2 tablespoons ras el hanout or
 Madras curry powder
3 tablespoons unsalted butter

1. To make the brine: In a large saucepan, combine all the brine ingredients and bring to a boil, then let cool.
2. Cool the brine and pour into a large vessel. Add the chickens and refrigerate for 30 to 36 hours.
3. Remove the chickens from the brine and rinse them off. Then hang to dry in the refrigerator until the skin has become translucent, about 4 days.
4. To make the lacquer: In a small saucepot, combine the honey, soy sauce, ras el hanout, and butter. Over low heat, allow the lacquer to heat up and melt for 10 minutes while whisking. Set aside to cool down.
5. Hang the chickens in the smoker. Smoke at 140° to 150°F for 2 hours; after the first hour begin lacquering the birds with a basting brush every 30 minutes until the cooking process is finished. After the first 2 hours, bring the smoker up to 170°F for 1 hour, then finish at 210°F for 1 hour, using a probe thermometer and removing the birds when the internal temperature reaches 145°F. Let the birds cool.
6. Serve whole and slice tableside.

Whole Smoked Lamb, Sheep, or Goat

At one time, mutton was considered one of the top choice meats in much of the Northeast region. In the 1930s, steakhouses such as Keens here in New York City proudly boasted selling thousands of roasted mutton chops per week. A few years ago, I made a pilgrimage out to Owensboro, Kentucky, where smoked mutton is a common local dish. There, they like to joke that there are more mutton smokehouses than people.

Whether it's North Carolina–style open-pit whole hog, burying goats underground for traditional Mexican *barbacoas*, hand-turning suckling pigs on a rotisserie over a fire like the *lechóns* of the Philippines, or spreading them on crosses over coal beds like the *cochon de lait* of Northeastern Louisiana or the *lechóns* of Argentina, there are many different cultural traditions for cooking whole animals. Many of the same rules and processes apply whether you are using pigs, lamb, sheep, goat, or venison.

Cooking over an open fire or embers is both nostalgic and important to me. I spent much of my youth backpacking in the wilderness and preparing meals, staying warm, and bonding over campfires. I learned how to roast vegetables, how to make flattops and Dutch ovens out of large stones and embers to bake breads and pizzas, how to cook stews by dropping in searing hot rocks, and how to carefully cook meats using nothing but a well-regulated fire or coal bed while keeping proper airflow and distance from the heat. Simply being around a fire now instantly brings me back to these memories and to the beautiful adventures and people that I miss very much.

For this recipe, you will need a few extra tools.

SPECIAL EQUIPMENT
Metal pointed-tip digging shovel
Firewood (any local hardwood)
20 feet of 4- to 8-gauge steel wire
Two 2- to 3-foot steel rods, posts, or rebar (unfinished), 1½ to 3 inches in diameter
One 5- to 7-foot steel rod, post, or rebar (unfinished), 1½ to 3 inches in diameter
1 medium stainless steel pot or long-handled camping pot
1 mallet or hammer
1 pair of heatproof gloves

SPICE MIXTURE

20 garlic cloves, peeled and crushed

6 rosemary sprigs, roughly chopped

¼ cup freshly ground black pepper

3 tablespoons ground juniper berries

3 tablespoons ground allspice

3 tablespoons ground coriander

2 tablespoons paprika

3 pounds kosher salt

2 pounds maple or brown sugar

One 70- to 100-pound lamb, sheep, or goat, cleaned and dressed

5 pounds cured fatback, cut into 1-pound chunks (the thicker the better)

2 medium juniper branches

1. To make the spice mixture: Combine all the ingredients in a bowl.

2. Lay the animal in a large, clean garbage bag. Rub the spice mixture evenly over the body, making sure to pack it into every crevice. Close the garbage bag and place it in a refrigerator or dark, cool place overnight to cure.

3. The next day, thoroughly rinse off the spices with cold water and let the animal air-dry in a shady place while you build the fire pit.

4. Use the digging shovel to build a fire pit about 3 feet wide by 5 feet long. Once finished, it's time to build your fire. For years, I've been using the same log cabin technique of building a small A-frame out of twigs and small tinder around a bundle of anything highly flammable like dried moss, leaves, grasses, or birch bark, then placing about 6 split logs around the sides and above it in a log-cabin-like formation. Simply light the inner bundle and you shouldn't have to do anything else.

5. Use the steel wire to tie together the 2 shorter rods perpindicular across the longer 5- to 7-foot center rod. It's important to choose thick-enough rods to withstand the weight of the animal you're cooking. Each of these 2 shorter rods will be used to secure the animal's front and back legs. The rod for the front legs should be aligned with the animal's head, while the rod for the back legs should be positioned just below its tail. It's very important to lash each connection securely, going up and around so the rods cannot slide up or down at all. Often, flat rods are used to create more friction and connect more seamlessly.

6. Lay the animal out spine side up. Using either force or a cleaver, break the ribs where they connect to the spine. Push down on the meat to butterfly

the animal. Using a sharp knife, completely remove the rib closest to the neck, on either side of the spine. Make an incision through the inside of all 4 legs at the thick upper thigh, splaying each as flat as possible. Last, make small incisions no more than ¼ inch deep in between all the other remaining ribs.

7. Lay the lashed rods flat on a table near the meat. Transfer the animal onto the rods so that the head is facing down over the end of the long rod, with its spine running lengthwise along the long rod. The four feet of the animal should be about where the two crossbars are. Use the wire to tie the end of each leg securely to the end of a crossbar, then tie once around the middle of the animal, securing it to the longer bar. Finish by tying each butterflied leg to the inside of the crossbars, to flatten and butterfly the animal completely.

8. After about 1 hour, the fire should settle into a nice, even coal bed. Make sure the embers are very hot and shoveled evenly throughout the pit. Place 1 pound of the fatback in a small pot and rest it on an even surface in the coal bed. Let the fat slowly render in the pot for a few minutes. When the fat is rendered, it can be moved to a warm spot near the fire.

9. Using a mallet or hammer, stake the animal in the ground roughly 2½ feet from the fire so that the head is up and the belly is angled down at about 45 degrees toward the fire. Do not let any part of the animal come in contact with the ground or fire. If the belly side of the animal begins to char, simply move and re-angle the animal or shovel some of the coals farther away. It's up to you to manage the temperature the best you can; you'll eventually learn how to judge it based on experience. Cook the animal for 4 to 8 hours, using the juniper branches as a brush to baste the animal with the rendered cured fatback every 20 minutes, until the internal temperature of both the lower hams and forefront shoulder reach 165°F. Then, using heatproof gloves (and a few buddies!), flip the animal so the skin side faces the fire at a similar angle. This is solely to crisp up the skin and, depending on how hot the fire is, will take anywhere from 45 to 60 minutes. The key here is keeping an even temperature. During the cooking process, depending on how fast the embers are cooling down, it's okay to add small amounts of wood to help feed the fire. As long as doing so doesn't cause flare-ups large enough to affect the animal, this is also a great way to add extra smoke flavor.

10. The amount of time it takes to cook a whole animal can vary greatly, based on many variables, including animal size, heat, wind, and outside temperature. On very cold days, when we did a poor job maintaining our fire, it has taken us up to 24 hours to cook a whole pig. On average, a whole sheep can be cooked in 5 to 6 hours. It's important that the heat from the fire and coal bed be kept consistent by constantly monitoring and feeding it as needed, as the final product should be cooked through and evenly caramelized.

11. When the meat is done, remove the animal from the fire and let it cool for 20 minutes. Remove from the rack to large cutting boards and slice the meat for your guests. We like to remove the hams, front legs, and head first, then remove the loins to be sliced separately, before chopping up everything, including the crackling, together.

7

RECIPES FOR THE GROWING SEASON

Sown in Frost

bare feet
freezing ice cold
scream howl cry and sigh
collapse and crash right through the snow
shattered. I tumble, we fall, so dark . . . so free . . .

empty.

bird, sound, green, grown and full of hope
life, leaves, flowers, love.
grasp . . .
grasping . . . now let go.

repeat.

Smoked Trout on Trout Lilies

Trout lilies pair well with smoked trout, especially since their growing season lines up nicely with the beginning of trout season in early spring, when the rivers are running highest. Sweet, floral, and mildly lemony, the lilies are a wonderful complement to smoked fish. Catch them popping up in woodland areas while they still have some light, before the trees fill in completely with leaves.

Makes 4 servings

1 tablespoon butter

Four 4- to 6-ounce Smoked Trout fillets (page 143), at room temperature

¼ cup Spicebush Berry Vinegar (page 99), or any other light vinegar, such as apple cider

¼ cup Birch Bark Syrup (page 93)

¼ grapeseed oil

Kosher salt

1 pound trout lily leaves and flowers, cleaned, roots trimmed (heartier greens like a frisée or even snap peas are a nice alternative if you can't source trout lily)

3 ounces Smoked Trout Roe (page 144)

Chive Salt (page 73) or other finishing salt

Freshly ground black pepper

1. In a large nonstick skillet, melt the butter over medium heat. Add the fillets, skin side down, and cook them for 2 to 3 minutes, basting with the butter, to get a nice, crispy skin and to heat for serving.
2. In a small bowl, whisk the vinegar, syrup, and oil until emulsified. Taste and adjust the dressing for salt. Gently and lightly dress the trout lilies.
3. To serve, arrange the flowers and leaves on a plate and sprinkle trout roe throughout. Set the smoked trout on top and finish with chive salt or a favorite finishing salt and black pepper.

Smoked Mackerel with Nasturtiums and Tarragon Cream

Mackerel often falls under the trash fish category here in the Northeast. In the past few years, however, we've begun to see a resurgence of them on menus. Oily fish, such as mackerel, need to be prepared very fresh and are perfect candidates for pickling or smoking.

Makes 4 servings

4 Brined Lemon wedges (page 72)
1 tablespoon grapeseed oil
6 to 7 ounces young nasturtium
  leaves
2 tablespoons butter

4 fillets Smoked Mackerel
  (page 140)
Kosher salt
½ cup Tarragon Cream
  (page 121)

1. In a small bowl, squeeze the brined lemon wedges of any remaining juice and whisk in the grapeseed oil to make a quick dressing. Remove the remaining meat and pith from the lemon rinds and julienne the rind to yield 2 teaspoons, reserving the rest. Lightly dress the nasturtium leaves and combine with the julienned rind.
2. Make a bed of the dressed nasturtium leaves on a plate.
3. In a medium saucepan, melt the butter over medium-low heat and gently warm the fillets. Remove from the pan and lightly season with salt.
4. To serve, spread a thick smear of tarragon cream on the plate next to the greens. Lay a smoked mackerel fillet over the cream (or slice each fillet into 1-inch pieces for easier consumption). Finish with reserved lemon rind.

Raw Artichoke Salad

I rarely see artichokes served raw in the Northeast, but they're quite common in many parts of Italy, especially when classically marinated. This recipe can also be used with lightly steamed and sliced cardoons, which are in the same family as artichokes and just as delicious.

Makes 3 or 4 servings

2 medium artichokes

2 cups grapeseed oil

Kosher salt

2 excess trout, cod, or mackerel skins (2 ounces) left over from other recipes (salmon skin would also work; so can bonito flakes as an easy store-bought replacement)

1 fennel bulb

2 tablespoons Concord grape vinegar or high-quality balsamic vinegar

3 tablespoons Smoked Herb Oil (page 98), made with rosemary

5 garlic cloves, roasted (see Note, page 190)

1 cup Chestnut Yogurt (page 131)

2 ounces Smoked Trout Roe (page 144)

Freshly ground black pepper

1. Peel away the tough outer layers of the artichokes. Using scissors, trim off the pointy tips from the soft inner leaves and separate them. Remove the fuzzy chokes underneath and reserve the artichoke hearts.

2. Pour the oil into a medium saucepan and bring it to 350°F over medium-high heat. Add the soft inner artichoke leaves and fry until they're nice and golden brown, about 1 minute. Drain on paper towels and season with salt.

3. Carefully add a trout skin to the hot oil, keeping it as flat as possible. The skin will start puffing up and turning golden brown. Cook until browned and crisp, about 2 minutes per side. Drain on paper towels and season with salt. Repeat with the second trout skin.

4. Trim the bottom of the fennel bulb and remove and discard the stalks (or keep for making stock). Reserve and pick the fronds. Slice the fennel bulb thinly on a mandoline and toss it in a bowl with the vinegar and rosemary

oil. Slice the raw artichoke hearts to ⅛ inch thick on the mandoline and add them to the bowl. Toss gently and let sit for at least 5 minutes (or up to 24 hours in the refrigerator).

5. In a bowl, mash the roasted garlic into a paste. Whisk in the yogurt until thoroughly combined.

6. Drain the vegetables in a colander, shaking lightly.

7. To serve, spoon the yogurt mixture onto a plate or layer at the bottom of a shallow jar or bowl and top with the artichoke-fennel salad, fennel fronds, and fried artichoke leaves. Break up the trout skins and place on top. Spoon a liberal amount of trout roe on each serving. Season to taste with salt and pepper.

Monkfish Pâté with Buckwheat Crackers

Monkfish liver and cod liver are incredibly underused in America, but they are delicious plated simply or served casually in a dip.

Makes 3 to 5 servings

CRACKERS
½ pound roasted buckwheat groats (kasha)
1 tablespoon amaranth flour
1 tablespoon rice starch
½ tablespoon kosher salt
2 teaspoons ground white pepper
1½ cups water

PÂTÉ
2 pounds monkfish liver (these livers are very large, so this recipe is scaled up to match the size of about 1 liver)

1 pound butter
2 shallots, roughly chopped
4 garlic cloves, roughly chopped
Kosher salt
½ cup good dry Riesling
½ cup Smoked Cream (page 116)
Ground white pepper
½ cup Knotweed Jam (page 89)
Greens from 1 bunch chickweed

1. To make the crackers: In a bowl, stir together the buckwheat, amaranth flour, rice starch, cornstarch, salt, pepper, and water. Cover and refrigerate overnight. Mix in a food processor for 2 minutes. Check the consistency periodically; you're looking for an off-white/gray spreadable paste. Mix in a little more water if needed.

2. Spray a dehydrator rack or silicone baking mat with cooking spray. Use a spatula to spread on a thin layer of the paste. (Alternatively, lay a piece of wax paper over the paste and lightly flatten with a rolling pin until the mixture is about ⅛ inch thick.) Dehydrate at 115° to 120°F for 6 to 8 hours

until they have completely dried and are cracker-like. Store the crackers in a sealed container at room temperature. Most of the time they will naturally break into smaller 1- to 2-bite pieces while tranferring or can be broken intentionally. They can be made up to 2 weeks ahead.

3. To make the pâté: Clean and devein the monkfish liver. In a large skillet, melt a third of the butter over medium heat. Add the liver, shallots, and garlic and season evenly with salt. When the livers are golden brown on both sides, deglaze the pan with the wine. Slice a little bit of the liver open to see if it's cooked through. It should still be a pale pink on the inside and just barely firm. When ready, remove from the heat.

4. Transfer the pan's contents to a food processor. Pulse until smooth, slowly adding the smoked cream and the rest of the butter, small, cubed, and at room temperature. (At Ducks we like a smoother mouthfeel, so we finish by running the mixture through a tamis or drum sieve. But a home pâté can be rough and country-style; the consistency of the pâté is up to you. Just avoid overworking the protein, so you don't end up with a gummy product.) Finish with additional salt and some white pepper to taste. Let the mixture set in the refrigerator until slightly firm.

5. To serve, spread the pâté roughly on the crackers and top with the jam. If you'd like to plate the dish more formally (as pictured opposite), spread a thin layer of the jam on a plate, then add generous spoonfuls of pâté on top. Toss on a few chickweed greens and finish with cracker shards.

Dandelion Kimchi

Some of the most potent wild medicines can often be found right in our backyards. Dandelions are a great example. I personally use the leaves to aid in circulation and hypertension. The root has also been shown to be helpful with the digestive system. This recipe is great on its own, or over steamed rice to subdue some of the bitterness.

Makes 8 to 10 servings

1½ pounds dandelions, greens and roots

1½ pounds lamb's-quarter, cleaned and cut into 3-inch pieces

7 small heirloom tomatoes, quartered

1 cup clam juice

1 tablespoon dark soy sauce

3 tablespoons kosher salt, plus more for fermentation

1½ tablespoons honey

½ tablespoon chopped garlic

1 tablespoon of Korean chile flakes

1. Slice off the dandelion taproots, then rinse and peel them. Thoroughly clean the dandelions stems and leaves and cut them into 3-inch pieces.

2. In a medium crock, combine the dandelion parts with the lamb's-quarter, tomatoes, clam juice, soy sauce, salt, honey, garlic, and chile flakes. Place a 2- or 3-pound crock weight or a plate with a gallon zip-top bag filled with water and 2 tablespoons of kosher salt on top. Cover the crock with cheesecloth and let it sit at room temperature (55° to 65°F is ideal) for 8 to 10 days, mixing each day. Generally, after 3 to 4 days you will begin to taste some of the lactic acid; as this matures, the saltiness and spice will subside to a more sour flavor. You will know it's finished once it has a similar sourness to a half-sour pickle or, if you have a pH tester, a pH of 4.3 or lower.

Steamer Clams with Rose Hip Brown Butter

Steamers, or "piss clams" as my grandfather would lovingly call them, are a family favorite in our house. One of the best parts of summer as a kid was sitting on my grandparents' hand-built deck overlooking the bay with a bucket of steamers and a bowl of melted butter. This recipe is a beautiful, rich, and aromatic nod to those memories on the deck.

Makes 2 to 4 servings

Kosher salt

2 dozen soft-shell clams or steamers

¼ cup olive oil

½ cup pickled whole rosebuds (see page 76), for garnish

1½ cups Rose Hip Brown Butter (page 120)

Sea salt

1. Soak the clams in a bucket of cold water with 2 tablespoons kosher salt for 20 to 30 minutes. Drain and rinse the clams in fresh water, then repeat this process twice more (three times total). The goal here is to let the clams clean themselves, as they expel sand and other matter from inside their shells.

2. Set a large steamer pot over high heat. Add the clams in a single layer. After 6 to 8 minutes, the clams will begin to open; keep a close eye and immediately remove them from the heat before they start to shrink. Keep them in the shell and drizzle the olive oil onto the meat of the clams. Stick the clams whole in the fridge, covered loosely with a piece of plastic wrap.

3. When the steamers are cool, shuck away the shells and peel off the rough, outer black membranes from the bellies of the clams and up the long necks.

4. To serve, place the clams in small jars or serving bowls. Insert the bellies of the clams first, so that the necks sticks out above the jar. Warm the rose hip butter and pour into the jar to cover the clam bellies. Garnish with the pickled rosebuds and a pinch of sea salt.

Roasted Bay Whelks in Toasted Oat Broth

These sea snails have taken over many of the clam, oyster, and mussel beds in Long Island. Many local fishermen have even begun harvesting and selling them overseas to make a living. Thankfully, if prepared right, this gorgeous whelk meat has a flavor that is delicate and sweet and adaptable to many recipes.

Makes 3 to 5 servings

SPECIAL EQUIPMENT
Electric hand drill and small drill
  bit (⅛ inch to ¼ inch)

BROTH
½ cup heirloom oats (I love Anson
  Mills oats!)
6 quarts water
4 dried shiitake mushrooms
1 small piece kelp
⅔ cup white wine vinegar
2 tablespoons soy sauce

½ tablespoon honey
Kosher salt

WHELKS AND GARNISH
4 medium to large local whelks—
  must be fresh and alive!
Violets or another edible, colorful
  flower
Smoked Herb Oil (page 98), made
  with lavender
Sea salt

1. To make the broth: Toast the oats in a hot, dry skillet over medium heat, stirring, until they begin to slightly smoke. They should start developing a golden brown color, but don't let them blacken. Keep the oats moving constantly and watch them closely.

2. In a large soup pot, combine the toasted oats, water, shiitakes, kelp, vinegar, soy sauce, and honey. Set over high heat and when big bubbles start popping, bring the heat down to a low simmer and cook until the liquid is reduced by half, 30 to 35 minutes. If it gets too thick, just add a little more water to thin, producing a nice creamy broth. Season with salt as needed. Strain the broth and cool to room temperature.

3. To cook the whelks: Bring a large pot of water to a boil and add the whelks. Cook them until you start to see them release white globs of fat, about 10 minutes (or slightly longer depending on their size). Immediately take

the pot off the heat and transfer the welks to a bowl of ice water to stop the cooking process.

4. Have ready a hand towel and a hand drill with a small bit. Hold the whelk securely in the towel with the opening toward you. Drill carefully through the top pointy side of the shell. Whelks are able to hold tremendous suction, and this small hole releases the pressure and lets you easily pop the meat out of the shell. You should see one large muscle, the belly of the whelk. Cut off the tube, or siphon. The remaining white, curved, cylindrical piece is what we're after. Remove the meat this way from all of the shells and place them in an ice bath to cool. After cooling, slice into thin pieces.

5. To serve, fill a shallow bowl with the room-temperature oat broth. Add the whelk slices. Finish with some of the violets, a drizzle of lavender oil, and a dash of sea salt.

Quahog Sashimi in Hibiscus Broth

Where my mother now lives in the North Fork of Long Island, most of the clams we get tend to be large and too chewy when cooked, but are fantastic raw. She recently planted a row of hibiscus flowers in front of the house where wild sea beans and sea rocket naturally grow, all of which is situated around the corner from a beautiful raw dairy farm. This recipe perfectly represents our ability to use what the land around us has to offer.

Makes 2 or 3 servings

BROTH

2 cups water

2 ounces dried hibiscus flowers

2 northern bayberry leaves

1 tablespoon white wine

1 teaspoon kosher salt

2 quahog clams (about ½ pound total)

3 ounces sea beans, cleaned and trimmed

1 cup grapeseed oil

1 tablespoon fermented black beans, store-bought or homemade (page 107)

4 tablespoons Smoked Butter (page 116), seasoned with salt and pepper

1. To make the broth: In a pot, combine the water, hibiscus, bayberry leaves, wine, and salt. Bring to a simmer over low heat and cook until the mixture is reduced by half, about 25 minutes. Strain out the solids and let the hibiscus broth cool to room temperature.

2. Clean and shuck the clams. Quahogs range in size and can be quite large and tough to open. All you are looking for in this recipe are the adductor muscles, which connect the top and bottom shells, and the "foot." The clam belly is not ideal for sliced sashimi, but is the perfect reward for getting the shells open—pop it right into your mouth. Thinly slice the clams as close to serving time as possible so that the meat is still glistening when it's plated.

3. In a pot of boiling water, blanch the sea beans until they turn bright green. It should take no more than a minute or so. Then shock them in ice water.

4. In a small saucepan, heat the oil over high heat until the surface glistens and it's hot enough to fry. Smash the fermented beans with the side of a knife so they're flattened like small chips. Briefly fry them in the oil until crisped, about 30 to 40 seconds or until they begin floating to the top, then set them to dry on paper towels.

5. In a shallow bowl or plate, spread the butter into a 3- to 4-inch round using the back of a spoon or an offset spatula. You'll want to create higher edges around the rim of the round to contain the broth. Position the clam sashimi and black beans inside the round of butter and top with the sea beans. Spoon the hibiscus broth over everything to finish.

Stuffed Squash Blossoms with Cockles and Peas

There is no better way to celebrate spring than with peas and squash blossoms. To make the dish perfect, add in the preserved cockles in thyme oil, one of the most umami-packed ingredients I've ever worked with. (If they can make it to the plate without being eaten first, it's a miracle.)

Makes 4 to 6 servings

SQUASH BLOSSOM STUFFING
2 medium summer squash, halved
   lengthwise
3 cups olive oil
Kosher salt
½ cup farmer cheese, store-bought
   or homemade (page 125)
Freshly ground black pepper

PEAS
1½ pounds sugar snap peas, cleaned
   and stringed
Kosher salt
6 ounces fresh English peas,
   shucked (just under 1 cup
   shucked)
2 tablespoons Smoked Cream
   (page 116)

STUFFED SQUASH BLOSSOMS
6 squash blossoms
2 cups all-purpose flour

¼ cup rice starch
2 eggs
¼ cup water
Kosher salt

SALAD
A handful of purslane (about
   6 ounces)
A handful of pea shoots (about
   6 ounces)
½ cup high-quality white wine
   vinegar or champagne vinegar
2 tablespoons olive oil
Kosher salt

FOR SERVING
35 Preserved Cockles in Smoked
   Thyme Oil (page 154)

1. To make the squash blossom stuffing: Prepare a smoker to 225°F. Lay the summer squash halves cut side up on a rimmed baking sheet and drizzle with 2 tablespoons of the olive oil and a few dashes of salt. Smoke for about 2 hours, then scoop out the flesh and roughly chop.

2. In a small bowl, mix the smoked squash with the farmer cheese until blended and season with salt and pepper to taste.

3. To prepare the peas: Run the snap peas through a juicer and refrigerate the juice for later.

4. In a medium saucepan, bring 3 cups water to a boil. Add a generous amount of kosher salt (2 tablespoons at least). Add the English peas and blanch until they are a vibrant green color, about 15 to 25 seconds, then immediately transfer to an ice bath. Drain the peas, then store in the fridge until you're ready to plate.

5. Whisk the reserved sugar snap pea juice with the smoked cream. Season with salt to bring out the vibrant flavor.

6. To make the stuffed squash blossoms: Stuff the blossoms two-thirds full with the stuffing mixture (1 to 2 tablespoons). You should be able to squeeze the tops of the petals together without the mixture overflowing. Combine the flour and cornstarch on a plate. In a shallow bowl, beat the eggs with the water. Dredge the stuffed blossoms in the flour mixture, then dip in the egg wash, and back in the flour again. Shake off any excess.

7. In a medium pan, bring 2½ cups of the olive oil to about 350°F over medium-high heat. (You can test the oil's temperature with a drop of flour. It should bubble but not smoke.) Working in batches, fry the stuffed blossoms until golden brown and crispy on all sides. Rest them on a drying rack or paper towels and lightly season with salt.

8. To make the salad: Toss the purslane and pea shoots with the vinegar, remaining olive oil, and a pinch of salt.

9. To serve, place the salad in the center of a shallow bowl to make a small platform for the squash blossom. Pour the pea cream over the greens until the bottom of the bowl is covered. Sprinkle the cockles and English peas around the plate and drizzle with the thyme oil. Finish with a fried squash blossom.

DOG DAYS

Pickled Razor Clams with Roasted Clam Vinaigrette

"I'd just walk right on out into the bay with my rake and basket and yell back to Granny in the kitchen, 'What kinda clams do ya wanna cook tonight? The big ones, littles, or monsters?' Clams were all over back then, so were scallops and the best oysters were just right down the beach. I'd bring sacks of scallops back up on to the deck to shuck. One in the colander and then one in my mouth. I'd be stuffed by the time dinner came around."

—BENJI SOKOBIN, MY GRANDFATHER

Shellfish has always been at the center of my family's love affair with food. For more than a century, it was a staple of most New Yorkers' diets. For me, it is a birthright of growing up on the coastline. One of my earliest memories with my grandfather was learning to rake hardshell clams and scallops and shovel pissers and razors. Though his old worn-down rake has long since been retired to the wall of the shed, I still use the same wire clam basket he taught me to use as a child.

Makes 3 to 5 servings

2 dozen razor clams, alive and fresh

Kosher salt

2 cups White Quick Pickle Liquid (page 38)

½ cup dry white wine

5 garlic cloves, roughly chopped

7 ounces scallions, chopped

1 handful sea rocket (baby arugula works, too), for serving

Chive Salt (page 73)

1. Check the clams to make sure they are still alive, fresh smelling, and intact. Place them in a large bowl of lightly salted water. The water should cover the

clams with about 3 inches to spare. Leave them for about 1 hour, changing the water twice to ensure the clams have thoroughly rid themselves of sand and grit.

2. Preheat the oven to 400°F.

3. In a large sauté pan, combine ½ cup of the pickling liquid, the wine, and the clams. Cover the pan, turn the heat to medium, and steam until the clams begin to open. Watch them closely. As soon as you see one open, remove it from the pan to cool. Continue until all the clams are removed. Reserve the pan juices.

4. Shuck the steamed clams and cut out the bellies (reserving the feet and outer muscles for later). Toss the bellies with the garlic, spread them on a baking sheet, and roast until golden brown, about 15 minutes.

5. Strain the pan juices through a cheesecloth or a sieve. Combine in a blender with ½ cup of the pickling liquid, the scallions, and roasted clam bellies with garlic. Blend on high until the mixture is perfectly smooth, adding more pickling juice as needed to loosen it up. The end product should be a deep green vinaigrette. Taste for salt.

6. Pour the roasted clam vinaigrette into a large bowl and add the reserved clam feet and muscles. Cover tightly with plastic wrap and let marinate in the fridge or a cool cellar for at least 10 hours, or up to 1 week for a more intense flavor.

7. To serve, spoon the clams into a shallow bowl and top with some vinaigrette marinade. Add a few strands of sea rocket and sprinkle with chive salt. This is an excellent dish to eat with a chunk of sourdough bread, or on its own in quick succession with a toothpick.

Matsutakes Porridge
with Smoked Eel Skin Broth

"Nobody besides Papa Benji would touch the eels. He'd drag in his eel traps here and there. Never a shortage of eel. They would be flopping around on the deck even after he'd whack 'em over the head with a wooden mallet. 'They wiggle because they just don't know they're dead,' he'd say. Gut them right down the middle and throw 'em into a big cylinder steel smoker he had. Always best straight up. Just the smoke, fat, and ocean. Delicious!"

—JANE QUICK, MY AUNT

You don't have to go too far back in time to find stories of smoking eel, a widespread tradition up and down the East Coast of North America. My grandfather harvested quite a bit of eel using traps he would set out in Orient, Long Island. When done correctly, it is one of the most remarkable and richest tasting traditional foods found here. I've met some pretty interesting eel farmers who have supplied us over the years at the restaurant, many of whom we've become quite close to. We consider eel one of the most treasured ingredients we serve in the restaurant.

Makes 6 to 8 servings

BROTH

1 gallon water

1½ cups dry white wine

2 tablespoons soy sauce

1 tablespoon pure dark maple syrup

1 medium branch fresh spruce (4 to 6 inches), needles intact

1 small piece kombu (about 2 ounces)

5 smaller or 3 large leftover smoked eel skins, heads on or off

6 garlic cloves

6 green cardamom pods

4 black cardamom pods

1 tablespoon black peppercorns

½ tablespoon kosher salt, plus more as needed

MATSUTAKES AND APPLES

5 fresh medium matsutake
  mushrooms

2 Northern Spy or Golden Russet
  apples

½ tablespoon butter

¼ cup dry white wine

Kosher salt

1 teaspoon ground white pepper

1 tablespoon Smoked Cream
  (page 116)

SQUID

4 to 6 ounces fresh squid, bodies
  only

2 tablespoons grapeseed oil

Kosher salt

½ tablespoon butter

GARNISH

Maldon sea salt

2 ounces young spruce buds or
  shoots

Wintergreen oil

1. To make the broth: In a large pot, combine the water and remaining broth ingredients. Bring to a boil over high heat, then reduce to a light simmer. Simmer until the liquid is reduced to about one-fifth of the original amount, about 4 hours. It should have a very decadent, rich flavor. Strain the broth into a bowl and season with more salt as needed.

2. To prepare the matsutakes and apples: Matsutakes can be difficult to clean, but an easy way is to take a damp paper towel and lightly grip them, twisting to pull off the outer membrane. Cut off the caps and lower fibrous parts of the stem. Reserve the upper, tender parts of the stem in a small covered bowl. Cut the caps and remaining lower stems into a medium dice.

3. Peel, core, and slice the apples, then cut them into dice to match the size of the mushrooms. In a small sauté pan, melt the butter over medium heat. Add the wine and reduce for 2 to 3 minutes. Add the diced apples and mushrooms, season with salt and the white pepper, and cook until tender, about 5 minutes. Pour the contents of the pan into a food processor, add the smoked cream, and blend the porridge until smooth. Adjust the seasoning if needed.

4. To prepare the squid: Clean and slice the squid bodies into very thin rings. Coat a nonstick or cast-iron skillet with the grapeseed oil and heat over high heat until it begins to smoke. Char the squid very briefly, no more than 2 minutes. While it's cooking, sprinkle with 2 or 3 large pinches of salt.

5. Warm the porridge in a small pot over medium heat and whisk in the butter. Pour it into a shallow bowl. Spoon a liberal amount of eel broth over the porridge, then place the charred squid rings on top. Generously shave the reserved matsutake stems over the bowl. Finish with a light sprinkle of Maldon salt and the spruce buds or shoots. Drizzle with a very light touch of wintergreen oil. The dish should be served warm.

THE PLANT-BASED SMOKEHOUSE

Whether you are a die-hard carnivore or a devoted vegan, there's no question that our health and our environment would benefit by eliminating large-scale farming and the production of animal-derived foods. I believe that a sustainable future relies not necessarily on the absence of meat altogether but on a drastic reduction, along with diversifying our diet and becoming more reliant on local food. Our restaurants, originally founded on a menu comprised mostly of smoked meats, have made a shift over the past few years toward more plant-based dishes—and with great success!

With many mass-farmed, hyper-processed ground meat substitutes on the rise, and the distribution of bio-engineered, laboratory-grown meats in our near future, I believe there is another path to be found that starts by simply adjusting the way we view whole vegetables and fruits. In our kitchens, we began by applying to produce many of the same techniques we've practiced for generations for meats.

Over the past few years we have experimented with different multistep combinations of fermenting, curing, quick pickling, poaching, steaming, smoking, dehydrating, frying, grilling, and roasting hundreds of different whole fruits and vegetables. The thought process is simple. For vegetables, this generally begins by softening or souring them first either through steaming, lacto-fermenting, or quick-pickling. For fruit, the process usually involves making them more savory and less watery, and, if the skin or rind is removed, encouraging the fruit to form a new skin that is dry enough to caramelize. In order to help promote the new skin's growth, we often work with higher alkalinity brines using ash or lye, which tend to react with the natural pectin found in the fruit.

I have included three basic examples of this process, all of which have become staples in our restaurants.

Watermelon Radish "Bresaola"

Last year we entered this recipe in a charcuterie contest under the pretense that it contained meat. We almost won. Out of all of our root vegetable experiments, this was one of my favorites. Though our original version was lacto-fermented, we found this simpler quick pickle version version to work great!

Makes 3 to 5 servings

BRINE

2 cups white vinegar

½ cup kosher salt

2 cups water

2 tablespoons cracked black peppercorns

2 tablespoons dried oregano

4 garlic cloves, chopped

4 large rainbow radishes, trimmed of leaves and excessive roots

2 tablespoons quality extra virgin olive oil

1 tablespoon Maldon sea salt

1. To make the brine: Whisk together the vinegar, kosher salt, water, peppercorns, oregano, and garlic. Place the radishes in a zip-top bag or a sealable container and pour over the brine to submerge them completely.
2. Let the radishes sit in the brine for 3 days, refrigerated.
3. Remove from the liquid and place in a 225°F smoker over your preference of smoking wood (we use oak) for 6 hours.
4. Set aside to cool. From here they can either be hung in a room set up for aging meat (page 40) for 20 to 30 days, until the water weight has reduced by about 30%, or for a quicker result, they can be placed in a dehydrator for 8 hours at 120°F.
5. To serve, slice the radishes paper thin and finish with the olive oil and Maldon salt.

See photo on page 241.

Smoked and Charred Carrots with Watercress

Every time I make this I still nervously smile, remembering all the chefs growing up who would have yelled at me for poaching these carrots into baby food. But the result is truly amazing!

Makes 3 or 4 servings

3 pounds medium carrots

½ cup white vinegar

4 bay leaves

6 garlic cloves, roughly chopped

1 tablespoon cracked black peppercorns

2 tablespoons kosher salt, plus more to taste

¼ cup olive oil

SAUCE

2 tablespoons kosher salt, plus more to taste

One 3- to 4-ounce bunch watercress, cleaned

Zest and juice of 1 lemon

3 tablespoons crème fraîche or sour cream

2 teaspoons rice or potato starch

Ground black pepper to taste

1. Rinse and peel the carrots; trim the greens if attached, leaving the stems. In a large saucepan, place the peels, carrot greens, vinegar, bay leaves, garlic, cracked black peppercorns, salt, and the peeled carrots. Fill with cold water until the carrots are covered by approximately 3 inches. Place the pan over medium-high heat.

2. When the liquid begins to boil, lower the heat and cover until carrots are just soft enough to cut through with the back of a knife but not falling apart. Carefully remove the carrots onto paper towels to cool and drain.

3. Toss the carrots with 2 tablespoons of the olive oil and place them on a rack in a smoker set to 140°F. Smoke for 4 to 5 hours, until they have lightly browned. Let cool.

4. Transfer the carrots to a dehydrator set at 120°F and dehydrate for 2½ hours, until they have noticeably shrunken in size but are still moist on the inside. Cool, then store in a covered container in the refrigerator until ready to use.

5. To make the sauce, in a large saucepan, bring 1 gallon of water and the salt to

a boil over high heat. Set a large mixing bowl filled with ice water on the side. Place the watercress in the boiling water for no more than 45 seconds, until it turns a bright green. Quickly remove the watercress and submerge it in the ice water. Drain, then place in the blender with the lemon zest and juice and 2 tablespoons of water. Blend until smooth. Add the crème fraîche and blend on low. Using a strainer, gently shake in the rice starch while the sauce is blending to give it a little more body and shine, then season with salt and pepper to taste.

6. Heat the remaining 2 tablespoons of olive oil in a large sauté pan over high heat. Place the carrots in the pan and sear for 3 to 4 minutes, until lightly charred, stirring gently.

7. To serve, place the carrots on a plate, top generously with watercress sauce, and finish with a sprinkle of salt.

See photo on page 241.

Whole Smoked Watermelon "Ham"

We've spent a lot of time working with root vegetables, but we could never replace the almost explosive mouthfeel and flavor that come from biting into a well-marbled piece of meat. We found what we were looking for by simply using higher-moisture fruits. This watermelon recipe has been fun because there are very few showpiece plant-based dishes that are comparable to large prime ribs, turkeys, or briskets and luckily farmers have already spent millions creating seedless watermelons!

Makes 3 to 5 servings

I whole seedless watermelon (3 to 5 pounds)

2 gallons water

1½ cups smoker ash or 1 tablespoon food-grade sodium hydroxide

1 cup kosher salt

⅓ cup dried oregano

2 tablespoons cracked black peppercorns

1 cup tamari

2 tablespoons olive oil, plus more for basting

6 garlic cloves

3 fresh rosemary sprigs

½ cup buckwheat flour (optional, to make gravy)

1. Using a sharp knife, carefully trim off the watermelon rind (which can always be pickled). In a container large enough to hold the watermelon, combine the water, ash, salt, oregano, peppercorns, and tamari. Submerge the watermelon and let it brine for 4 days.

2. Remove from the brine, rinse lightly, and let air dry in the refrigerator for 2 to 4 hours, until the outside feels completely dry.

3. Spread 2 tablespoons of the olive oil in a roasting pan large enough to hold the watermelon but not oversize. Set the watermelon in the pan. Place the garlic and rosemary sprigs along the sides of the watermelon. Heat a smoker to 225°F and smoke the watermelon for 4 hours. Remove the melon and lightly score the surface of the top and sides in a diamond pattern (as on a ham), going no deeper than ¼-inch below the surface. Baste with some of the remaining oil and juices from the pan and return to the smoker for 3 hours, rotating the pan every hour.

Whole Smoked Watermelon "Ham" with Watermelon Radish "Bresaola" (page 237) and Smoked and Charred Carrots with Watercress (page 238)

4. Preheat the oven to 400°F. Remove the pan from the smoker, baste again, and roast until the melon is evenly golden brown, with a light char starting to form.

5. Set the watermelon in a serving dish. If you like, whisk the extra juices from the pan slowly into the buckwheat flour and simmer until thickened into gravy. Slice the watermelon tableside, pour the gravy on top, and serve.

Bluefish Salad

For a long time, bluefish was considered to be a trash fish in the Northeast. Our grandparents prepared bluefish for as long as I can remember; it always had a place on the table. Late summer to early fall is when the smaller "snappers" begin circling the bays and inlets in frenzies. What follows is a fun preparation utilizing some of the pickled berries we normally have stored from earlier in the year. Once smoked, however, this salad is perfect to eat with simply a little sour cream, watercress, dill, and lemon. It's also great as a dip with fresh sourdough or crackers for any occasion.

Makes 2 to 4 servings

2 medium fillets Smoked Bluefish (page 140), picked apart into large chunks

¼ cup Smoked Cream (page 116) or store-bought crème fraiche

½ cup buttermilk

¾ cup lavender oil, store-bought or homemade (see Note), can also be replaced with simply good quality extra virgin olive oil

½ cup apple cider vinegar

1½ ounces pickled green strawberries, sliced lengthwise (see page 74)

1½ ounces pickled green tomatoes, diced

1½ ounces pickled gooseberries (see page 74), halved

⅓ cup chopped mint, chopped

Kosher salt and freshly ground black pepper

A handful of fresh purslane or similar green, for garnish

In a large bowl, lightly toss the fish, cream, buttermilk, lavender oil, and vinegar. Drain the pickled fruit, add to the bowl along with the mint, and toss gently. Season with salt and pepper to taste.

Note: Combine a few food-grade lavender stalks with a mild oil, like grapeseed or high-quality canola oil, and let sit for a few days to infuse.

Sour Corn on the Cob with Duck Liver Butter and Shad Bottarga

"There's really all sorts of ways to eat corn after harvest. Course, dryin' it is most common. My family soured a lot in jars, with just salted water and time. Soured corn was a staple on our dinner table through the winter months. It also made great chum for fishing catfish. As it still does."

—ED QUICK, MY UNCLE, FROM MISSOURI

My uncle's family had come to the Ozarks via central Louisiana. Both corn and freshwater fish were meal staples in his home in Missouri. He'd tell me stories of mythical catfish, of noodling creatures much larger than most men. In my mom's family, and for many who grew up close to the water, shad roe was considered a delicacy. The same roe that used to be discarded is now more expensive than the whole fish itself! It's most similar in size, flavor, and texture to the mullet roe often used in traditional Italian and Croatian bottarga. This recipe combines these two essential components in one beautifully, rustic dish.

Makes 6 to 12 servings

SOUR CORN

3 gallons water

4 cups kosher salt

12 ears peak-of-season corn, insides shucked but a few larger outside husks left on

2 young spruce tree branches, with needles attached, rinsed

FOR SERVING

¾ cup Duck Liver Butter (page 119)

4 sacs Shad Bottarga (page 149), shaved

2 lemon wedges

1 cup chopped fresh flat-leaf parsley

1. To make the sour corn: In a plastic container, mix the water and salt until the salt has dissolved. Drop the corn and spruce branches into the brine. Cover with a heavy plate or pot lid to help keep the corn completely submerged.

Let the corn sit at room temperature for 5 to 7 days; it should taste sour and almost a little cheesy. (You can then drain the corn and keep it in cold storage for up to 4 months to continue souring.)

2. When ready to serve, rinse the corn in cold water. Grill it over wood coals (oak or any fruitwood works here) until nicely and evenly charred.

3. Coat the corn well with the duck liver butter and generously top with shaved bottarga and a squeeze of lemon. Sprinkle with the chopped parsley.

Smoked Sea Scallops with Black Garlic, Pear, and Spearmint

A perfectly rich yet bright dish for early scallop season. Similar preparations can be made with less sauce and more shaved pear using raw bay scallops when in season.

Makes 3 to 4 servings

1 head Black Garlic (page 104)
1½ cups Smoked Cream (page 116)
1 tablespoon dry white wine
½ tablespoon kosher salt, plus more to taste
Ground white pepper

1 tablespoon butter
12 to 16 medium to large Smoked Scallops (page 151)
2 small red Bartlett pears
Spearmint leaves, for serving

1. Extract the black garlic cloves and puree in a blender with ½ cup of the cream until smooth. Blend in the remaining cream, wine, and salt and transfer to a medium saucepan. Bring the mixture to a simmer over medium-low heat and reduce until it takes on a medium nappe consistency (coats the back of a spoon), about 20 minutes. Season with salt and white pepper to taste. Set aside.
2. In a nonstick skillet, melt the butter on medium low heat. Add the smoked scallops and warm them for 2 to 3 minutes.
3. Halve and core the pears, then shave them lengthwise on a mandoline into ⅛-inch-thick slices, leaving the skin on.
4. To serve, pour the cream into shallow bowls. Add 3 or 4 scallops to each bowl, top with the pear slices, and sprinkle with spearmint leaves.

Hen of the Woods with Elderberries

Also known as maitake mushrooms, hen of the woods can take on many
different flavors. Few other mushrooms change quite as much based on their
age and terroir. The younger, darker ones are often as fragrant and nutty as
the acorn-filled oaks they grow under. As they open up later in the season, the
mushrooms can take on a fruitier, citrusy flavor. All of the ingredients in this
recipe are thought to hold tremendous medicinal value, making it a perfect meal
for early winter, to ward off colds and sickness.

Makes 6 to 8 servings

ROASTED MUSHROOMS
2½ pounds hen of the woods
    mushrooms
½ cup Smoked Herb Oil (page 98),
    made with oregano
Kosher salt

SEAWEED SAUCE
2 ounces wild dulse or sugar kelp
    seaweed (if dried, rehydrate
    before weighing)
2 ounces fresh mint leaves
I cup distilled white vinegar

Grated zest and juice of 2 lemons
2 tablespoons soy sauce
3 ounces hen of the woods
    mushrooms
½ cup Smoked Herb Oil (page 98),
    made with thyme
Kosher salt

FOR SERVING
Leaves from I small bunch fresh
    mint
2½ tablespoons Pickled Elderberries
    (page 74)

1. Preheat the oven to 350°F.
2. To make the roasted mushrooms: Clean the mushrooms and trim off the
   woody base, leaving the rest of the mushrooms whole. Brush the mushrooms
   with the oregano oil, season with kosher salt, place them on a small baking
   sheet, and roast them for 15 minutes, or until tender.
3. To make the seaweed sauce: In a blender, combine the dulse, mint, vinegar,
   lemon zest, lemon juice, soy sauce, and mushrooms. Blend until smooth and
   whisk in the thyme oil. Season with salt to taste.
4. To serve, toss the roasted mushrooms with the seaweed sauce and serve warm.
   Sprinkle the fresh mint leaves and elderberries over the top.

Boudin Noir with Roasted Jerusalem Artichokes and Beach Plum Preserves

There's nothing quite as satisfying as eating gathered around a warm fire on some of those first chilly camp days of the year, especially after a long day of hiking. This is one of my favorite hearty meals to make over a campfire.

Makes 8 to 10 servings

1 cup coarse sea salt

3 pounds Jerusalem artichokes, washed

3 to 5 pounds Boudin Noir (page 188)

3 tablespoons dry white wine or Riesling

2 cups Beach Plum Preserves (page 86)

½ cup julienned fennel

2 tablespoons butter

Kosher salt and freshly ground black pepper

2 bunches fresh wood sorrel, cleaned (or regular sorrel, roughly chopped)

2 tablespoons fresh oregano leaves

1. Build and light a small fire in a fire pit using any nearby dry wood. Let it burn until a nice coal bed has formed. Push a handful of embers to the side of the pit and crush them into smaller pieces. Evenly spread about ½ cup of the coarse sea salt into a layer on top of the crushed embers, then tightly pack in the Jerusalem artichokes. Pour the remaining ½ cup coarse sea salt over the artichokes and cover with a light layer of additional crushed embers.

2. Hang the boudin over the coal bed, either from a sturdy rod or on a metal camping grill. Make sure to place it far enough away so that it's warming but in no danger of burning.

3. Cook the artichokes until tender. Check them after 10 minutes and test with a metal skewer; they should yield easily. Place the roasted artichokes in a metal bowl covered tightly with plastic wrap or in a Tupperware container

with a lid. Let them steam for 5 to 10 minutes; this will make the outer layers easier to remove. Using a kitchen cloth or clean rag, rub the artichokes to peel off the charred skins.

4. Place a medium cast-iron pan over the coals and pour in the wine and plum preserves. Stir until combined. Add the artichokes, fennel, and butter, then mix and season with salt and pepper to taste. When the butter is melted, toss in the fresh sorrel and oregano.

5. Slice the links of boudin and serve over the artichokes.

Venison Gravlax with Apricot and Chanterelles

Some of my favorite memories from living in Colorado for much of my early twenties involved local honey, wild game, and wandering fields of wild sagebrush in the foothills, which were perfect grounds for chanterelle foraging. This recipe brings me back to my Colorado days.

Makes 4 to 6 servings

6 dried apricots halves

2 cups warm water

2 tablespoons raw honey

½ cup Sage Cream (page 122)

10 to 12 thin slices (¼ inch or thinner) Venison Gravlax (page 183)

6 to 8 ounces Pickled Chanterelles (page 79)

Seasonal edible flowers, for serving

1. Rehydrate the apricots in the warm water for 20 minutes.
2. In a blender, combine 2 of the apricots, the honey, and ⅓ cup of the warm water used to hydrate the apricots and blend. Set the syrup aside.
3. Remove the 4 remaining apricots from the water and cut into small pieces.
4. To serve, spread a thick layer of the sage cream on a plate. Add the gravlax slices, the apricot pieces, and the chanterelles. Drizzle the apricot syrup over the plate and sprinkle with flowers.

Smoked Squirrel Brunswick Stew

Our own twist of one of the most traditional American game meat dishes. For this recipe we use squirrel, but you can easily substitute other small game. Get the most out of these little critters with this easy and delicious one-pot meal.

Makes 6 to 8 servings

6 to 8 squirrels, cleaned and quartered (heads removed), or 2 cleaned rabbits, or 1 large cleaned woodchuck

Kosher salt and freshly ground black pepper

1 pound cured fatback, cut into 2-inch lardons

2½ tablespoons Acorn Flour (page 103; can be substituted with buckwheat flour)

2 tablespoons sassafras leaf powder

2 teaspoons cayenne pepper

4 garlic cloves, roughly chopped

1 yellow onion, roughly chopped

⅓ cup Smoked Ketchup (page 90) or tomato paste

1 gallon chicken stock (can be substituted with water)

6 Pickled Oysters (page 156)

1 pound okra

3 ears Sour Corn (page 244), cut into thirds

6 ounces pole beans, ends trimmed

Any fresh herbs you have on hand (I prefer a savory herb like oregano), for garnish

1 loaf sourdough bread, for serving

1. Season your woodland creature of choice with salt and pepper. Smoke them over oak wood for about 1 hour at 170° to 185°F.

2. In a large cast-iron pot, kettle, or Dutch oven, render the fat from the lardons over medium-high heat. When browned on all sides, remove and drain on paper towels. Reduce the heat and add the acorn flour to the pork fat in the pan to make a rustic roux. Stir with a wooden spoon, constantly moving it so that the flour doesn't burn. Add the sassafras leaf powder, cayenne, garlic, onion, and ketchup and cook for 3 to 5 minutes, stirring often. Slowly add the stock or water, stirring well to combine.

3. Roughly chop the oysters and smoked meat. Add them, along with the reserved lardons, to the pot. Cover and lightly simmer over medium-low heat until the meat becomes just tender, about 1½ hours.
4. Slice the okra lengthwise. Add the okra, corn, and pole beans to the pot and cook for 30 minutes over low heat. The stew should be rich, thick, and hearty.
5. Finish the dish with fresh herbs. Serve with thick-cut sourdough bread.

8

RECIPES FOR
THE COLD SEASON

Winter solitude
In a world of one colour
The sound of the wind

—MATSUO BASHŌ

Pickled Okra Salad with Mint Dressing and Shaved Monkfish

As the price of monkfish has risen over the past few years, it has become more and more important for us to learn how to utilize and preserve every part of the fish, from the tail and cheeks to the liver, stomach, and intestine. Once it's preserved, we can use the monkfish to season salads and other dishes throughout the whole year!

Makes 4 servings

4 ounces fresh spearmint leaves (from 1 bunch) or regular mint

¼ cup Black Locust Flower Vinegar (page 99)

1 teaspoon sesame paste (tahini)

¾ cup grapeseed oil

Kosher salt and freshly ground black pepper

6 ounces pickled okra, mix of green and purple if possible

4 ounces small to medium pickled shishito peppers

½ tablespoon white benne seeds (sesame seeds)

1 pound Dried Monkfish (page 150)

1. In a food processor, combine the spearmint leaves, vinegar, and sesame paste and blend until smooth. Slowly pour in ½ cup of the grapeseed oil and blend until emulsified. Season the mint dressing with salt and pepper to taste.
2. Preheat a grill to high heat. Clean and slice the okra lengthwise. In a bowl, toss with 2 tablespoons of the grapeseed oil and season with a large pinch of salt. Grill the okra slices until nicely charred, 4 to 5 minutes, depending on how hot your grill is. Don't be afraid to let them blacken on the surface. Remove them to a baking sheet to cool.
3. Feel for any woody bits on the shishitos and cut them off. Halve the larger peppers lengthwise and keep the smaller ones whole. In a bowl, toss with the

remaining 2 tablespoons oil and salt to taste. Char on the grill, similar to the okra. In a bowl, toss both charred veggies with the benne seeds.

4. Slice the monkfish proscuitto-thin. You should be able to hold it up to the light and see through it.

5. To serve, plate a small pile of the veggies, drizzle with the mint dressing, and generously layer with the sliced monkfish.

Acorn Squash in Clay

You can find people cooking in clay muds all over the world. Often it's as simple as having access to a plentiful free material, but it also imparts incredible flavor and added minerals. In many traditional areas where squash is a mainstay, like for some of the indigenous groups of Mexico and the United States, the first squash of the season is often ceremoniously wrapped in corn husks or larger leaves, then buried under the earth with hot coals to bless the harvest.

Side note: Many of the indigenous groups in North America grow squash as part of the "three sisters," which include squash, beans, and corn. After the corn is picked, the beans are planted so that they can grow up the empty corn stalks, allowing just enough light to grow squash on the ground below, whereas the broad squash leaves help suppress weeds as well as encourage the growth of topsoil by trapping in moisture, creating a system of symbiotic crops that grow with one another. This is one of the earliest and most traditional forms of permaculture in the Americas.

Makes 3 or 4 servings

ACORN SQUASH

1 medium acorn squash

2 tablespoons olive oil

3 tablespoons Seaweed Butter (page 118)

2 pounds premixed, food-safe red clay (see Note)

1 bunch or handful of alfalfa straw (see Note)

Kosher salt

1 teaspoon cayenne pepper

2 teaspoons dried ground ancho pepper

1 tablespoon fish sauce or garum, store-bought or homemade (page 158)

CRISPY BURDOCK

1 medium to large burdock root

2 cups neutral frying oil, such as grapeseed

Kosher salt

GARNISH

½ tablespoon chopped fresh sage leaves

2 teaspoons dried ground sumac berries

1. To prepare the acorn squash: Cut 2 inches off the top (stem end) of the squash and scoop out the seeds. Reserve the top. (Rinse the seeds, let them

air-dry, then toss with a the olive oil and lightly toast in the oven or in a skillet for a snack later on.)

2. With a large fork, puncture the acorn flesh from the inside, careful not to poke holes through the skin. Using your hand, take half of the seaweed butter and coat the inside of the squash, including the inside of the top. Place the top back on the squash.

3. Preheat the oven to 300°F.

4. Roll out the clay into a round that's large enough to completely enclose the squash. Be sure to move the flattened clay as you're rolling it out so it doesn't stick to the work surface. Place the straw in a nice, even layer in the center of the clay, leaving a 3-inch border clear around the edges. Pat the straw down lightly so that it sticks to the clay. Sprinkle 3 tablespoons of salt evenly over the straw. Place the acorn squash in the center, bring up the sides of the clay around the squash, and smooth it over the top to encase the squash entirely. Use a little water and a flat knife to seal up any seams and smooth the clay around the squash.

5. Cook the squash on a baking sheet for 3 hours. (Or, if you have a fire pit, you can cover the squash with the coals of an open fire and cook for 2 hours.)

6. To prepare the crispy burdock: About 30 minutes before the squash is done, trim and peel the burdock root. Use a vegetable peeler to pull the flesh of the burdock into long strips.

7. In a small saucepan, heat the oil to about 350°F. Working in 2 or 3 batches, fry the burdock strips until golden and crispy, about 4 minutes, moving them around with chopsticks to make sure they don't stick to one another. Remove the strips from the oil and set onto paper towels; season to taste with salt.

8. When the squash is done, carefully crack the top of the clay with a hammer. Watch out for steam! Very carefully, remove the top of the squash. Spread the rest of the seaweed butter around the inside of the squash.

9. Serve the squash with the fried burdock strips, garnished with the sage and sumac. This can be eaten straight out of the squash itself, or sliced to share.

Note: I purchase my clay from SOS Chefs, my favorite local spice shop by our restaurants in the East Village; it can also be purchased online.

Note: I prefer dried alfafa straw, which can be purchased at your local farm, feed store, or online.

WINTER SOLSTICE

Duck Breast with Pawpaw Jam and Black Walnut Crème

"One of my favorite dishes to make while entertaining was Duck à l'Orange. We'd go down and buy our ducks whole from Crescent Farm. Oh, gosh, what an awful smell! The family there has been running that farm since the 1600s. You know back then that's what the island was famous for—it was all duck farms and potato farms. If you've lived here long enough, most likely you had something to do with one of the two. That's of course unless you made your living from the sea."

—MURIEL SOKOBIN, MY GRANDMA

In her heyday, my grandma loved to entertain. She was trained in classic French gastronomy, and her menus read like storybooks as classically beautiful as anything from Julia Child. Her recipes revolved around ingredients sourced from local farms near Orient Point and the Great Peconic Bay, just a few yards from her kitchen. This is an homage to her.

Side note: Pawpaw has made a big comeback over the recent years. Once a commonly grown fruit in this region, it had long since been forgotten by farmers, most likely due to its short harvest season at the end of summer. Its custard-like consistency and its flavor, resembling a mix of a banana and apple, make it a unique but approachable ingredient for the Northeast. People often compare it with soursop or cherimoya.

Makes 4 servings

2 tablespoons butter
4 Smoked Duck Breasts (page 184)

½ cup Black Walnut Crème
   (page 123)

½ cup Pawpaw Jam (recipe follows)   Fennel flowers (optional)

1. In a nonstick skillet, melt the butter over medium heat. Add the duck and lightly sear each side for 2 to 3 minutes while bringing the interior to room temperature.
2. Spread the black walnut crème on four plates and top with pawpaw jam and fennel flowers, if using. Lay a whole finished duck breast on each plate next to it. Serve with steak knives.

— Pawpaw Jam

Makes 4 cups

4 ripe or overripe pawpaw fruits
½ cup white wine
½ tablespoon raw honey
2 teaspoons sea salt
Zest and juice of 1 lemon
Leaves from 4 fresh tarragon sprigs
2 tablespoons unsalted butter

1. Peel and seed the pawpaws. Roughly chop them and add them to a blender with the wine, honey, salt, and lemon zest and juice. Blend thoroughly.
2. Pour the mixture into a small saucepan over medium heat. Add the tarragon and reduce to one-third the original amount, about 20 minutes. Remove from heat and discard the tarragon. Whisk in the butter and let cool.
3. Store in a sterilized jar and refrigerate for up to 1 year.

Pork Shank with Fermented Black Beans and Dried Tomatoes

Our ode to the red-eye gravy and hams of times past!

Makes 8 servings

½ cup tamari

2 quarts chicken stock

½ cup fish sauce or garum, store-bought or homemade (page 158)

¾ cup Fermented Black Beans (page 107)

2¼ cups cold-brew coffee

1 cup sun-dried tomatoes, roughly chopped

½ ounce dried spruce or pine needles

8 pieces pork shank (about 1½ pounds each)

1 tablespoon Smoked Butter (page 116)

Cooked grains, such as farro or barley, for serving

Spruce shoots (optional), for garnish

1. In a large roasting pan, combine the tamari, chicken stock, fish sauce, ½ cup of the fermented beans, 2 cups of the coffee, ⅔ cup of the tomatoes, and the spruce needles. Add the pork shanks, turn to coat, and marinate in the refrigerator overnight.

2. Remove the pork shanks from the marinade (strain and reserve the liquid) and lightly rinse them. Smoke the shanks over hickory at 225°F until lightly browned, 4 to 5 hours.

3. Preheat the oven to 250°F.

4. Place the smoked shanks in a roasting pan with the bone up. Pour the strained marinade on top, cover the pan with foil, and oven-braise until the shanks are just shy of fork-tender, 2½ hours. Let them cool slightly in the liquid, then remove them and keep warm. Pour the liquid into a saucepot and simmer over medium heat until the cooking juices turn into a thick, sticky jus, reduced by about two-thirds, for about 45 minutes.

5. Heat a large cast-iron skillet over medium-low heat. Add the butter, the remaining ⅓ cup tomatoes, and the remaining ¼ cup fermented beans. Stir and let the flavors combine. Deglaze the pan with the remaining ¼ cup coffee

and a generous splash of pork jus. Place the shanks in the skillet and baste thoroughly with the glaze before serving.

6. Plate the shanks over your choice of grain, finishing with a few tablespoons of the sauce and the spruce shoots, if using.

Grits with Pickled Oysters and Fermented Apricot Sauce

Good-quality grits and grains can be difficult to find, but in recent years we have seen a resurgence in heritage species. Being able to source freshly milled grains is a true luxury, but for the home, I find it to be a worthwhile investment to buy a cheap electric or hand mill.

Makes 3 or 4 servings

GRITS

1 quart chicken or duck stock, plus more as needed

1 cup coarse yellow grits (I prefer Anson Mills)

Kosher salt

½ cup Smoked Cream (page 116)

¼ pound (1 stick) butter, cut into ½-inch cubes

Freshly ground black pepper

FERMENTED APRICOT SAUCE

2 tablespoons brandy

3 cloves soft Black Garlic (page 104)

4 Fermented Apricots (page 109)

3 tablespoons crème fraîche or sour cream

Kosher salt

OYSTERS AND GARNISH

10 Pickled Oysters (page 156), roughly chopped

½ cup fresh sage leaves, chopped

1. To make the grits: In a large saucepan, bring the stock to a boil over high heat and pour in the grits, whisking rapidly to keep them from sticking to the bottom of the pan. (Alternatively, the grits can be soaked overnight and then cooked in stages of adding stock and thickening, similar to a risotto.) After 2 to 3 minutes of whisking, the grits should begin to thicken the stock. Reduce the heat to low, cover, and cook, whisking every few minutes to keep the grits from burning. Taste for seasoning; depending on how salty your stock is, you may need to add a tablespoon or two of salt. Continue to cook the grits, whisking every few minutes, for 35 to 45 minutes total. The grits will go through several stages of cooking, from firm and separated granules, to releasing a translucent filmy starch, and finally to a creamy porridge. If the

mixture becomes too thick, add a small amount of water or more stock as needed.

2. Whisk the smoked cream and cubed butter into the grits, trying to incorporate as much air as possible. Season to taste with salt and pepper. The grits should not feel gummy but rather airy and creamy to taste. I tend to enjoy grits a bit looser than usual.

3. Meanwhile, make the fermented apricot sauce: In a small saucepan, combine the brandy, black garlic, and apricots over medium heat. Simmer and stir the mixture for 5 minutes, then let it cool to room temperature. In a blender, blend it to a smooth puree. Pour the mixture into a bowl and fold in the crème fraîche. Season with salt to taste.

4. To serve, spoon the grits into individual bowls and top with the chopped pickled oysters, fermented apricot sauce, and sage.

HOLIDAYS AND CELEBRATIONS

Whole Rabbit with Preserved Morels, Pickled Ramps, and Chile Ash Paste

This recipe is perfect for a family feast or a special occasion. It's excellent served with a bowl of grits or polenta to round it out.

This process is how we tend to cook smaller whole animals and vegetables, but it doesn't work quite as well with larger whole animals, when you're faced with different cooking times and temperatures for each part of the animal.

Makes 4 to 6 servings

RABBITS AND BRINE
2 whole rabbits (3 to 3½ pounds each), head on, cleaned and gutted
¼ cup lightly packed brown sugar
2 tablespoons honey
¼ cup kosher salt
2 teaspoons pink curing salt #1 (aka insta-cure #1)
1 gallon water

FOR SMOKING AND CONFITING
½ cup pure dark maple syrup

3 gallons master fat (see Note), at room temperature
1 bunch thyme sprigs
15 garlic cloves, peeled
10 juniper berries

FOR SERVING
Cooked grits or polenta (optional)
Morels in Smoked Juniper Oil (page 102)
Pickled Ramps (page 75), as you like
¼ cup Chile Ash Paste (page 110)

1. To brine the rabbits: In a container big enough to submerge the rabbits in 1 gallon of brine, combine the brown sugar, honey, kosher salt, pink salt, and water. Add the rabbits to the brine and submerge completely. Brine in the refrigerator overnight.

2. To prepare the rabbits for smoking: Rinse the rabbits thoroughly in cold water and lay them on a rack, splayed open and belly side down. Let them air-dry in a cool room until the skin is tacky to the touch, 2 to 4 hours. About halfway through the process, coat the backs of the rabbits with the maple syrup.

3. Prepare the smoker at 140°F and smoke the rabbits for 1 hour. We prefer oak or birch, but any local wood works. Brush an even coat of master fat over both rabbits, about ½ cup on each.

4. Increase the temperature on the smoker to 170°F and smoke for 1 hour. Brush the rabbits with another ½-cup coat of master fat.

5. Lay a generous handful of thyme on top of each rabbit and continue to smoke for an additional 1½ hours. It is important to keep the skin moist, brushing it with fat whenever you feel it's needed, keeping it constantly glistening. Let the rabbits cool to room temperature.

6. Preheat the oven to 250°F.

7. In a 6- or 8-inch-deep hotel or roasting pan, submerge the rabbits in the remaining master fat along with the smoked thyme, garlic, and juniper berries. Cover the pan tightly with foil and place in the oven. Confit the rabbits until the meat on the sides of the bodies becomes fork-tender (it's okay to pull off the foil to check it), about 2 hours.

8. Let the rabbits cool to room temperature in the fat, then store them with the fat in any sealable container in the fridge for up to 2 months. Check every once in a while to make sure they're still completely submerged in the fat and that no visible, funky bacteria is growing on them.

9. To cook, bring the rabbits to room temperature in the fat so that you can extricate them without breaking them apart. Very carefully, hold and press the whole rabbits between two grill plates or grates. This is the key to allow you to flip them carefully without breaking. The less you are moving the rabbit itself independent of the grate, the less likely it will break. We use a Japanese ceramic grill in our restaurants, but a standard charcoal grill works well, too. Light the grill and wait until the coals are evenly hot—a coal chimney helps. Char the rabbits over hot coals or embers, belly side down, for 4 to 5 minutes, then carefully flip so the top side is facing down. Cook for another 4 to 5 minutes. while continually basting them with fat.

10. Serve on a cutting board, over a bed of grits or polenta if you like, with the morels, ramps, and chile ash paste.

Note: To make "master fat," combine half bacon fat and half duck fat. Render in a saucepan over low heat until liquid. Remove from the heat and whisk every few minutes as it cools back into a solid.

Tomahawk Rib Eye with Black Trumpets

At the restaurants, after cold-smoking, we'll often try to age these steaks for 60 to 70 days. If you have the opportunity to talk directly to the farmer or butcher, choose a cow older in age from a more flavorful breed (we love Jerseys!). We have a lot of luck getting meats from our dairy farmers, who will often sell in farmers' markets as well. This will easily be the best steak you have ever had. Hands down.

Makes 2 or 3 servings

30 to 35 ounces tomahawk rib eye steaks, 2½ to 3 inches thick, cut from an older cow

½ cup rendered beef fat or kidney fat (see Note)

Kosher salt

3 tablespoons butter

1 bunch thyme

Freshly ground black pepper

1½ cups Fermented Black Trumpets (page 84)

2 tablespoons fresh currants, for serving

1. Cold-smoke the rib eye at 40°F for 6 to 8 hours. Nothing will visibly change in the meat, but the longer you smoke it, the heavier the smoke flavor will be. Rub it lightly with 3 tablespoons of the beef fat and let it sit overnight in the fridge, or it can hang for up to 90 days.

2. Let the rib eye come to room temperature and season with salt. Select an ovenproof skillet that is large enough for the meat to lie flat (it's okay if the bone is sticking up).

3. Preheat the oven to 350°F.

4. Set the skillet over medium-high heat and add the butter. Add the steak and sear, basting often, until golden brown, about 8 minutes. Flip the rib eye and add the thyme straight to the skillet. Cook and baste for another minute or two.

5. Place the skillet in the oven and cook for about 20 minutes. Stick a metal cake tester or skewer into the thickest part of the meat and test it against your bottom lip. The tester should be room temperature. If it's cold, put the skillet back in the oven and test again after a few minutes. If it's hot, invent a time

machine. When the temperature is perfect, remove the rib eye from oven and the skillet so as not to overcook, then season it with pepper. Let it rest on a rack at room temperature for about 15 minutes.

6. Slice off the fat cap and cut it into smaller pieces for your hungry guests while they wait for the dish to be plated. Cut the meat across the grain into slices ⅔ to 1 inch thick.

7. To serve, arrange a few slices on a plate and sprinkle with the black trumpets and currants. Finish with salt to taste.

Note: To render beef fat, place 2 pounds of diced beef fat and ½ cup water in a small saucepan over medium-high heat. The fat will begin rendering after a few minutes. Let simmer for 20 minutes, allowing the water to cook off completely. Adding the water at the beginning will prevent the fat from browning. Once cooled, use as needed.

Smoked Goat Neck with Curried Cracked Oats and Cranberries

After spending some time in Nepal, I came to love *paya*, a rich, sticky curry broth with braised goat or sheep feet often served for breakfast. When we opened our first restaurant, Ducks Eatery, this was one of the first dishes I wanted to bring to the menu. Unfortunately, many Americans tend not to love gelatinous textures when it comes to meat or fish, so we went back to our butchers to look for other cuts. They offered us a bag of frozen goat and mutton necks that they couldn't sell. After six years, it still remains our most popular dish!

Makes 4 servings

MARINADE

3 quarts water

¼ cup fish sauce or garum, store-bought or homemade (page 158)

¼ cup soy sauce

¼ cup massaman curry powder

2 tablespoons honey

1 tablespoon pure dark maple syrup

2 tablespoons kosher salt

2 tablespoons freshly ground black pepper

1 tablespoon ground sumac

2 tablespoons minced garlic

2 tablespoons minced shallot

4 fresh northern bayberry leaves

GOAT NECKS AND THE REST

2 whole goat necks (1½ to 2 pounds each)

3 tablespoons butter

½ cup cranberries (fresh or frozen), roughly chopped

½ cup dry Riesling

½ cup rolled oats, lightly toasted in a dry saucepan over medium heat for 2 to 3 minutes

3 tablespoons fresh chervil leaves

2 tablespoons cilantro (delfino if you can source it!)

Kosher salt and freshly ground black pepper

1. To make the marinade: In a large container or hotel pan, combine the water and the remaining marinade ingredients.
2. To prepare the goat necks: Submerge the goat necks in the marinade, cover, and marinate in the refrigerator for 24 hours. Remove the necks and reserve the marinade.

3. Prepare a smoker to 225°F with a mixture of oak and maple and lay the necks on a rack with the top (curved fat cap) facing up. Smoke until dark golden brown, 5 to 6 hours.

4. Preheat the oven to 250°F.

5. Place the necks (fat cap facing up) in a deep roasting pan (3- to 4-inch-high sides). Whisk the reserved marinade until thoroughly combined and pour it into the roasting pan, lightly covering the necks. Wrap tightly with foil and roast until the necks are just shy of fork-tender, 2 to 3 hours. Remove the necks to a baking sheet, pour the remaining marinade into a large saucepan, and simmer over medium heat until reduced by half, 6 to 8 minutes.

6. Heat a cast-iron skillet over medium-high heat. Add 1½ tablespoons of the butter. Gently place the necks in the skillet and baste with the butter until they start to brown. Add ¼ cup of the cranberries and baste for another minute. Add the Riesling and bring the sauce to a boil to cook off the alcohol. Reduce the heat to a simmer, add ½ cup of the reduced marinade to the skillet, and baste the necks with the sauce until it thickens.

7. On a large plate, mix the toasted oats, chervil, cilantro, and remaining ¼ cup cranberries. Remove each neck from the skillet and lightly roll on the plate to coat in the oat mixture. Stir the remaining reduced marinade and the remaining 1½ tablespoons butter into the sauce in the skillet. Season with salt and pepper to taste. Drizzle skillet sauce over the goat necks and serve.

Our Famous Smoked Beef Brisket

"Pops made and smoked brisket well. He had come from southern Hungary in the late 1800s. Though back then we never called it brisket, just beef. They would cut up the forequarter into pieces and cook them. The customers would ask for beef fatty or beef lean. Fatty was what we call brisket now. Poppy would always have something pickling in big wood drums out on the fire escape . . . tongues, brisket, geese, veggies. Any extra pickled fat would be used to fry French fries."

—FRANCES HOROWITZ, MY GRANDMOTHER

My father's family came here to the Lower East Side of New York City from the southern countryside of Hungary, near Romania, also known as Transylvania. My great-grandfather Harry "Pops" Zinn owned a kosher delicatessen for many years in New York City. His wife, Ida, did most of the cooking; having been sold into servitude at a young age in Hungary, she had learned to cook out of necessity. She cooked with her hands, never with a recipe but by intuition and feel. My delicatessen is named after them: Harry & Ida's Meat and Supply Co. and Luncheonette.

Many professional BBQ pit masters all over the country consider whole briskets to be the most difficult category in competition. This is because the brisket, which is part of the pectoral muscles on the cow, is actually made up of two completely different types of meat, informally known as "fatty" and "lean," each with different ratios of fat that cook at varying times and temperatures. It has taken us years of trial and error to master a cooking process that lends itself to both parts of the brisket. Today, our award-winning smoked brisket at the restaurant is juicy and full of flavor and melts in your mouth.

Makes 10 to 12 servings

1 whole beef brisket (11 to 16 pounds; see Note)
½ cup kosher salt

½ cup cracked or butcher-grade black peppercorns
½ tablespoon brown sugar

I teaspoon Hungarian paprika

½ teaspoon cayenne pepper

½ teaspoon garlic powder

½ cup fish sauce or garum, store-bought or homemade (page 158)

½ cup apple cider vinegar

1. Place the brisket on a cutting board with the fat cap facing down. You will be able to see and feel where the two different muscles meet. Locate the small curved piece on one side that is made up entirely of fat. Using a boning knife, cut around the small piece of fat, being careful not to cut into any of the meat itself. (This fat can be rendered and stored in the freezer for later use.) Any excess silver skin can be removed as well.

2. Flip the brisket so the fat cap is on top. You will see there will be a small piece of hard, pure fat on one side of the meat. Carefully cut it out to allow the brisket to flatten.

3. Using the boning knife, begin to shave off fat from the top of the brisket until the fat cap is only ¼ to ½ inch thick.

4. Flip the brisket again—fat cap on the bottom—and season it with the salt. It is very important that the salt evenly coat the meat, but the amount becomes intuitive with experience. I like to describe it as if I were seasoning it to look like the static on a broken television screen; I even train people what side the salt should fall from the chef's hand while seasoning to ensure consistency. We are pretty heavy handed at Ducks, using about ¼ cup for each side (a total of ½ cup), assuming some of it will fall off the brisket as you're applying it.

5. In a medium bowl, combine the cracked black peppercorns, brown sugar, paprika, cayenne, and garlic powder. Use approximately half of the mixture to liberally coat the top of the brisket. It is very important that you do not clump or mound the seasoning mixture, as that will cause it to burn.

6. Turn the brisket over again—fat cap facing up—and salt and season the top in the same way. Once you have finished, place the brisket uncovered in cold storage, to build a proper pellicle; allow it to sit until the skin takes on a slightly tacky feel, 8 to 10 hours. This will also allow the salinity of the rub to further permeate the meat.

7. I divide my brisket cooking into 3 stages: 1) penetrate the meat with smoke, 2) caramelize the bark or exposed surface of the meat, and 3) break down the inner fat until tender.

8. Place the brisket—*always* fat cap up—in the smoker at 225°F. I like to use

oak, often with a bit of hickory for added flavor. Oak tends to be very reliable in keeping a consistent temperature, though wood use traditionally varies by region. Smoke for 2½ hours.

9. Fill a spray bottle with the fish sauce and vinegar. Crank the smoker up to about 285° to 300°F, depending on how indirectly your smoker's heat source is (you do not want sparks of fire landing on your meat). Cook the brisket, spraying it every hour during this stage to aid in the caramelization, until a beautiful, firm, charred-looking bark has formed around it. (This is not to be confused with a carbonized look, which is often a sign of too much seasoning.) This can take anywhere from 2 to 4 hours.

10. For the last stage of cooking, the brisket gets wrapped. At Ducks Eatery, we find that traditional peach butcher paper works best at letting the brisket steam in its own juices while keeping the bark at the right consistency. Tear off two long pieces of butcher paper, each about three times the length of the brisket. Arrange them in a "T" and place the brisket—fat cap up!—in the center. Wrap one piece top to bottom, tucking it back under on the other side of the brisket, and wrap the other right to left around the brisket.

11. Once it's firmly wrapped, with any loose ends of the butcher paper resting underneath the meat, place the brisket back in the smoker and reduce the heat to about 270°F. Smoke the wrapped brisket for 3 to 6 hours. I know my brisket is done by feel and smell, but a surefire indicator is sticking a metal skewer into the meat where the two different muscles meet. As soon as the skewer is able to puncture the brisket deckle easily, the brisket is ready!

12. Keeping the brisket wrapped, place it in an insulated cooler to rest for at least 1 and up to 3 hours before serving. It will still be nice and hot when it's ready to slice.

13. Remember that the brisket has two different muscles, and each muscle must be cut at a different angle in order to properly slice it across the grain. Carefully slice through the brisket along the diagonal line where the two muscles meet. Once they are separated into "fatty" and "lean" pieces, it will be easier to identify the grain in each muscle. Cut it across the grain into slices ¼ to ½ inch thick and serve. This will be the best brisket you've ever had! Try it with the BBQ sauce on the next page.

Note: Choose a brisket from a good cow (meaning high quality, not the opposite of a naughty cow). You are looking for an even, large white fat cap that extends across the entire top and side. Make sure that the cap is thick but not too lopsided in height from the larger point (deckle) to the flat (lean).

Hot Willie's BBQ Sauce

Makes 2½ cups

I cup Smoked Ketchup (page 90)

I cup pure dark maple syrup

I cup apple cider vinegar

⅓ cup hoisin sauce

2 tablespoons honey

2 tablespoons fish sauce or garum, store-bought or homemade (page I58)

¼ cup lightly packed brown sugar

I cup water

3 tablespoons guajillo chile powder

2 tablespoons ancho chile powder

I tablespoon Spanish paprika

I tablespoon smoked paprika

I tablespoon garlic powder

I tablespoon onion powder

½ tablespoon ground cumin

½ tablespoon ground juniper berries

½ tablespoon ground celery seed

½ tablespoon ground northern bayberry leaf

½ cup freshly ground black pepper

2 teaspoons cayenne pepper

2 whole limes, shaved zest and juice

½ tablespoon fresh makrut lime leaves (aka "kaffir lime")

In a medium saucepan, whisk together all the ingredients. Simmer over medium-low heat until it starts to thicken, about 45 minutes, then set aside to cool. Keep the sauce for months in the fridge.

THE LONG FREEZE

Cod Roe Fritters with Lichen

Here in the Northeast there is still an unfortunate amount of fish roe that is thrown away at the markets every day, despite how many great uses there are for it. My favorites include spicy cod roe seasonings and flounder roe taramasalata and pâté.

Lichen is still one of the great mysteries of the botany world. We're just barely beginning to understand the incredible symbiotic relationships they hold with the oxygen and flora around them. We do know, however, that they were historically eaten around the world by First Nation groups and relied upon as a source of vitamin C during the winter, in places where they could still be foraged under the snow.

Makes 3 or 4 servings

COD ROE FRITTERS

2 teaspoons pure dark maple syrup

4 eggs, separated

6 ounces cod roe, very finely minced

2 ounces pork fatback, very finely minced

1 cup acorn flour or buckwheat flour

½ teaspoon kosher salt

1 teaspoon freshly ground black pepper

2 cups lard (see Note), for frying

½ cup all-purpose flour

STRAWBERRY-SAGE CREAM

6 pickled green strawberries (see page 74)

3 tablespoons Smoked Cream (page 116)

½ tablespoon chopped fresh sage

FOR SERVING

2 big handfuls Reindeer Lichen (2 to 3 ounces; see page 106)

2 teaspoons caraway seeds, lightly toasted in a dry saucepan for 2 minutes

1. To make the cod roe fritters: In a medium bowl, whisk the maple syrup and egg yolks. Add the roe and fatback and whisk again to combine. In a small bowl, mix the acorn flour, salt, and pepper. Working ¼ cup at a time,

mix the seasoned acorn flour into the roe/fatback mixture until it reaches a consistency that allows you to form 2- to 3-inch balls with your hands.

2. In a small saucepan, melt the lard over medium-high heat and bring it to 350°F.

3. Grab three small bowls. In one bowl, whisk the egg whites with 1 tablespoon water to make an egg wash. Place ¼ cup of the all-purpose flour in each of the other two bowls. One at a time, dip a fritter into the flour in one bowl, shaking off the excess. Next, dunk it in the egg wash, coating it thoroughly. Finish with another coating of flour in the third bowl, shaking off the excess again.

4. Drop the fritter into the hot frying oil. It's best to fry only a few fritters at a time so as not to overcrowd the pan. Fry until golden brown, then flip, 2 to 3 minutes on each side. Drain on a rack or paper towels. (Reserve the hot lard.)

5. To make the strawberry-sage cream: In a blender, blend the pickled strawberries, smoked cream, and sage until smooth.

6. Toss the lichen with a few teaspoons of the hot lard and the toasted caraway seeds. To plate, set 2 or 3 fritters on a plate or shallow bowl. Top with strawberry cream and fluffy tufts of caraway lichen.

Note: You can use the "master fat" described in the Note on page 270, or save the fat trimmed off the brisket fat cap for Our Famous Smoked Beef Brisket (page 279) and render it for use here.

Skate Wing with Crab Apple Crème

It amazes me to hear people still refer to skate as a trash fish. While it is no longer widely considered as such, many chefs don't love to work with skate because it can be painstaking to clean and can sometimes smell of ammonia if not processed or frozen immediately. The recipe that follows uses dried skate, which imparts tremendous depth of flavor and lets us use the skate at a later time without the risk of the dreaded ammoniated smell. This is the ultimate finger-food bar snack!

Makes 4 servings

4 cleaned skate wings
2 cups dark aged soy sauce (find at any Japanese market or substitute regular soy sauce)
3 egg yolks
½ cup Crab Apple Butter (page 91)
2 pinches of cayenne pepper

1 cup grapeseed oil
Kosher salt
Pinch of ground sumac
⅓ cup "master fat" (see Note, page 270)
1 teaspoon minced Brined Lemon peel (page 72)

1. Carefully look over the skate wings and remove any skin, cartilage, or bone. Place the wings in a large, shallow bowl or hotel pan. Pour the soy sauce on top and lightly massage it into the wings.

2. Lay out the wings on a dehydrator rack. Make sure the whole skate is spread out and that the fingers are not touching. Dehydrate at 140°F overnight. If you plan on serving this within a few hours, you can pull it off while it's a bit soft. If you plan on storing it, let it dry for another 10 to 12 hours. The drier version can be kept for months in cold storage.

3. In a bowl, whisk the egg yolks until pale and slightly thickened. Add the crab apple butter and a pinch of cayenne, combine well, then whisk in the oil until the mixture takes on a mayo-like consistency. Season with salt, the remaining pinch of cayenne, and the sumac powder.

4. (If you're using the harder dried version of the skate, rehydrate it in warm water before grilling.) Oil and prepare the grill, making sure there's an even

layer of hot embers. We use oak, but any hardwood will work well. Carefully lay out the skate wings on the grill. As soon as they start crackling, baste them carefully with the master fat. Be careful of flames from the dripping fat! Rotate the wings often as they cook for 2 to 3 minutes on each side; you want even charring and blistering over very high heat on all sides, while continually basting with fat.

5. When the skate is charred to perfection, remove it from the heat and serve while still warm. Slice along the length of the fingers into pieces 1 to 2 inches wide and fan on a plate, with the fingers fanned toward the rim of the plate. Add a dollop of the crab apple crème and serve topped with a sprinkle of the minced lemon peel.

Warm Smoked Eel in Sassafras Syrup

This is my ode to the Hudson Valley. Though the eel population has had a rough few years, we've begun to see a resurgence as of late, with a few marine biologists even working to breed them. We prefer to source the larger eels that are mature enough to have bred. Eel, sassafras, and ramps are some of the First Nation staples of the Northeast.

Makes 2 servings

RAMP CUSTARD

2 ounces (about 1 cup) Pickled Ramps (page 75), drained and roughly chopped

½ tablespoon honey

1 tablespoon rice starch

1 cup whole milk

2 eggs, lightly whisked

Kosher salt

Freshly ground black pepper

TARRAGON VINAIGRETTE

Leaves from 1 bunch tarragon

¼ cup white wine vinegar

¼ cup grapeseed oil

SMOKED EELS

4 tablespoons butter

2 fillets (about 1 pound each) Smoked Eel (page 146)

¾ teaspoon kosher salt

FOR SERVING

2 tablespoons Sassafras Syrup (page 95)

2 teaspoons lavender flowers

1. To make the ramp custard: In a food processor, combine the chopped ramps, honey, and rice starch. Add ½ cup of the milk and process until smooth. Pour the mixture into a medium saucepan and add the remaining ½ cup milk. Bring the mixture to a simmer over medium-high heat, whisking occasionally to keep it from clumping. Remove from the heat and set aside to cool slightly. Whisk a few tablespoons of the warm mixture into the eggs to temper them, then vigorously mix the eggs back into the milk mixture. Return the pan to a low heat, then slowly raise the temperature to medium while continuously stirring so that the mixture thickens into a custard, 2 to 3 minutes. Add salt and pepper to taste.

2. To make the tarragon vinaigrette: Juice the tarragon leaves to get 2 teaspoons of juice. Add the vinegar and whisk in the grapeseed oil and salt.

3. To prepare the smoked eels: In a small saucepan, simmer 2 tablespoons of the butter over medium-low heat, skimming the surface when it begins to foam, until it smells slightly nutty and the color is light brown. Remove from the heat. It will turn a dark brown color and have a strong nutty taste. As it cools to room temperature, it will begin to thicken into a loose paste.

4. In another saucepan over low heat, melt the remaining 2 tablespoons of butter. Add the eel fillets and gently warm them, carefully flipping halfway through. Season with the salt.

5. To plate, lay down a thick layer of ramp custard, then place the eel fillets on top. Finish by drizzling with the tarragon vinaigrette and the sassafras syrup. Garnish with the lavender flowers.

Mussels with Maple-Chile Oil

This dish is a blend between a traditional Spanish *conserva* and candied mussels. These little treats have been a staple on the Ducks Eatery menu since the very beginning!

Makes 4 to 6 servings

MAPLE-CHILE OIL
1½ cups extra virgin olive oil
¼ cup pure dark maple syrup
2 dried shiitake mushrooms
4 garlic cloves, peeled
1 tablespoon kosher salt
1 teaspoon ground cayenne

MUSSELS
4 dozen Smoked Mussels
(page 153)

FOR SERVING
½ cup picked sumac buds (or 1 tablespoon grated lemon zest)
1 small bunch flowering chives, flowers reserved and chives chopped (up to 1 cup)
Smoked Butter (page 116)
Bread (a French baguette works well here)
Maldon sea salt

1. To make the maple-chile oil: In a small saucepan, combine the olive oil, maple syrup, shiitakes, garlic, salt, and cayenne. Bring to a low simmer over low heat and cook, stirring occasionally, for 10 minutes to thoroughly emulsify the maple into the oils. Set aside to cool and let sit for 24 hours. Strain through a cheesecloth. (This oil can be made well in advance and stored in a sealed container at room temperature for up to 1 year.)

2. To prepare the mussels: Add the mussels to the infused oil and set aside in cold storage or the refrigerator to marry the flavors for at least 24 hours or up to 2 weeks before serving.

3. To serve, place the mussel in a small jar, topped with the sumac buds and chive flowers. Plate with smoked butter spread on bread and a dash of sea salt and a sprinkling of chopped chives.

Beef (or Other) Tartare with Olives

As with our steaks, using an older cow for a tartare offers more flavor and is generally preferred. This recipe incorporates a flavor profile from northeastern Italy and has been one that's inspired me since I began cooking as a kid. This combination of sweet and briny ingredients tends to pop up on my menus a few times a year in various forms. (For a simpler version, see the Note opposite.)

Makes 2 to 4 servings

OLIVE MOSS AND OLIVE CREAM

½ cup pitted green olives, chopped (can substitute caperberries)

2 tablespoons Smoked Cream (page 116)

TARTARE

1½ pounds beef, lamb, venison, or moose loin (heart is also a great sub)

½ cup vanilla oil (see page 94)

1 large chicken or duck egg yolk

6 white anchovies, roughly chopped

8 large fresh basil leaves, finely chopped

Kosher salt and ground white pepper

FOR SERVING

3 basil leaves, finely chopped

1 tablespoon sumac syrup (page 96; or, when in season, sliced fresh Muscat or Concord grapes)

Fresh country bread

1. To make the olive moss and olive cream: Juice the olives, reserving both the juice and pulp. (If you don't have a juicer, you can blend the olives in a blender with ½ cup of water. Cook the mixture in a sauté pan over high heat for 5 to 7 minutes, until reduced by half, then let cool.) Spread the pulp on a silicone baking mat and dehydrate for 3 hours. If you do not have access to a dehydrator, turn the oven to the lowest setting and bake the pulp, checking often. Once it's fully dried, break the mixture into little bits of "moss." Whisk the olive juice into the smoked cream.

2. To make the tartare: Pick your protein. Since you're making tartare, it must be very fresh! If you're using wild game, make sure to clean it thoroughly and check for visible light-colored worms and parasites.

3. Dice the protein into ¼-inch cubes; I prefer a rougher-textured tartare over

the traditionally ground method, but you can cut up to your size of choice. In a large bowl, mix the meat with the vanilla oil, egg yolk, anchovies, and basil. Season liberally with salt and pepper, tasting as you go.

4. To plate, make a rough circle of the olive cream and gently position the tartare on top. Sprinkle with the basil leaves and olive "moss" and drizzle with the sumac syrup. Serve with bread.

Note: For a simpler version of the tartare, mix the protein with chopped olives and an egg yolk, perhaps with a dash of ground sumac.

ACKNOWLEDGMENTS

The amount of work it takes to write a book is more than humbling. I would like to start by thanking my sister and partner, Julie Horowitz, as this book would not have been begun or finished without her relentless hard work and dedication through thick and thin as an artist, writer, and editor. My parents, for their unwavering support and love through the good and the bad. My father, for giving me the thirst for knowledge within the natural world, and my mother, for showing me its beauty. To my cousin, Johnny, for the countless life rafts. Thanks to Kim; my brother, Jake; Ari; and the rest of my family for their support.

To the teachers, guides, friends, and mentors I've had along the way, teaching me bit by bit through the forests of the Northeast and the Rocky Mountains to the jungles of Central America and Southeast Asia. To the instructors and support system at Naropa

My sister, Julie

My great-grandmother Ida and her dog, Mustard

Pulling in a fishing net

University and Academy at Swift River, for showing me where to search.

For the many adventures it's taken in order to feel this worn down so young, thanks to my brothers Charlie "Patchy" Schultz and John "Mac" Mahaffey—spiraling up, down, or side to side, but always out of control, as if there was ever a choice. In the words of Dylan, "Something is happening here and you don't know what it is." A warm salutation to Stu and the rest of the Easy Keys band.

To the other chefs in my life whom I have worked with and looked up to, including David Milburn, Jaime Young, and my hard-hitting prep team and cooks who sacrifice themselves every day in our restaurant and others.

To my grandmother, for sharing with me her love of cooking and what it means to make good food.

To my grandfather, for sharing with me his love of the sea and Native American culture. For teaching me a sense of self-reliance, how to swing a hammer, tie a knot, and cast a rod, how to laugh more seriously than your friends, the art of stealing other people's lobster roe from across the table, how to slurp down a good oyster with enough horseradish to kill a small bird, and most important above all . . .

RESOURCES

FOOD HISTORY AND ANTHROPOLOGY

The Food History Reader by Ken Albala. 2014: Bloomsbury Academic, New York, NY.

The Cambridge World History of Food by Kenneth F. Kiple and Kriemhild Coneè Ornelas. 2000: Cambridge University Press, Cambridge, UK.

High on the Hog: A Culinary Journey from Africa to America by Jessica Harris. 2011: Bloomsbury USA, New York, NY.

Gastropolis: Food and New York City by Annie Hauck-Lawson and Jonathan Deutsch. 2009: Columbia University Press, New York, NY.

HOMESTEADING AND PERMACULTURE

The One-Straw Revolution: An Introduction to Natural Farming by Masanobu Fukuoka. 2010: New York Review Books, New York, NY.

The Self-Sufficient Life and How to Live It by John Seymour. 2003: Dorling Kindersley, London, UK.

Ceramic Houses and Earth Architecture: How to Build Your Own by Nader Khalili. 1990: Cal-Earth Press, Hesperia, CA.

Permaculture: A Practical Guide to a Sustainable Future by Bill Mollison. 1988: Island Press, Washington, DC.

The Resilient Farm and Homestead: An Innovative Permaculture and Whole Systems Design Approach by Ben Falk. 2013: Chelsea Green Publishing, White River Junction, VT.

CURING, SMOKING, AND CHARCUTERIE

BOOKS

The Art of Making Fermented Sausages by Stanley Marianski. 2009: Bookmagic, LLC, Seminole, FL.

Meat Smoking and Smokehouse Design by Stanley, Adam, and Robert Marianski. 2009: Bookmagic LLC, Seminole FL.

Charcuterie: The Craft of Salting, Smoking, and Curing by Michael Ruhlman and Brian Polcyn. 2005: W.W. Norton, New York, NY.

Charcutería: The Soul of Spain by Jeffrey Weiss and Sergio Mora. 2014: Surrey Books, Chicago, IL.

UNIVERSITIES AND COURSES

Penn State Meat and Agricultural department HACCP training

Iowa State University, www.meatscience.ag.iastate.edu/shortcourses

EQUIPMENT

Ole Hickory Smokers Pits, www.olehickorypits.com

Backwoods Smoker, www.backwoods-smoker.com

Cabelas, www.cabelas.com

The Sausage Maker, www.sausagemaker.com

Butcher Supply, www.butchersupply.net

AquaLab Technologies (for water activity meters), www.aqualabtechnologies.com

FERMENTING AND PICKLING

BOOKS

Vinegar: The User Friendly Standard Text Reference and Guide to Appreciating, Making and Enjoying Vinegar by Lawrence Diggs. 1989: Author's Choice Press, Lincoln, NE.

Wild Fermentation: The Flavor, Nutrition, and Craft of Live-Culture Foods by Sandor Katz. 2016: Chelsea Green Publishing, White River Junction, VT.

The Art of Fermentation: An In-Depth Exploration of Essential Concepts and Processes from Around the World by Sandor Katz. 2012: Chelsea Green Publishing, White River Junction, VT.

The Noma Guide to Fermentation by David Zilber and René Redzepi. 2018: Workman Publishing Company, New York, NY

EQUIPMENT AND CULTURES

Ohio Stoneware, www.ohiostoneware.com

Northern Brewer, www.northernbrewer.com

The Brooklyn Kitchen, www.thebrooklynkitchen.com

GEM Cultures, Inc., www.gemcultures.com

Cultures for Health, www.culturesforhealth.com

The Cheesemaker, www.thecheesemaker.com

SOS Chefs of NY, www.sos-chefs.com

FORAGING, HERBAL MEDICINE, AND WILDERNESS SURVIVAL

BOOKS

Tom Brown's Field Guide to Wilderness Survival by Tom Brown. 1983: Berkley Books, New York, NY.

Identifying and Harvesting Edible and Medicinal Plants in Wild (and Not So Wild) Places by Steve Brill and Evelyn Dean. 1994: William Morrow, New York, NY.

The Country Almanac of Home Remedies: Time-Tested & Almost Forgotten Wisdom for Treating Hundreds of Common Ailments, Aches & Pains Quickly and Naturally by Brigitte Mars and Chrystle Fiedler. 2014: Fair Wind Press, Beverly, MA.

Advanced Bushcraft: An Expert Field Guide to the Art of Wilderness Survival by Dave Canterbury. 2015: Adams Media, Avon, MA.

COURSES AND GUIDES

"Wildman" Steve Brill,
www.wildmanstevebrill.com

Off the Wall Excursions, Louisiana
(225) 247-2543

Tom Brown Jr.'s Tracker School,
www.trackerschool.com

MYCOLOGY

Mycelium Running: How Mushrooms Can Help Save the World by Paul Stamets. 2005: Ten Speed Press, Berkeley, CA.

Mushrooms Demystified by David Arora. 1979: Ten Speed Press, Berkeley, CA.

National Audubon Society Field Guide to North American Mushrooms by Gary H. Lincoff. 1981: Knopf, New York, NY.

The Complete Mushroom Hunter: An Illustrated Guide to Finding, Harvesting, and Enjoying Wild Mushrooms by Gary Lincoff. 2010: Quarry Books, Beverly, MA.

BUTCHERING, HUNTING, AND GENERAL PREPARATION

La Technique: An Illustrated Guide to the Fundamental Techniques of Cooking by Jacques Pépin. 1976: Times Books, New York, NY.

After the Hunt: Lousiana's Authoritative Collection of Wild Game and Game Fish Cookery by John D. Folse. 2007: Chef John Folse & Company, Gonzales, LA.

The Complete Guide to Hunting, Butchering, and Cooking Wild Game by Steven Rinella and John Hafner. 2015: Spiegel & Grau, New York, NY.

Whole Beast Butchery: The Complete Visual Guide to Beef, Lamb, and Pork by Ryan Farr and Brigit Binns. 2011: Chronicle Books, San Francisco, CA.

The Butcher's Apprentice by Aliza Green and Steve Legato. 2012: Quarry Books, Beverly, MA.

INDEX

Note: Page references in *italics* indicate photographs.